Queerness in Heavy Metal Music

While the growing field of scholarship on heavy metal music and its subcultures has produced excellent work on the sounds, scenes, and histories of heavy metal around the world, few works have included a study of gender and sexuality. This cutting-edge volume focuses on queer fans, performers, and spaces within the heavy metal sphere and demonstrates the importance, pervasiveness, and subcultural significance of queerness to the heavy metal ethos.

Heavy metal scholarship has until recently focused almost solely on the roles of heterosexual hypermasculinity and hyperfemininity in fans and performers. The dependence on that narrow dichotomy has limited heavy metal scholarship, resulting in poorly critiqued discussions of gender and sexuality that serve only to underpin the popular imagining of heavy metal as violent, homophobic, and inherently masculine. This book queers heavy metal studies, bringing discussions of gender and sexuality in heavy metal out of that poorly theorized dichotomy.

In this interdisciplinary work, the author connects new and existing scholarship with a strong ethnographic study of heavy metal's self-identified queer performers and fans in their own words, thus giving them a voice and offering an original and ground-breaking addition to scholarship on popular music, rock, and queer studies.

Amber R. Clifford-Napoleone is Associate Professor of Anthropology and Curator of Nance Collections at the University of Central Missouri, USA.

Routledge Studies in Popular Music

Queerness in Heavy Metal Music
Metal Bent

Amber R. Clifford-Napoleone

Routledge
Taylor & Francis Group
LONDON AND NEW YORK

First published 2015 by Routledge

2 Park Square, Milton Park, Abingdon, Oxfordshire OX14 4RN
711 Third Avenue, New York, NY 10017

Routledge is an imprint of the Taylor & Francis Group, an informa business

First issued in paperback 2017

Library of Congress Cataloging in Publication Data

Clifford-Napoleone, Amber R., 1974– author.
Queerness in heavy metal music : metal bent / Amber R. Clifford-Napoleone.
    pages cm. — (Routledge studies in popular music ; 5)
Includes bibliographical references and index.
    1. Homosexuality and music. 2. Heavy metal (Music)—History and criticism.
    3. Gender identity in music. I. Title.
ML3838.C55 2015
781.66086'64—dc23   2014043518

ISBN: 978-0-415-72831-7 (hbk)
ISBN: 978-0-815-36558-7 (pbk)

Typeset in Sabon
by codeMantra

To the queer fans of heavy metal, wherever you are.

Contents

List of Figures

List of Tables

Acknowledgments

I have always been fascinated by acknowledgments pages. I read them constantly, looking for connections between people and ways to thank those whose influence appears in your work. Being faced with writing one is, however, a daunting task.

First, there is a long line of writers and artists whom I have never met who deeply influence my thinking, writing and research. For their work: Michel Foucault, Esther Newton, Gayle Rubin, Leslie Feinberg, Leo Bersani, S. Bear Bergman, Pat Califa, Dorothy Allison, George Chauncey, Jose Esteban Munoz, Rob Halford, Joan Jett, L7 and everyone who helped create the Riot Grrl movement, Rammstein, Trent Reznor, Charlie Parker, Amy Ray, Allen Ginsberg, Lawrence Ferlinghetti, and the writers of *Velvet Goldmine*.

Second, I want to thank some brilliant cultural writers, thinkers and archivists for their assistance. No story about GLBTQ people would be complete without the dedicated work of members of the community. My thanks to the Leather Archives and Museum in Chicago, Illinois, its Board, its Executive Director Rick Storer and his staff. My work was greatly changed when I was granted the LA&M Visiting Scholar award in 2013, and I sincerely hope that I do the LA&M and its important work justice. Thanks also to the staff of the Lesbian Herstory Archives in Brooklyn, New York, a home for our history and a staff that does better work for scholars from a distance than some professionals deliver in person. My deepest thanks to the staff of the Kirkpatrick Library at my home institution, the University of Central Missouri, and specifically to Robert Hallis for his support of this project and all of my other interests in making sure heavy metal music and its cultures are remembered and maintained. Last but not least, Elizabeth Levine, Emily Ross, and especially Andrew Weckenmann at Routledge for their patient fostering of this project from concept to page.

Third, I believe that any academic work, whether in the classroom or in print, is always a collaboration. On the heels of completing my dissertation in 2007 I embarked on this project, and on a whim I proposed to present a paper at the International Congress on Heavy Metal and Gender in Cologne, Germany. Little did I know that paper and conference would lead me to my life's work, and to a group of friends with whom I tour the world. So deepest thanks to Florian Heesch for Cologne, to Brian Hickam for his friendship and for his dedication to preserving metal history, to Deena Weinstein, Jeremy Wallach, and Keith Kahn-Harris for leading the charge and never giving up the faith, to Karl Spracklen for his ISMMS leadership and his dancing, Nelson-Varas-Diaz and Eliut Riverra-Segura for Puerto Rico and for applauding every time I shock someone, Toni-Matti Karjalainen for brilliant photography and the epicness that will be Helsinki in 2015, and Niall Scott for being my Dutch/English/Texan philosophical hell-raiser. And for all those who enjoy an inside joke: thanks to everyone who enjoyed the services of my minivan cab driving in Bowling Green for some of the funniest conversations I have ever had.

In 2011 I was lucky enough to be selected for the NEH Seminar on Ethnomusicology and Global Music. I had no idea that what was one of the hardest years of my life would find me in a dorm at Wesleyan, listening to Tuvan throat singing and contemplating my work. The people I met there changed my work, and my life, in incredible ways. Deepest and heartfelt thanks to Ali Colleen Neff and Kwame Harrison, who have never ceased to cheer me on, to Luis-Manuel Garcia for his fabulous scarves and his even sexier thoughts on affect, to Heather MacLachlan and our long talks about gay chorus and metal music, the brilliant Jesus Ramos for keeping my leftist feet on the ground, Rebekah Moore for teaching me what applied really means, and the ever-funny Jeremy Grimshaw who has kept me smiling no matter what happened. Though she was not at Wesleyan, a very special thanks to Angela Glaros: we have seen each other through grad school, dissertation, hiring, conferences and board meetings, and now we find ourselves at those same conferences herding our own students in those directions. High five.

My colleagues and friends at University of Central Missouri have supported my work, and my family, through incredible victories and terrible defeats. Without them this work would have been absolutely impossible. First to Dr. John Sheets and Dr. Joy Stevenson, who took a bewildered 14 year old kid under their wing. Thank you for seeing me through every misstep, listening even when I was making a bad decision, and teaching me how to be a true teacher. To the professors I learned from, who taught me to be a scholar: David Rice, Bill Foley, Arthur McClure, Gene Twomey, Pat Ashman, Carol Heming, Mary Ellen Rowe, Susan Pentlin, Roy Stubbs, LeRoy McDermott, and Jim Loch. To Julie Willett and Randy McBee at Texas Tech University, who let me explore not just the underside of history, but my role in remembering it. Thanks to my colleagues in the Department of History and Anthropology, especially Eric Tenbus and Sean Kim, for supporting this project from the beginning. Special thanks to Carol Benton and Wendy Geiger for seeing me through the challenges of an academic life, for endless and really blue humor, and unscheduled club meetings in the hallway. A salute to Janice Putnam for our walking appointments, our coffee talks, and for teaching me how to say no. Hats off to the crew in American Studies at University of Kansas, especially Sherrie Tucker who has never stopped supporting my work. Rock Chalk. And a special note to Vivian Richardson, whom I've worked with for nearly 25 years. I know that my work on one side of the street has taken away from my work on the other side of the street, and your unbelievable work has never gone unnoticed. Thank you.

I am an anthropologist. It gives me great joy to say that, and serving as a teacher, and a researcher, in Anthropology is not just my vocation, it is my avocation. There is nothing about my work, or my life as an academic, that would be possible without John Sheets and Jeff Yelton. Thank you John, for showing me what it means to be a teacher-scholar, and for allowing me to pass on the incredible kindness you did for me and my family when you took me under your wing. Jeff, without your unwavering support and your incredible work, I would not have been able to accomplish anything. I laughingly refer to you as my partner in anthropological crime, but all joking aside, our partnership is one of the greatest developments of my life, and I am proud to call you my friend. And my thanks to the newest addition to this little lineage, Hannah Marsh, who is more than happy to talk for five hours about heavy metal music as long as we include cranial vault thickness. Welcome to the family.

To my students: you keep me fresh and on my toes, you teach me more about the world than I could ever hope to learn alone, you keep me guessing. May you always remember how brilliant you are, and never lose sight of the promise that your future holds. Well done.

Last but never least, my family. There is an old saying from the GLBTQ activist world: "close friends and chosen family." I have not seen this anywhere in a long time, but it sits on the dresser in my home as a reminder of the importance of what we anthropologists would call fictive kin for GLBTQ people. I have a few friends that I long ago chose as my family, and they have never strayed no matter the circumstances. John, Krisana and their son John Gareth, I love all of you more than I can say, and thank you for sheltering me when the world got too hard. Niko Herzog, who drank beers and shot pool with me the night Matthew Shepard was found, his wife Lisa and their two boys Milan and Viktor. Niko, who knew that first day in Lubbock that we would be like two old guys on a barstool one day. Thank you for always being there, no matter how far that took you. And To Dennis and Brian, just one thing: thanks for helping me breathe.

Nothing could begin to describe my family, a band of war weary travelers who only lock arms and stare down the next attack. For my sister Rachel, you are astounding, a force to be reckoned with, a woman of pure steel with a core of nothing but light. For my nephew Nate, a smart, funny, kind young man with a heart beyond all measure. For my mother Myrna, a woman for whom no words exist, who has accepted more loss and yet remains steadfastly with open arms. Most of all my wonderful wife Tara M. Napoleone, whom I love so much I married her twice. I never fail to be amazed at your unflinching care, your willingness to defend no matter the odds, your amazing intellect and your strength, and your ability to go to hundreds of heavy metal shows and act happy. Mi familia, long may you run.

This book, and all of my work from this day forward, is dedicated to my father Jim and my brother Austin. I had the kind of father most kids wish they had, and would give anything for him to hold this book in his hands. Daddy, I hope I did you proud. My brother Austin was the first person I came out to, the first person to meet my future wife, the first person to read my work. We wrote collaboratively for most of our lives, and losing him is the loss of part of my own voice. Austin, I hope my work meets with your approval, and that the edits are few. What else could I be? All apologies.

Introduction

Figure 0.1 Image of crowd at heavy metal concert. Photo by author.

The heavy metal glam band Pink Stëël released its debut album, *Enter the Pink*, in 2003. The band was a play on all the stereotypes about 1980s hair metal bands such as Motley Crüe and Twisted Sister but with a new edge: they billed themselves as "harder than Liza, gayer than Kiss."[1] Their camp reproduction of hair metal looked awfully familiar and their lyrical dependence on gay male experiences blatantly obvious. Hanson Jobb, the lead vocalist of murkily German origins, told *HX Magazine*: "Heavy metal is for everyone. The beauty, the leather, phallic worship of a Fender Stratocaster guitar … wait a minute. It's *so* the gayness. It's gayer than young Nathan Lane at choir camp."[2] Pink Stëël's first release, "Converter," suggested the band would convert listeners' sexual orientation: "You think you're straight/But just you wait!CONVERTER."[3] Heavy metal band Torche, led by out gay male singer Steve Brooks, was asked in a 2009 interview how he happened to be a gay singer in an "aggressive and manly" genre. "So is being gay," Brooks replied. "Metal is the gayest form of music out there. You can quote me on that. You know, guys wearing leather and studs, beating each other up in the pit, getting all sweaty with each other, growing their hair real long, wearing makeup. ... That's all pretty gay."[4] When Paul Masvidal and Seth Reinert of the influential metal band Cynic came out in a 2014 article in *The Los Angeles Times*, both men discussed their place in the supposedly hypermasculine and heterosexual work of heavy metal. "I see all those old dudes out there just banging their heads to our records," Reinert told reporter August Brown, "and I have to think, 'That stuff you're banging your head to? That is some gay, gay metal man'."[5] Two days after the interview appeared, owner of Kuletski guitars Vik Kuletski made a homophobic remark on his Facebook page aimed at Masvidal.[6] Within two days, heavy metal guitarists began to cancel their contracts with Kuletski.[7] Six days after Masvidal and Reinert's interview was published on May 8, two members of the Dutch heavy metal band Exivious posted a YouTube video song entitled "Vik in the Closet" with the lyrics "Vik Kuletski/Why don't you get in touch with your feelings?"[8] If heavy metal is the aggressive, manly, ubermasculine, and homophobic musical community it is believed to be, how does Pink Stëël thrive? If heavy metal is as hateful as its stereotype suggests, why are Brooks, Masvidal, and Reinert defended, even welcomed, by heavy metal fans?

Heavy metal is queer, and not in the popular culture bastardization of the word that equates queerness with stupidity. The histories, development, style, even some of the most influential heavy metal musicians in the genre are, in fact, queer-identified. In the scenes and spaces of heavy metal, queer-identified people created and supported a place to belong. In her exploration of queer belonging, critical geographer Elspeth Probyn wrote: "It is desire embodied in an object that is the condition for belonging as gay or lesbian."[9] For queer fans of heavy metal, desire is embodied in the hypermasculine performances and hyperfeminine video vixens of heavy metal. It is embodied in the status of heavy metal as forbidden, marginal, and taboo. Queer belonging in heavy metal means to desire power, and anger, and control, and blatant sexuality – the same desires as metal's straight fans but with different bodies and different perspectives. Metal scholars can truly begin to understand those desires, those aspects that make heavy metal what it is, only by disconnecting the discussion of masculinity from the white, male, heterosexual body. Only by refocusing the study of heavy metal away from its projection as heterosexual masculinity can we truly begin to unpack the ways in which heavy metal fans consume and enact their heavy metal desires. As a heavy metal fan, a lesbian woman, and a scholar of heavy metal, my examination in *Queerness in Heavy Metal* is an attempt to queer heavy metal. Hopefully, this work will allow scholars, performers, and fans in heavy metal to realize metal is not, and has never been, all about the straight boys.

Queerness in Heavy Metal has two major goals. First, this book is intended to queer heavy metal studies and bring discussions of gender and sexuality in heavy metal out of a poorly theorized dichotomy. Beginning with foundational texts such as Robert Walser's *Running with the Devil* and Deena Weinstein's *Heavy Metal*, heavy metal scholarship has focused almost solely on the roles of heterosexual hypermasculinity and hyperfemininity in fans and performers.[10] The dependence on that narrow dichotomy has limited heavy metal scholarship and has resulted in poorly critiqued discussions of gender and sexuality that serve only to underpin the popular imagining of heavy metal as violent, homophobic, and inherently masculine. *Queerness in Heavy Metal* focuses on queer fans, self-identified queer performers, and the aspects of heavy metal cultures that are borrowed from queer culture(s). With this in-depth excavation of gender and sexuality in metal, I intend to both queer heavy metal and interrogate previous scholarship in metal music studies.

The second goal of *Queerness in Heavy Metal* is to give self-identified queer fans of heavy metal a voice. In 2009 I released an online ethnographic survey of self-identified queer heavy metal fans worldwide. Included in the survey was a request for individuals to consent to an interview. The survey resulted in data from over 500 respondents from around the world and a continuing project collecting interviews for the majority of those respondents. Rather than rely on second-hand information, this interdisciplinary work connects scholarship in secondary works with a strong ethnographic study of heavy metal's queer fans in their own words. In addition, my interviews are conducted online or on site, resulting in ethnographic study in several locations in the United States and around the world. This study is not simply a theoretical one; it is one that presents a broad queer perspective on heavy metal based on ethnographic work.

Three terms in use in this book are particularly important. *Queerness in Heavy Metal* is transdisciplinary. It is written for metal studies scholars, scholars of gender and sexuality, and the all-important fans and performers of heavy metal. Consequently, there are particular terms in use that may not translate across all disciplines. At the same time, the uses of some terms are more specific than might be suspected. First, this book depends on the word "queer." It should be noted, however, that unless otherwise stated, queer is not intended to denote queer theory, queer studies, or any other designation of the word "queer" as a theoretical tool. Instead, my use of queer is to denote individuals who self-identify as non-normative in terms of sexual orientation, gender identity, and gender presentation. Queer has multiple meanings, both historical and political, that make it highly problematic. Its use here is meant precisely as a way of discussing non-heteronormative behavior and performance in heavy metal scenes. The association of the word "queer" with musical scenes is hardly unknown. Chauncey (1994) discussed the use of queer to denote masculine gay men in the music halls of early New York. Biographer David Hadju (1996) suggested queer meant "unusual" or "eccentric" in 1920s jazz scenes, and its use to describe same-sex sexuality was not unheard of. Historian Nan Alamilla Boyd (2007), in her study of Los Angeles, positioned queer as a signifier of any behavior marked by sexual and gender transgression of dominant norms. If the word "queer" is used in this text as an indication of a theoretical, methodological, or political tool, it is indicated.

Second, "heavy metal" is a term that is just as problematic as queer, though perhaps not as well known. In truth, the definition and boundaries of heavy metal have taken up hundreds of books and no doubt millions of debates among performers and fans. While there is a great deal of debate about the first heavy metal recording, or even the history of the term "heavy metal music," there is broad agreement that heavy metal as a sonic production came from working-class industrial cities such as Detroit in the United States and Birmingham in England. Moore (2010) additionally states heavy metal arose from deindustrialization and a crisis in working-class male masculinity in the 1970s and 1980s.[11] Heavy metal describes first a sonic production marked by a cacophony of thick sound, amplified distortion, instrumental solos that encourage virtuosic performance, and the use of the tritone. While heavy metal began with a cadre of bands in England and America, it is today a global phenomenon of bands, fans, and networks of clubs, music stores, and festivals. The heavy metal scene, while varied across cultures and national borders, is nonetheless "spread across the globe, across race, sex, and class."[12] In order to understand the global effect of heavy metal as it pertains to queer-identified folks, I have categorized heavy metal as a minor transnationalism. According to Lionnet and Shih, minor transnationalisms are creative networks developed by minority people "produced and performed without necessary mediation by the center."[13] Heavy metal, which exists as a creative system, provides minority people with a system of disruption that avoids the center. Though the concept of community is still under debate in metal music studies, there is broad agreement that identifying as a metalhead brings with it the minor transnationalism of belonging in metal scenes. As Wallach, Berger, and Greene wrote in 2011: "By tapping into and channeling discontent, the music [heavy metal] opens these social formations up to critique and offers fans the opportunity to forge identities rooted in the music itself, its affective positions, and the global community of heavy metal musicians and fans."[14] The survey and interview data utilized in this book are international in scope with one focus: queer fans of heavy metal. Because heavy metal was categorized as a minor transnationalism, I did not examine questions of race, class, or ethnicity in this work. Asking specific survey questions about race was impossible, since the cultural construction of race (and class for that matter) varies widely from one culture to another. There are other scholars in metal music studies doing excellent work on race (see Dawes 2013, Fellezs 2013), the ethnicity of local scenes (see Baulch 2007, Wallach 2008), and other categories of difference (Wallach et al. 2011) and as metal studies develop, that work will continue to grow. The focus of this book, however, is solely on queer-identified people and their lives in heavy metal.

The third and final term requiring discussion is leather/BDSM. Just as the history and usage of queer and heavy metal as singular terms are historically problematic, leather/BDSM as a singular term is fraught with potential problems. Nonetheless, the history and style of heavy metal, and in my estimation the history of queer-identified politics, are inextricably linked to leather/BDSM. Leather has been used as a fabric for clothing since ancient times, but individuals identifying with/as leather is a post-World War II practice. In the second half of the twentieth century, identifying as leather came to symbolize or identify individuals practicing the erotics of BDSM: bondage and discipline (B/D), dominance and submission (D/s), and sadism and masochism (S/M).[15] While leather originally referred to leathermen (gay males who practiced BDSM), in the late twentieth century, leather/BDSM spread well beyond gay male enclaves into normative households and popular culture. Its growth precipitated an increase in the number of erotic and sexual practices now considered leather/BDSM. At the same time, identification as leather/BDSM caused a new revolution in both sexual terms and political ones. Even Foucault wrote about BDSM as a site of "queer praxis."[16] "True leatherfolk see black leather not as a stylish affectation," wrote Mark Thompson, "but rather as a still daring symbol of cultural transgression and personal transformation."[17] This cultural transgression became inextricably linked to heavy metal and was pivotal to the development of a queerscape in heavy metal.

Queerness in Heavy Metal is organized in five chapters, each presented as a specific aspect of the heavy metal queerscape. In "Heavy Metal Queerscape," the first chapter, I present the theoretical foundations of the work. This chapter introduces my theory of heavy metal as a queerscape, a theory developed from the work of Gordon Brett Ingram combined with aspects of critical geography, cultural studies, and queer theory. Queerscape theory presents heavy metal as a subcultural sphere that imbricates with queer culture. Consequently, queer fans of heavy metal occupy two marginal positions at the same time and are discursively produced by both. I suggest that, through heavy metal and queer identities, queers in heavy metal create desire-zones within heavy metal sites. Aspects of those desire-zones that are created by heterosexual metal fans are then reterritorialized as masculine and heterosexual. Though heavy metal may appear to be a masculine, heterosexual space, it is resolutely a queer space. This chapter also presents a critique of gender and sexuality study in existing heavy metal scholarship. Scholarship in heavy metal is relatively young but prolific. Beginning with foundational texts by Walser and Weinstein, metal studies developed into a unique field over the last two decades. Most scholarship, however, is focused on the history and genres of heavy metal or on specific events and fan groups.

Metal history is by far the largest of these categories, and includes recent auto-biographies by metal performers such as Ozzy Osbourne and Zakk Wylde. Discussions of specific genres are also quite prolific, especially in specialized genres such as death and black metal and the ever-popular guide to recordings. Among the best known works in this subfield are Moynihan's *Lords of Chaos* (2003) and Kahn-Harris's *Extreme Metal* (2007), and recording guides such as the recently published *Eddie Trunk's Essential Hard Rock and Heavy Metal* (2011). Aside from books, heavy metal studies has a growing base of films, including those by Sam Dunn (*Global Metal, Metal: A Headbanger's Journey*, and *Metal Evolution)* and Moretti's *Heavy Metal in Baghdad*. Most recently there is a growing interest in the study of heavy metal cultures, including LeVine's *Heavy Metal Islam* (2008) and Hecker's *Turkish Metal* (2012). The popular heavy metal press Bazillion Points has published Laina Dawes's *What Are You Doing Here* (2013), an autoethnographic and interview-based work on African American women in heavy metal. Despite the growing body of work and interest in the study of heavy metal cultures, however, there is little scholarship on sexuality or gender in heavy metal. Though Walser's *Running with the Devil* addresses gender and sexuality, it does not include an in-depth analysis of sexuality or non-normative gender, and is at this point a classic monograph that does not reflect recent work in the fields of gender and sexuality studies. *Queerness and Heavy Metal* is intended to fill the void of recent scholarship on gender and sexuality in heavy metal, and fits in with the heavy metal studies turn towards cultural questions.

The second chapter, "Black Leather," explores the heavy metal style and its roots in queer-identified cultural practices. Specifically, this chapter's focus is on the queer formations of heavy metal through leather/BDSM communities. In this chapter I will consider the hallmarks of heavy metal style, especially black leather and equipage such as whips, and examine their movement from queer-identified leather enclaves to heavy metal enclaves. My goal is to demonstrate, through ethnographic data and analysis of images, that heavy metal style was borrowed from the leather/BDSM community: metal style is leather's child. In addition, I argue that queer leather style and heavy metal style are still in conversation, influencing each other constantly.

The third chapter, titled "Outsider Togetherness," is about queer fans themselves. The title of the chapter is drawn from a quote by a survey participant who described his position as a queer fan of heavy metal as a "feeling of outsider togetherness." In this chapter, I present an in-depth analysis of the stories, beliefs, and experiences of queer heavy metal fans in heavy metal scenes as presented in my qualitative study. A focus of this chapter will be the many ways in which queer fans believe their overlapping identities (queer individual and heavy metal fan) perform with each other and against each other. I will also explore queer fans' affect in the metal world and how they consume heavy metal music and its productions. This chapter focuses on the fans themselves, how they identify as both queer individuals and heavy metal fans and what those identities mean in relation to the sounds and performances of heavy metal.

"Everyone Knows," the fourth chapter of the *Queerness in Heavy Metal*, will particularly focus on gender identity in performance. When is the performance of gender purely a performance and when is it the discursively formed performance of gender? Can the two ever be separated? This study centers gender as a field of disruption in heavy metal but looks instead to the work of performance studies in order to understand the role that gendered performance plays in the heavy metal queerscape. The chapter focuses on an in-depth reading of the heavy metal performers that surveyed queer fans most frequently identified: Rob Halford, Gaahl, Joan Jett, Otep Shamaya, Mina Caputo, and Marissa Martinez. In this scheme, these performers are not simply the vehicles for the representation of gender. They are, in fact, agents who use their bodies in performance as a way to trouble gender for the audience. *Queerness in Heavy Metal* will explore the ways in which individuals were subjected to the regulatory definitions of gender and the methods those individuals use to disrupt and interrupt those definitions.

The fifth and final chapter is titled "Eat Me Alive," taken from the title of a Judas Priest song. The song, listed by the Parents Music Resource Center's "Filthy Fifteen" in the 1980s, was considered a prime example of the dangers of rock music. The chapter focuses on consumption, and the ways in which consumption of heavy metal music, performances, and bodies are integral to the queerscape. Consumption is a common term in cultural studies, often focusing on popular culture as commodity supplied for a consumer. In this chapter, however, consumption is positioned as a way to understand queer fans of heavy metal as consumers not only of music but also of performances, audiences, artists, bodies. Drawing on studies of queer consumption, queer-identified musical performance, and representations of the corporeal, I posit that consumption includes methods queer fans use to consume space: geographical space, body space, and mind space. Through a discussion of queer metal fans' use of heavy metal as a text of desires, I examine queer modes of consuming heavy metal as a hallmark of the queerscape.

Finally, a word about my subject position and methodology. My first heavy metal recording was a bootleg copy of Black Sabbath's germinal album *Paranoid*, specifically the song "Fairies Wear Boots." I was a child, and have been a heavy metal fan every moment since then. Heavy metal was the music that saw me through the ups and downs of puberty, the challenges of academia. Even my coming out in 1998 happened with heavy metal playing in the background. I consider myself a hardcore heavy metal fan and, though such language tends to occasionally ring antiquated in the twenty-first century, an out and proud lesbian academic. Does that make me the same as other queer metal fans? Does being a lesbian make me a prototypical lesbian? Insider knowledge does not mean singular knowledge, and though my subject position as a queer fan of heavy metal has surely guided my work, it in no way makes my experience *the* queer metal fan experience. It did, however, provide me with cultural knowledge of two groups that are not easily open to the world at large. I argue, along with anthropologist Kath Weston, that my "hybridity blurs the distinction between researcher and research" because any decided attempt at separating my identity as a queer heavy metal fan would artificially distance myself from the subject and my informants.[18] "The Native Ethnographer, in the full glory of her hybridity, confronts the conventional definition of anthropology as the study of (hu)man, or even the study of cultural differences, with the possibility that the field might be more appropriately conceptualized as a site for the *production* of difference," wrote Weston.[19] My study is focused on just that: the production of queer fans in heavy metal, the production of queer-scapes in heavy metal scenes and spaces, how those two social and cultural differences are negotiated by those they encompass.

NOTES

1. Pink Steel, "About," http://www.pinksteel.com/home.html. Accessed August 17, 2014.
2. *HX Magazine*, "Mincing Metal: Hanson Jobb and Udo Von DuYu rock out as Pink Steel," *HX Magazine*, June 16, 2004, 24–25.
3. Pink Steel, "Lyrics," http://www.pinksteel.com/lyrics.html. Accessed August 14, 2014.
4. Chad Radford, "Torche's Steve Brooks talks about Atlanta, Harvey Milk and what makes metal so gay," *Creative Loafing Atlanta*, July 31, 2009, http://clatl.com/cribnotes/archives/2009/07/31/torches-steve-brooks-talks-about-atlanta-harvey-milk-and-what-makes-metal-so-gay.
5. August Brown, "Cynic's Paul Masvidal, Sean Reinert are out as ready to be loud," *Los Angeles Times*, May 8, 2012, http://www.latimes.com/entertainment/music/la-et-c1-gay-heavy-metal-20140508-story.html#page=1.
6. Robert Pasbani, "Vik Guitars Owner Posts Homophobic Remarks, Gets Denounced by Members of Periphery, Scar Symmetry," MetalInjection, May 13, 2014, http://www.metalinjection.net/latest-news/drama/vik-guitars-owner-homophobic-remarks-gets-denounced-by-periphery-scar-symmetry.
7. Graham "Gruhamed" Hartmann, "Periphery Cut Ties," *Loudwire*, May 14, 2014, http://loudwire.com/periphery-cut-ties-vik-guitars-homophobic-remarks-against-cynic/?trackback=tsmclip.
8. Exivious, *Vik In the Closet*. YouTube video. https://www.youtube.com/watch?v=4wPGmcTnCUg. Accessed May 14, 2014.
9. Elspeth Probyn, "Queer Belongings: The Politics of Departure," in *Sexy Bodies: The Strange Carnalities of Feminism*, edited by Elizabeth Grosz and Elspeth Probyn (London: Routledge 1995): 6.
10. Robert Walser, *Running with the Devil: Power, Gender, and Madness in Heavy Metal Music* (Middletown: Wesleyan University Press, 1982) and Deena Weinstein, *Heavy Metal: The Music and Its Culture* (New York: DaCapo Press, 1991) are considered the two foundational texts in the nascent field of heavy metal music studies.

11. Ryan Moore, *Sells Like Teen Spirit: Music, Youth Culture, and Social Crisis* (New York: New York University Pressm 2009): 80.
12. Rosemary Lucy Hill, "Hard Rock and Metal in the Subcultural Context: What Fans Listening to the Music Can Tell Us," *Leisure Studies Association Newsletter* 98 (July 2014): 67.
13. Françoise Lionnet and Shu-mei Shih, eds., *Minor Transnationalism* (Durham: Duke University Press, 2005): 5.
14. Jeremy Wallach, Harris Berger, and Paul D. Greene. "Affective Overdrive, Scene Dynamics, and Identity in the Global Metal Scene," in *Metal Rules the Globe: Heavy Metal Music Around the World*, edited by Jeremy Wallach, Harris Berger, and Paul D. Greene (Durham: Duke University Press, 2011): 26.
15. Bert Cutler, "Partner Selection, Power Dynamics, and Sexual Bargaining in Self-Defined BDSM Couples." PhD diss. (Institute for Advanced Study of Sexuality, 2003): 14–15.
16. David Halperin, *Saint Foucault: Towards A Gay Hagiography* (New York: Oxford University Press, 1995): 85.
17. Mark Thompson ed., *Leatherfolk: Radical Sex, People, Politics, and Practice* (Los Angeles: Daedalus Publishing Company, 1991; 3d, 2004): xx.
18. Kath Weston, "The Virtual Anthropologist," in *Anthropological Locations: Bounds and Grounds of a Field Science*, edited by Akhil Gupta and James Ferguson (Berkeley: University of California Press, 1997): 174.
19. Ibid., 179.

1 Heavy Metal Queerscape

A queer methodology, in a way, is a scavenger methodology that uses different methods to collect and produce information on subjects who have been deliberately or accidentally excluded from traditional studies of human behavior. The queer methodology attempts to combine methodologies that are often cast as being at odds with each other, and it refuses the academic compulsion toward disciplinary coherence.

—Judith Halberstam[1]

I am not sure when I became a metalhead, just as I am not sure when I became a lesbian. The two were always there, part of my life, and I never experienced any incongruity between those two parts of my identity. When my wife and I were first dating, however, I took her to a Ministry club show. It was the first metal crowd I had taken her to and I was very excited about showing her what I considered my people. When we arrived I asked if she was OK and she was very nervous, bordering on scared. I told her nothing would happen, that my people would not be concerned at all about her or about us being there together. I asked what she was afraid of. It was of being attacked, or in danger, being around a rough crowd who might beat her up over her dreadlocks and her girlfriend. I was shocked. I had never thought about how my metal family might be thought of as dangerous to her. I had never been attacked at a show, as long as you do not count the occasional mosh pit injury. I was at once surprised and amazed. I even went so far as to say: "But this is Ministry. It's not like we're at a Slayer show or something." Why was I so sure we were safe among the very fans who outsiders consider dangerous, threatening, and inherently homophobic? How were these metal fans my people? How did I come to identify heavy metal with queerness?

The study of heavy metal music, both as a sound and a scene, continues to grow and develop. Many scholars have examined the role of popular music in reifying dichotomous gendered discourses, as well as the link between musical discourses and gendered identities. Too frequently, however, such scholarship in heavy metal has focused on the role of masculinity in reifying hyperfemininity in females and hypermasculinity in males. Academic studies of heavy metal focus on the inherent masculinity in the sounds and performances of heavy metal. Is the masculinity of heavy metal extended only to straight male fans? This focus is especially prevalent in examinations of rock and heavy metal as a male rite of passage, or continued critiques of the marginalization of female performers in heavy metal. Also in play in analyses of heavy metal is the presence of gay male performers and fans. Rob Halford's "coming out," the homoerotic performance of glam metal, the use of accessories such as leather harnesses and spiked bondage gear – all of these and other events in the production of heavy metal have served to create a conception of masculine sexual expression despite their queer origins. Is this expression of masculinity extended to fandom or restricted to the performers themselves? Further, where are queer fans in this field of sexual expression? If heavy metal is indeed a field of desires and possibilities for sexual expression, then where are the lesbian women, the feminine men, the transgender fans and performers? I suggest those fans, indeed a space for those fans, exist within heavy metal. The academic writing about heavy metal, however, presupposes a heterosexist and heterosexual fan base for heavy metal and consequently ignores the creation of a queerscape in heavy metal. This study seeks to fill that void through an excavation of the queer origins, performances, and fans of heavy metal music.

Given the obvious masculinist and heterosexual aspects of heavy metal, why focus on queers in heavy metal? Our theoretical and academic understanding of heavy metal relies on masculinity and heterosexuality as though they are static and immutable, as though they are the very core of heavy metal itself. Consequently, the masculinist and heteronormative qualities of heavy metal are not excavated or interrogated. The result is that academic interest in heavy metal avoids queerness not because such identities do not exist within heavy metal cultures but because the static nature of the scholarship ignores queerness in an effort to reify masculinity. That is in itself problematic because the reification of masculinity and heteronormativity makes those qualities invisible. As gender scholar Judith Halberstam wrote: "Masculinity … becomes legible as masculinity where and when it leaves that white male middle-class body."[2] This is especially true when the queer body is subjectified and masculinity becomes one of many possibilities for the application of masculinity as a performance rather than an identity. Instead of centering masculinity and heterosexuality as a given, unchaining the masculinity of heavy metal from the heterosexual body makes it clear heavy metal is not inherently masculine at all. That masculinity is only a performance, an illusion that has come off the stage and entered scholarship. That assertion may come as a surprise to those who live outside the heavy metal world, a strange international amalgamation of sounds, styles, and aesthestics all wrapped up with a bow of authenticity. The heavy metal world, however, is inherently a queer world of BDSM style and symbolism, leather subcultural cues, overt visual and lyrical images of "abnormal" sexual behavior, and performers who defy heteronormative cultural norms of appearance and behavior. The performed masculinity of the heavy metal scene is nothing more than a drag show.

What this drag shows signifies for queer fans, however, is far different. Rather than see queerness in heavy metal as a simple reproduction of the masculine (a key move made by heavy metal scholars to portray metal fans as always male, heterosexual, and cisgendered), I propose heavy metal fans are engaging in a complicated Deleuzian assemblage of gender, sex, sexuality, performance, style, and affect. This complex and mutual imbrication of identities plays itself out in the sounds, lyrics, and spaces of heavy metal, an equally complex and dense assemblage. In essence, queer heavy metal fans occupy an overlap of assemblages, a cultural zone where identities are constantly in flux, reified and recoded by a multitude of gazes, defined and neither queer nor metal, or both, or none. "Displacing queerness as an identity or modality that is visibly, audibly, legibly, or tangibly evident," wrote Jasir Puar, "assemblages allow us to attune to intensities, emotions, energies, affectivities, textures as they inhabit events, spatiality, and corporealities."[3] As Leo Bersani suggested in his influential essay "Is the Rectum a Grave?" this study seeks to define the edges of distinction between the effects of gendered and sexualized queer styles on the supposedly heterosexual world of heavy metal and their significance to the queer heavy metal fans who practice them.[4] I argue, in the same vein as Avery Gordon's work on *un*visible haunting, that gendered and sexualized queer styles, performances, and self-identified queer fans have always operated in the heavy metal landscape, the reality behind the mirage of masculinity. Mirages are the result of light bending and displacing images on the horizon, but their interpretation is a function of the mind: we see water where none exists. Mirage in heavy metal bends in the light of queer cultures, styles, and people. Heterosexual masculinity appears to come into view. I propose, however, that queerness in heavy metal is not the mirage but the reality. It is masculinity that is the mirage, the shimmering image we interpret as the reality. We simply never get close enough for the mirage to fade away, and as the tumescence of heavy metal masculinity rises, we keep our distance and allow the masculinity mirage to become accepted reality. "It is the self that swells with excitement at the idea of being on top," wrote Leo Bersani, "the self that makes of the inevitable play of thrusts and relinquishments in sex as argument for the natural authority of one sex over another."[5]

This masculinity mirage that argues for the authority of heterosexuality in heavy metal is essentialized in the growing canon of heavy metal scholarship. While there are queer performers and fans in heavy metal scenes, they appear seldom in heavy metal scholarship. Instead, scholars typically focus on the performed masculinity and heterosexuality of heavy metal as factual, and reify it by excluding other possibilities. In order to maintain this heteronormativity, heavy metal scholars underpin their work with three primary assumptions: rock (and consequently heavy metal) is sexually exclusive, fans are assumed to be heterosexual, and queer performers and fans are positioned as oddities. Through these three assumptions, scholars of heavy metal render the queerness of heavy metal as the mirage, placing the greatest authority in the male, heterosexual, and cisgender interpretations of heavy metal.

The first of these key assumptions is that heavy metal is sexually exclusive. According to this assumption, heavy metal is the domain of males and anyone (performer or fan) who is not male is an exception or a poseur. This assumption is omnipresent in heavy metal scholarship and is taken largely from the works of Deena Weinstein and Robert Walser. Weinstein's positioning of the "masculinist code" in heavy metal and Walser's discussion of exscription are frequently included in the assumption that heavy metal is sexually exclusive. For example, in Sheila Whiteley's groundbreaking work on gender and music, *Sexing the Groove*, Whiteley explored the role of masculinity in rock music genres. "Rock's function," wrote Whiteley, "is to confer masculinity: to enter the domain of rock is a male rite of passage."[6] Another key example is from "Rock and Sexuality," an essay by Simon Frith and Angela McRobbie. According to Frith and McRobbie:

> The male consumer's identification with the rock performer, his collective experience of rock shows which, in this respect, are reminiscent of football matches and other occasions of male camaraderie – the general atmosphere is sexually exclusive, its euphoria depends on the absence of women.[7]

One other aspect of the male exclusivity assumption pushes the concept even further by suggesting the female in heavy metal and rock is, in fact, a plaything of the male. Robert Walser's discussion of exscription suggests the female form in heavy metal is either eliminated or subverted to conform to the heterosexual male gaze.[8] Weinstein posits female fans cater to masculinity through actions such as the "bitch goddess" and the "groupie." Interestingly, other scholars have taken these concepts to present non-masculine behaviors as systems of support for male exclusivity. "The woman is solely accepted provided she stimulates masculinity standards," wrote Klypchak, "and caters to a system of definition designed to privilege males."[9] By marking the female as male reification embodied, scholars make no effort to understand the masculinity itself. At the end of this assumption lies one conclusion: authentic heavy metal fans and performers are male and anything else is not real. As Davies wrote in her article "All Rock and Roll Is Homosocial": "The sexist discourse operating with respect to female performers makes it clear that the world of 'serious' music is ideologically a very masculine one, and that female fans are unwelcome."[10]

The second assumption in heavy metal scholarship is that fans and performers are heterosexual. This assumption goes beyond sexual exclusivity and posits heavy metal also depends on sexualized and gendered exclusivity. Heavy metal scholars rely primarily on sex as an indicator of exclusivity and then consider sexual exclusivity as clear evidence that queerness is also nonexistent. Under this argument, the need to consider queerness as a part of heavy metal is rendered impossible. If women are excluded, then by proxy, queer individuals must be excluded. Essentially, queerness is marked as female and therefore disqualified. Denski and Sholle present this argument when they suggest that when heavy metal performers "take up styles that imply female or homosexual identity," fans recognize this performance as purely masculine."[11] The authors further exclude queerness and support the exclusivity of masculinity in their explanation of gender in metal: "Heavy metal may shift some outward signs of gender, but it leaves untouched the constructed core of identity of binary sex, and unchallenged the asymmetrical dominant power relations of gender."[12] In his study of gender in heavy metal, Brad Klypchak studied homosexuality in heavy metal but only as an occasional and public exception to a genre-based rule. As Klypchak wrote: "Metalheads are assumed to be heterosexual, embracing the traditional orientation and attitude of the dominant whole."[13] An important part of this gendered assumption in heavy metal scholarship is an inherent homophobia that scholars identify with heavy metal. In his history of heavy metal, Phillip Bashe explained that metal's focus on individuality and perseverance made metal homophobic. "Headbangers are notoriously homophobic," wrote Bashe, "and generally regard any act that does not go in for metal's mucho-macho posturing as beneath contempt."[14] Krenske and McKay actually marked heavy metal as a "heterosexist formation."[15] In their study of a heavy metal club in Queensland, Australia, they even went so far as to identify a group they termed "metal wenches": women who were not bitch goddesses but rather females whose "bodies were normally concealed underneath an androgynous mode of dress."[16] In essence, the authors suggest androgyny made these "wenches" interlopers who somehow concealed their gender from the metal scene. Their status as failed females and failed metal fans reveals the importance of negation and failure to discuss gender and sexuality in the heavy metal canon. As Halberstam posited in the book *The Queer Art of Failure*, in this interpretation butch lesbians and androgynous folks in heavy metal are seen as failures: failed females and failed heavy metal fans.[17] Perhaps the most obvious use of homophobia as a way to support gender exclusivity is in the work of Simon Reynolds and Joy Press. In their book *The Sex Revolts*, Reynolds and Press wrote that rock (and consequently metal) marks anything other than heterosexual maleness as "abject" and therefore a potential pollutant. In their examination of lesbian women in punk and the Riot Grrl movement, the dependence on male, cisgendered masculinity in heavy metal scholarship truly reveals itself. According to Reynolds and Press, punk pioneer Suzi Quatro was "the archetypical male impersonator," Joan Jett's "black leather image was pure macha," and neither brought "anything new, different, to the stock rock posture."[18] The authors go even further in their analysis of the Riot Grrl band L7, an openly queer band the authors term "almost a caricature of hard rock":

> A sort of politically correct version of the Runaways, L7 show that trying to be as hard as the boys is just a dead end. Surely, women have more to offer rock than just the same old hardened, repressed armature

of cool? Are L7's notorious antics – like the incident at the 1992 Reading Festival where singer/guitarist Donita Sparks pulled her tampon out of her vagina and hurled it into the crowd – really that much of an improvement on heavy metal's ritual feats of misbehavior?[19]

In their discussion of L7 as failed rock musicians, Reynolds and Press fail to examine the way that queer women performing masculinity opposed the presupposed heterosexual core of heavy metal. Is the problem that L7 and Joan Jett bring nothing new to cock rock or is it that scholars fail to deconstruct the tumescence of cock rock itself? The problem with such analysis is that the reliance on heterosexual exclusivity reveals scholars have not adequately examined the cultural and social capital of heterosexual masculinity inherent in such concepts. In other words, is it heavy metal itself that "leaves untouched the constructed core of identity" or is it the scholars who study heavy metal?

The third and final assumption of heavy metal scholarship is that queerness, where it is public and visible, is purely an anomaly. Scholars of heavy metal mark a few queer performers, the ones most public and most visible, as somehow courageous anomalies of an inherently homophobic scene. Even if those performers had clearly marked themselves as queer, the scholarship suggests those signs were somehow misunderstood by fans as hypermasculine (or, in the case of lesbian performers, bastardized masculine) behavior. This is the core of Robert Walser's discussion of exscription and gay male fans. While Walser briefly discusses the status of gay male fans, his discussion of those fans completely focused on the members of the Gay Metal Society, a now defunct group in Chicago. According to Walser, gay male fans "sometimes forthrightly celebrate the homoeroticism that is latent" in heavy metal and "may see metal videos as erotic fantasies."[20] Clearly, Walser sees any gay male readings of heavy metal as fleeting and incongruous with heavy metal authenticity. This is further evident in Walser's brief discussion of homosexuality and the band Accept: "Some of Accept's lyrics are explicitly homosexual if studied closely; despite this, the band is quite popular among heterosexual, often homophobic, men."[21] Walser's treatment of queerness in metal is clear. Queer fans are a self-organized anomaly and despite overt queerness, some straight fans deign to enjoy possibly queer lyrics. Many additional examples of this subjectification of queer performers exist (see previous discussion of Suzi Quatro and L7, for example). The prime example in current heavy metal scholarship is Rob Halford, longtime heavy metal performer and lead singer for the influential band Judas Priest. Halford publicly announced his sexuality as a gay man in an interview on MTV News in 1998. Since then, Halford has appeared as a subject in practically every academic discussion of gender in hard rock and heavy metal. What is most interesting about the coverage of Halford's sexuality, however, is the seeming surprise on the part of heavy metal scholars. For example, Brad Klypchak wrote: "Having publicly declared his lifelong homosexuality in 1998, Halford acknowledged himself as a closeted gay man working in the homophobic metal world."[22] This surprise at a seeming public announcement of "lifelong homosexuality" stemmed largely from Halford's performances themselves. Halford is known in heavy metal history as one of the originators of the leather and spikes appearance now so synonymous with heavy metal scenes, an appearance he premiered in 1978. His use of leather, spikes, and harnesses was not from biker culture, however; it was taken entirely from the gay leather subculture of San Francisco, a fact Halford admitted in the same 1998 interview in which he came out. After all, two weeks after Halford's interview, Judas Priest bandmate Ian Hill said of Halford's sexuality: "It must have been the worst kept secret in rock and roll."[23] Despite the clear visual cues and queer subcultural symbols of this "worst kept secret," heavy metal scholars continue to insist Halford's sexuality was unknown, and his appearance was read by fans as hypermasculine biker culture. According to Klypchak:

> As a leading figure throughout metal's development, Halford's artistic involvement with Judas Priest offers insight at the ways in which both audience and performer functioned within the climate of heteronormativity, to selectively interpret homoeroticly-loaded cues in such a fashion that metal's hegemonic masculinity went unthreatened.[24]

This leaves behind interesting questions. Was it performers and fans who selectively interpreted such subcultural cues or the scholars who now choose to point to Halford as an anomaly, a successful masculine pretender in homophobic heavy metal, thus engaging in selective interpretation? Did queer fans read Halford's performances as "homoerotically-loaded cues" or as signposts for a queer space in heavy metal? Is heavy metal's masculinity truly unthreatened when a performer commonly referred to as the Metal God announces his masculinity is offered to other men?

SCENES, SUBCULTURES, AND THE QUEERSCAPE

An important aspect of understanding the overlapping assemblages of queer heavy metal is the interrogation of common tropes in the study of popular music: scenes and subcultures. Though numerous studies of popular music have focused on scenes and/or subcultures, I argue those reference points are too bounded to be applicable to the queering of heavy metal. Though both concepts provide better understanding of popular music in its sociocultural milieu, they do not provide a good framework for understanding the discursive and political status of queer individuals or the role masculinity plays in reifying heterosexual power in heavy metal. Scenes have been vital to the study of music, especially the cultural and social power of musical communities. As Mark Olson pointed out in his essay "Everybody Loves

Our Town," however, scene is too often reduced to scenery.[25] A scene is not simply the backdrop for the performance of heavy metal, it is the cultural space within which newcomers are initiated, educated, and transformed into insiders. As Will Straw suggested, scenes are cultural sites where cultural practices are in operation.[26] As such, the scenes of heavy metal are not simply the stages and mosh pits where metal is performed, it is all the spaces where individuals are enculturated as headbangers and metalheads. In fact, musical scenes are the spaces where "music signifies collective ideas, images and meanings."[27] Music scholar Lawrence Grossberg further elaborated on scenes when he suggested a musical scene is less defined by the sound than the social interactions that render such scenes authentic. For Grossberg, scenes are always and only situational, relying on fans and their differentiation.[28] "Audiences are constantly making their own cultural environment," wrote Grossberg, "from the cultural resources that are available to them."[29] Heavy metal, therefore, has many scenes depending upon the local cultures, peoples, and practices that define authentic heavy metal fandom in those places. Consequently, heavy metal scenes are everywhere and constantly shifting, and the ability of queer fans to take part in those scenes depends not on their ability to hide their sexuality and/or gender but on their ability to learn, adapt, and conform to the practices and signifiers of the local scene. Using the concept of the scene, it becomes quite clear why someone like Rob Halford is not an anomaly: he simply adopted the practices and signifiers necessary. The best example of this is in a forward Halford wrote for Philip Bashe's 1985 book *Heavy Metal Thunder*. "In concert, heavy metal is larger than life, so we performers try to be larger than life ourselves, as a sort of visual representation of the music," wrote Halford. "How else can I look other than the way I do? In what other costume could I perform heavy metal?"[30]

While scenes are vital to the understanding of popular music, they are much different than subcultures. Subcultures suggest two things: deviance from hegemonic norms, and behaviors regulated by the subculture's members themselves.[31] Perhaps the most important scholar in the study of subculture is Dick Hebdidge, whose work on style reframed the understanding of subcultural groups in music scenes. One can be both a member of a subculture and part of a scene. According to Hebdidge, subcultures require regulated behaviors but those behaviors are not constant. In his work on punk, Hebdidge wrote that while punk was constructed to signify chaos, it only did so based on a carefully ordered style that punk individuals policed themselves.[32] At the same time, subcultures are constantly shifting as the deviance and regulation shifted. As Hebdidge wrote: "It [a subculture] can form a unity which is either more or less organic, striving toward some ideal coherence, or more or less ruptural, reflecting the experience of breaks and contradictions."[33] When applied to queers as heavy metal fandom, subcultures can provide a way to understand the ways in which queer fans consume heavy metal music and operate in heavy metal spaces. For instance, scholar of gender Judith Halberstam proposed subcultural belonging in heavy metal provided a space for queer girls to experiment with their own masculinity by associating themselves with a strongly masculinist subculture.[34] In his study of lesbian fans of kd lang, geographer Gill Valentine wrote that young lesbian fans of lang's music created subcultural spaces where they could live out their identity vicariously through lang's songs.[35] Are young queer women looking to the subcultural space of heavy metal, with its deviance and order, as a way to live vicariously through the bodies and performances of hypermasculinity? At the very least, understanding heavy metal as a subculture provides a way for queer heavy metal fans to oppose the mainstream and experiment with their own gender and sexuality,while providing them with a sense of belonging. As Angela McRobbie wrote of young queer men in her essay "Settling Accounts With Subcultures":

> Does subcultural elevation of style threaten the official masculinity of straight society, which regards such fussiness as sissy? Does the skinheads' pathological hatred of 'queers' betray an uneasiness about their own fiercely defended male culture and style? Are subcultures providing relatively safe frameworks within which boys and young men can escape the pressures of heterosexuality?[36]

While both scenes and subcultures provide a space for individuals to experiment with their gender and sexuality, these two spatial systems do not necessarily provide for queer consciousness. In both cases, one must follow the order and enculturation of the scene or subculture. Consequently, queer fans can find themselves as subcultural queers in a heavy metal scene or subcultural metalheads in a queer scene. Where do these two spaces overlap and, when they do, how do queer metal fans negotiate the rules of each spatiality? Queer individuals must constantly negotiate their identity situationally, and often find themselves in hostile spaces and places. The same is true of heavy metal fans. When the two clash, however, it presents an interesting problem. How does a queer individual negotiate heavy metal fandom if their scene is homophobic and hostile? How do queers in heavy metal scenes and subcultures become subjects of scholarship if one's identity as a metal fan seemingly renders one's queer identity invisible? Essentially, this contested territory between the two identities creates two levels of marginalization: marginalization as a queer subject due to dominant masculinized heteronormativity and marginalization due to membership in the alternative social networks of heavy metal. This contested territory, this overlapping space between two margins, is queerscape.

The only way to deconstruct the many ways in which heavy metal is inherently queer is by pointing to queerness within heavy metal spaces. Especially in recent years, spatial metaphors have gained prominence in cultural studies. The use of terms such as interstitial, borderlands, boundaries, and locations are all reflections of the use of space as a metaphorical way of discussing power.[37] In the study of popular music such as heavy metal, the debate about spatial metaphors centers on the meanings of scenes, subcultures, and scapes. While each of these spatial arrangements offers the possibility of better understanding queerness in heavy metal, I argue queer heavy metal fans create a queerscape within the myriad scenes and subcultures of heavy metal. I do not think there is simply one formation of heavy metal. Rather, there are layers of subculture and scenes overlapping each other and within each of those layers is a queerscape. In fact, within this queerscape lies a field of possibilities that allow queer fans to reterritorialize heavy metal and to then resist the heteronormative and homophobic aspects of heavy metal so obvious to outsiders.

Understanding heavy metal as a queerscape allows scholars to understand the overlap between heavy metal identity and other marginalized identities, as well as creating the possibility for unchaining masculinity from the white male body. "A queerscape," wrote scholar Gordon Brent Ingram, "is essentially a sum total of subjectivities, some more closely linked, for a time, than others."[38] Originally proposed as a theory for architecture and the activist creation of public spaces, Ingram coined the term "queerscape" to explain a critical theory of queers in space. For Ingram, the goal of a theory of queerscapes was key to rethinking the common dichotomy of queer spaces as ephemeral or ghettoized. In addition, Ingram proposed queerscapes as a way of understanding the myriad ways in which same-sex desires are deployed, imagined, actualized, performed, and discursively produced in both exclusive and heteronormative places.[39] Perhaps most importantly, Ingram saw the queerscape as a space in which sexual minorities could engage in world-making. As Ingram wrote:

> The queerscape embodies divergent and sometimes competing and even conflicting strategies to make contact, to survive homophobia, and to make room for a diverse set of social and cultural experiences often grouped under the rubric of 'community.'[40]

José Esteban Muñoz, another scholar trying to deal with connections between space, performance, and identity, suggested minoritarian subjects used disidentification to construct an identity and correlating community. As Muñoz wrote: "Disidentification is about recycling and rethinking encoded meaning."[41] In the queerscapes of heavy metal, queer heavy metal fans are constantly recycling, reforming, and constructing new meanings for their mutually imbricated identities. The site at which the microphysics of spatiality and queer identity come together is inside the scenes, subcultures, and scapes of heavy metal music. The power of the queerscape to allow sexual minority individuals space for exploration, mutual defence, and world-making is not only part of heavy metal scenes, it is inherent in the heavy metal ethos: us against them, we stand together, the metal community.

This study of the queerscape of heavy metal will focus on three key aspects of such a queerscape: the desire-zones of the queerscape, the sounds and lyrics of heavy metal music and how they operate as part of a queerscape, and the symbolic borders (such as style) of the queerscape. As a site of resistance, spaces where the heavy metal queerscape appears develop into what Deleuze and Guattari termed "uncertain desire-zones."[42] These zones contain subordinate groups who seek to defend territory by representing an alternative to hegemonic social systems.[43] In other words, queer heavy metal fans and performers represent a counter-heteronormative possibility. Nurtured and created by the fans, queerscapes exist in clubs, concerts, and record stores without overtly challenging the heteronormative façade of heavy metal. Queer heavy metal fans and performers do not exist outside the mainstream or solely inside a queer enclave. Instead, they occupy a space, both literally and figuratively, of uncertain desire-zones in the queerscape. By existing in this uncertainty, queers in heavy metal maintain an anonymity that "gives the person the possibility to choose between what to reveal and what to conceal in any particular context."[44]

While the queerscape of heavy metal may not be visible to straight fans, it is visible to the queer fans who locate themselves in the places, sounds, and popular press of heavy metal. One example is an article in the September 2006 issue of *Decibel* magazine entitled "A Rainbow in the Dark." "So what's it like," asks the author in the introduction, "to actually be a homosexual *and* be into metal?"[45] The author interviewed several queer heavy metal performers and fans, including Rob Halford. In response to a question about his ability to negotiate his sexuality in supposedly homophobic heavy metal scenes, Halford explained:

> I never suffered any in-band intolerance or friction or nasty comments or that type of thing. I've certainly experienced it from some of the early tours with other bands and road crews. I heard it behind my back and I saw it. It didn't affect me. I was like 'Fuck you then.' There are still stereotypes that all gay men are effeminate and weak and queeny. Of course, nothing could be further from the truth, which is why I think it's unfortunate that that type of portrayal is still given to the straight general public. In my world, you couldn't have anything stronger or more masculine and intense.[46]

Clearly, according to Halford his sexual orientation was not new in 1998. In fact, his bandmates and other members of his heavy metal world knew about his sexuality. As Halford explained, however, belonging to the world of heavy metal brought his sexuality and his masculinity together. His two marginalized identities overlapped in his performance as a heavy metal singer. While heterosexual and mainstream heavy metal fans may have interpreted Halford's performance as the penultimate straight man's performance of power, Halford saw both his identity and his performance as the penultimate gay man's power. Only examining the queerscape in terms of desire-zones, as spaces where one's desires are also counter-hegemonic representations of a group territory, can we understand such performance as something more than a simple heavy metal masculine mirage.

The role of the sounds and lyrics of heavy metal music within the queerscape is to serve as a sonic representation of the queerscape itself. Though Ingram coined the term "queerscape" to deal directly with lived space, in this project I stretch queerscape to include sonic and symbolic space. Sonic and lyrical aspects of heavy metal in effect communicate the queerscape outside and beyond the space itself. It becomes a link to community, a memento of desire-zones, and a representation of the identity of queer folks in a heavy metal space. The music validates the queerscape and the individuals within the queerscape, as it provides a way to produce meanings and identities. In a play on Foucault's theory of heterotopia, scholar Josh Kun explains the power of music for minoritarian groups as audiotopia. According to Kun, audiotopias are spaces produced by music that offer listeners a way to imagine a different future. Such audiotopias begin in lived space and are then carried beyond that space by listeners and performers to different spaces and places. In addition, without the music the need for the space would not exist, thereby denying minoritarian groups a space in which to interact. The songs and sounds become signposts that mark both one's identity as a metal fan and one's identity as a queer person and lead the fan in and out of the queerscape. As Kun wrote:

> Sonic spaces offer effective utopian longings where several sites normally deemed incompatible are brought together, not only in the space of a particular piece of music itself, but in the production of social space and the mapping of geographical space that music makes possible as well.[47]

The third important pillar of the heavy metal queerscape is its symbolic borders. While lived spaces and places have physical borders, metaphorical spaces have symbolic borders. These borders operate as gatekeepers to identify insiders and outsiders and allow the queerscape to operate within a heavy metal culture that not only ignores but practically denies its existence. Such symbolic borders include style, coded language, the heavy metal pose, and the stereotypical symbols of queer communities. For example, the ubiquitous heavy metal T-shirt and leather jacket are practically a uniform of the heavy metal world. In queer communities, leather can have very specific meanings pertaining to one's gendered and sexual identity. In metal communities, it is the thing that marks you as metal the signifier. What if a metal fan in a leather jacket then puts a black handkerchief in their back pocket? Flagging black, in the coded queer world of hankies and bandanas, is a symbol of BDSM. If we consider the leather and studs pose of metal sprang from metal performers who purchased concert attire from queer-owner leather shops in New York and San Francisco, how do we explain the heterosexual acceptance of those symbols? And how do queer fans and performers who understand these symbols as symbolic borders separate queerscape markers from those symbols assimilated by heteronormative metal? By studying and understanding symbolic borders or the queerscape, such as coded language, leather, and flagging, the symbolic borders of the queerscape become more visible.

NOTES

1. Judith Halberstam, *Female Masculinity* (Durham: Duke University Press, 1998): 13.
2. Ibid., 2.
3. Jasbir K. Puar, "Queer Times, Queer Assemblages," *Social Text* 23, No. 3 (Fall-Winter 2005): 128.
4. Leo Bersani, "Is the Rectum a Grave?" in *Is the Rectum A Grave? And Other Essays* (Chicago: University of Chicago Press, 2010): 12.
5. Ibid., 25.
6. Sheila Whiteley, "Introduction," in *Sexing the Groove: Popular Music and Gender*, edited by Sheila Whiteley (London: Routledge 1997): xix.
7. Simon Frith and Angela McRobbie, "Rock and Sexuality," in *On Record: Pop, Rock, and the Written Word*, edited by Simon Frith and Andrew Goodwin (New York: Pantheon 1990): 375.
8. Walser, 114.
9. Brad Klypchak, *Performed Identity: Heavy Metal Musicians Between 1984 and 1991* (Berlin GE: VDM Verlag Dr Mueller, 2007): 194.
10. Helen Davies, "All Rock and Roll Is Homosocial: The Representation of Women in the British Rock Music Press," *Popular Music* 20, No. 3 (October 2001): 313.
11. Stan Denski and David Sholle, "Metal Men and Glamour Boys: Gender Performance in Heavy Metal," in *Men, Masculinity, and the Media*, edited by Steve Cray (London: Sage 1992): 49.
12. Ibid., 55.
13. Klypchak, 238.
14. Philip Bashe, *Heavy Metal Thunder: The Music, Its History, Its Heroes* (Garden City, NY: Dolphin Books, 1985): 7.
15. Leigh Krenske and Jim McKay, "'Hard and Heavy': Gender and Power in Heavy Metal Music Subculture." *Gender, Place and Culture* 7, No. 3 (2000): 290.
16. Ibid., 330.
17. Judith Halberstam, *The Queer Art of Failure* (Durham: Duke University Press, 2014): 95.
18. Simon Reynolds and Joy Press, *The Sex Revolts: Gender, Rebellion, and Rock 'n' Roll* (Cambridge: Harvard UP 1995): 244. Reynolds and Press took their concept of *macha* from the work of Dan Graham, who suggested women in rock used a "macha stance," an inversion of the male macho principle. See Dan Graham, *Rock My Religion: Writings and Projects 1965-1990*, ed. Brian Wallis (Boston: MIT Press, 1994).
19. Ibid., 248.

20. Walser, 115–116.
21. Ibid., 116.
22. Klypchak, 20. Halford's coming out is discussed in more detail in Chapter 4.
23. MTV News, "Judas Priest Speaks About Rob Halford's Sexual Openness." MTV Mews online, February 5, 1998, http://www.mtv.com/news/articles/1429869/judas-priest-speaks-about-rob-halfords-sexual-openness.jhtml.
24. Klypchak, 191.
25. Mark J.V. Olson, "'Everybody Loves Our Town': Scenes, Spatiality, Migrancy," in *Mapping the Beat: Popular Music and Contemporary Theory*, edited by Thomas Swiss, John Sloop, and Andrew Herman (Malden, MA: Blackwell 1998): 271.
26. Will Straw, "Sizing Up Record Collections: Gender and Connoisseurship in Rock Music Culture," in *Sexing the Groove: Popular Music and Gender*, edited by Sheila Whiteley (London: Routledge 1997): 9.
27. Sara Cohen, "Men Making A Scene: Rock Music and the Production of Gender," in *Sexing the Groove: Popular Music and Gender*, edited by Sheila Whiteley (London: Routledge 1997): 28.
28. Lawrence J. Grossberg, "Reflections of a Disappointed Music Scholar," in *Rock Over The Edge: Transformations in Popular Music Culture*, edited by Roger Beebe, Denise Fulbrook, and Ben Saunders (Durham: Duke UP 2002): 49.
29. Grossberg, "Is There A Fan," 53.
30. Bashe, *Heavy Metal*, ix.
31. Richard A. Peterson and Andy Bennett, "Introducing Music Scenes," in *Music Scenes: Local, Translocal, and Virtual*, edited by Andy Bennett and Richard A. Peterson (Nashville: Vanderbilt University Press, 2004): 3.
32. Dick Hebdidge, "Style As Homology and Signifying Practice," in *On Record: Pop, Rock, and the Written Word*, edited by Simon Frith and Andrew Goodwin (New York: Pantheon 1990): 56.
33. Ibid., 65.
34. Halberstam, Female Masculinity, 322.
35. Gill Valentine, "Creating Transgressive Space: The Music of kd lang," *Transactions of the Institute of British Geographers*, (New Series), 20, No. 4 (1995).
36. Angela McRobbie, "Settling Accounts With Subcultures: A Feminist Critique," in *On Record: Pop, Rock, and the Written Word*, edited by Simon Frith and Andrew Goodwin (New York: Pantheon 1990): 74.
37. Michael P. Brown, *Closet Space: Geographies of Metaphor From the Body to the Globe* (London: Routledge 2000): 3.
38. Gordon Brent Ingram, "Mapping the Shifting Queerscape: A Century of Homoerotic Space-Taking and Placemaking in Pacific Canada," paper presented to the Do Ask Do Tell: Outing Pacific Northwest History conference, Washington State Historical Museum, Tacoma, Washington, 1998, http://gordonbrentingram.ca/scholarship/wp-content/uploads/2008/12/ingram-1998-mapping-the-shifting-queerscape-space-taking-placemaking-in-pacific-canada-presented-in-tacoma.pdf: 43.
39. Gordon Brent Ingram, "Ten Arguments For a Theory of Queers in Public Space," paper presented to the Queer Frontiers Conference, International Lesbian and Gay Archives, University of Southern California, Los Angeles, California,1995, http://gordonbrentingram.ca/scholarship/wp-content/uploads/2008/12/ingram-1995-ten-arguments-for-a-theory-of-queers-in-public-space-presented-at-queer-frontiers-los-angeles.pdf: 7–9.

40. Ingram, "Mapping the Shifting Queerscape," 11.
41. José Esteban Muñoz, *Disidentifications: Queers of Color and the Performance of Politics* (Minneapolis: University of Minnesota Press, 1999): 31.
42. Muñoz, *Disidentifications*, 99–100.
43. Ibid., 114.
44. Catarina Frois, *The Anonymous Society: Identity, Transformation and Anonymity in 12 Step Associations* (Newcastle: Cambridge Scholars Publishing, 2009): 152.
45. Anthony Bartkewicz, "A Rainbow In The Dark," *Decibel* 23, September 2006: 64.
46. Ibid., 68.
47. Josh Kun, *Audiotopia: Music, Race and America* (Berkeley: University of California Press, 2005): 23.

2   Black Leather

Anything that bestows a sense of power to someone who feels generally powerless has to be attractive.[1]

Jus' lay me out toss on the charcoal lighter/An' fire me up smell the leather burn.

—Joan Jett, "Black Leather"[2]

Heavy metal fans sometimes refer to the uniform: jeans, t-shirt, and black leather jacket. This uniform, an amalgamation of styles, classes, cultures, and time, is also the ostensible signpost of masculinity. But how did this uniform develop and why does it serve as a supposed symbol of masculinity? And how do queer heavy metal fans today read black leather? This chapter, "Black Leather," explores the heavy metal style and its queer antecedents. Specifically, this chapter's focus is the queer formations of heavy metal through the leather and BDSM communities in queer culture. In this chapter I will consider the hallmark of heavy metal style – black leather – and examine if and how that traveled from queer leather enclaves to heavy metal enclaves. I will also present the heavy metal performance space, whether club, concert, or record store, as a space for queer cruising and sexual experience. Much of this chapter will be based on research at the national Leather Archives and Museum, where I was named Visiting Scholar for 2012–13. Using their collections, I will reconstruct the influence of queer leather subculture on heavy metal. My goal is to demonstrate, through ethnographic data and analysis of images, that the heavy metal style was borrowed from the leather community: metal style is leather's child. In addition, I argue queer leather style and heavy metal style are still in conversation, influencing each other constantly. This conversation is historical, cultural, and connects heavy metal with multiple outsider subjects. "The black leather jacket has always been the uniform of the bad, Hitler's Gestapo, the Hell's Angels, the Black Panthers, punk rockers, gay bar cruisers, rock'n'roll animals and the hardcore mutations of the eighties all adopted it as their own," wrote historian Mick Farren.[3]

My other goal in this project is to bring the history and culture of leather into the canons of sexuality, gender studies, and popular music studies. Whether due to the lack of understanding, sheer ignorance, or more likely a pointed refusal to include what is often stereotyped as misogynist and violent sexuality in academic writing, the exclusion of leather culture is epic in its proportion. The cultural milieu of leather, most strongly associated with gay men and masculine lesbian women who identify as BDSM, has shaped popular music since the end of World War II. Its influence is not stylistic alone but can also be found in performative posturing and theatrics, lyrical content, and in the identities of fans who read something more than heterosexual, missionary-position sex in the work of their rock idols. Though many scholars have written on the silencing of GLBTQ voices (and ears, I argue) in the academic study of popular music, there is no exploration of the incredible influence of queer folks, especially leather and/or BDSM identified queer folks, on popular music itself. John Gill, for example, has worked extensively on the idea of a "code of silence" in popular music that caused queer fans to seek coded meanings.[4] Scholar Robert DeChaine's work on queercore band Pansy Division, an important band in an overtly political music movement, suggested queercore bands worked "within the system in order to sabotage and undermine the cultural values which it holds up as normative and 'correct'."[5] Each of these examples, and hundreds of others, continue to place queerness as a background rather than the landscape itself. Rather than listening and watching for absences of queerness, it is time to see a queerscape on which popular music built its house. This is no more evident than in heavy metal, where queers have played a formative role in style, substance, lyrics, performance, and indeed the creation of the genre itself. How interesting that heavy metal is constantly portrayed as a bastion of straight and disenfranchised white males when its very foundations sit on a queerscape of gay performers, queer leather culture, and the influence of queers as promoters, performers, and especially fans. In his book on heavy metal, Robert Walser wrote:

> Metal is a fantastic genre, but it is one in which real social needs and desires are addressed and temporarily resolved in unreal ways. These unreal solutions are so attractive and effective precisely because they seem to step outside the normal social categories that construct the conflicts in the first place.[6]

I argue that indeed, some of these "unreal solutions" are unique in that they work as a disidentificatory practice. Rather than identify only as a metalhead, by identifying as a queer metalhead one both identifies and disidentifies with the conflict in place. When a queer fan sees a gay performer in heavy metal, or sees a performance that includes overtly homosexual practices on stage, or goes to a show in leather, they are at once challenging and conforming to heavy metal culture. Who is the interloper in such a space? When industrial metal band Rammstein comes on stage in bondage gear, with two band members on all fours being led on a leash, is it still a heterosexual male space? Whose "unreal solutions" are truly at work? In this chapter I will examine the history and development of a long-standing conversation between gay male music promotion, leather culture, and heavy metal. I plan to demonstrate the many ways in which heavy metal is a queerscape and metal's positioning as a bastion of male heterosexuality is in fact the only unreal solution in play.

THE ORIGINS OF BLACK LEATHER STYLE

There is little doubt that black leather as a style of clothing began at the end of World War II. Though German pilots wore head-to-toe black or brown leather in World War I, it remained the domain of military and police uniform until World War II.[7] Its growth as a stylistic sign came after World War II, when a surplus of leather jackets made for European and American soldiers were released into the open market. This simple market tool – the sale of military surplus – happened to coincide with three major social movements in American culture: the rise of motorcycles, the coalescing of gay cultural enclaves, and rock and roll. All three of those social movements were inextricably linked to the thousands of young men returned from service in World War II seeking male camaraderie and an escape from the shockingly mundane life in postwar America. According to one historian, the average age of a World War II veteran was only 26, and these young men doubtless suffered from what we would now call post-traumatic stress disorder. They no longer fit the mold of pre-war American masculinity.[8] Typically associated with the Gestapo, black leather was already marked as threatening. Interestingly, the Gestapo and SS black leather uniforms were also associated with homosexuality. Heinrich Himmler, leader of the SS, was responsible for much of the Nazi program against homosexuality, and he engaged in frequent discussions about homosexual men in the SS and Gestapo. At the same time, as historian Geoffrey Giles has explained, the Nazi heterocentrism leaned heavily on images and concepts of strongly homocentric, all-male organizations and homosocial behaviors of the mechanized German military.[9] This image, of the muscled young man in black leather, in the company of other men and astride a motorcycle, quickly became part of a postwar masculine ethos. Black leather became an "expression of revolt," a symbol of a new masculinity that called for long hair, denim, and the T-shirt.[10] While motorcycles were not new (Harley Davidson started production in 1903, the first motorcycle races in America began in 1909 near Los Angeles), it was the historical juncture of World War II, young veterans, and motorcycles that began the image of black leather as culturally threatening. Black leather's association with criminal behavior and licentiousness, however, started in 1947.

Hollister, California, was a long-term site of motorcycle racing. The home to a board track and dirt runs in the 1920s and 1930s, Hollister's population of 4,500 welcomed motorcycle racing as a major source of revenue. The racers of the 1930s, however, were not the same young men who returned to California after World War II. When motorcycle weekends at Hollister resumed for the Fourth of July weekend in 1947, the city opened bars and taverns and expected to welcome serious racers to the runs at nearby Memorial Park. Instead, hundreds of young veterans descended on Hollister, drinking and gathering in the streets and ignoring the American Motorcycle Association races. The city blocked the streets and called out more police, including forty California Highway Patrol Officers. Bikers were arrested for public drunkenness and disorderly conduct, but the unnecessary panic on the part of the police resulted in tear gas and the eviction of the bikers from Hollister.[11] The event would have easily have been forgotten if not for a *Life* magazine cover that month.[12] On July 21, 1947, *Life* ran a 115-word article on the Hollister incident titled "Cyclist's Holiday: He and friends terrorize a town." Above was one image captured by *San Francisco Chronicle* photographer Barney Petersen, showing cyclist Eddie Davenport on a Harley Davidson surrounded by broken beer bottles, drunk in the saddle, wearing what could easily be construed as service khakis.[13] This singular image introduced the biker outlaw to America and became the template for what would become a cultural fascination. Though Davenport wore khakis in the 1947 photograph, when the Hollister photograph and the supposed riot became the inspiration for Frank Rooney's 1951 short story *The Cyclist's Raid*, the lead character wore a black leather jacket. Two years later, Rooney's story became the film *The Wild One* and Marlon Brando was the new Davenport, wearing jeans, a leather and canvas military cap, and a black leather motorcycle jacket by Schott in New York.[14] The khaki and cap-wearing veteran was gone and the black leather outlaw had arrived.

The link between World War II veterans and the gay community in the 1940s is well documented. The attraction of gay men to post-World War II motorcycle and leather clubs was no doubt because of the power of the motorcycle, the outlaw image, and most of all the new image of masculinity that appeared. After Hollister and Brando's skulking leather biker outlaw image, the new masculinity was overtly sexualized and associated with the industrial and mechanical power of war machinery and the motorcycle. As John Preston wrote in *The Leatherman's Handbook*:

> One of the enticements of leather for many men was its connection with an ultimate heterosexual symbol of masculinity. … It wasn't just that those men represented the fantasized outlaw; they were also an unquestionably sexual male image. Part of the attraction of a motorcycle was the power and vibration of the big engine between a man's legs.[15]

According to Gayle Rubin, this overlap quickly identified itself with leather as a community marker.[16] Gay men gave biker black leather an erotic power and increasingly associated black leather with gay male masculinity.[17] It also associated black leather with roughness and power, and defied the public stereotype of effeminate homosexuals by linking gay men to postwar masculinity.[18] Last but certainly not least, leather became the symbol of camaraderie. "Leather came to mean more than a gay masculinity," wrote Gayle Rubin. "It also connoted brotherhood and group solidarity, on the one hand, and a kind of rebellious individualism on the other."[19] The Satyrs, the first gay organization in the United States with an official charter, was founded in 1954 in Los Angeles as a gay motorcycle club. Los Angeles and southern California, home to the Mattachine Society and a queer scene that would continue to inform queer culture and politics for the forseeable future, quickly spun out other gay motorcycle clubs: Oedipus in Los Angeles, Warlocks in San Francisco. Soon, gay motorcycle clubs were across the country.[20] The rise of black leather's association with motorcycles was, without doubt, inextricably linked to the growth and development of queer cultures in the post-World War II landscape. Gay motorcycle clubs led to the development of sadomasochism leather bars in cities with gay motorcycle clubs because the clubs provided a safe atmosphere for gay men to enact their BDSM desires in a safe space. As Mark Thompson wrote:

> The heavy leather garb of the biker (dictated by reasons of safety as much as anything else) became synonymous with the overt masculine attributes of its wearers. It was only natural, then, for S/M code and ritual to be informed by the lore of these black-jacketed riders.[21]

BLACK LEATHER AND ROCK MUSIC

The origins of rock music, and especially heavy metal, began in both America and England. Though the antecedents of rock and metal music have deep roots in everything from Mississippi Delta three-bar blues to London's glitter rock of the 1970s, the leather style of rock and metal is likely descended from an Atlantic crossing by two musicians: Gene Vincent and Eddie Cochran. Vincent was born Vincent Craddock in Virginia in 1935, while Edward Raymond Cochran was born in Minnesota in 1938 and raised by Oklahoma parents escaping the Dust Bowl. Both had early hits in America as rockabilly pioneers but found their biggest early audiences in England where their music had a greater following. Vincent joined the U.S. Navy in 1952, an underage enlistee who joined with his parents' permission. He was in an accident while riding a Triumph motorcycle in 1955, leaving him out of the military and permanently injured.[22] Cochran dropped out of high school to pursue music and made several early appearances wearing brown aviator bomber jackets. While in England, Vincent and Cochran found themselves in the midst of a burgeoning subculture of rockers, not unlike the greasers of America's Midwest. The rockers were themselves an off-shoot of American motorcycle culture that developed after Hollister and attracted young postwar veterans interested in rebelling against authority, British norms, and the good old days of the pre-World War II empire.[23] Rockers wore denim pants, black leather jackets, wallets with wallet chains, and white scarves. Vincent and Cochran came from postwar America where James Dean's *Rebel Without A Cause* (1955) had renewed a debate in America about rebellion, leather, teenagers, and questioning authority. Vincent appeared on stage in black leather in early 1960 at the request of Larry Parnes, the English tour manager handling Vincent and Cochran's double-bill tour of England. According to one scholar, Parnes was the "man who put rock'n'roll on the map in England."[24] He ran rock promotions for many young men in England's growing rock music scene, including Tommy Steele and Billy Fury. In fact, it was Parnes who put his performers on stage in leather jackets, starting with Billy Fury.[25] Parnes was open about his homosexuality, had managed clothing stores and factories before becoming a manager, and encouraged Vincent and other singers under his management to play up their sexuality on stage. Vincent wore black leather, not the bomber brown of previous appearances: black leather pants and shirt, black gloves, a white scarf, and boots that pulled over the leg brace he wore as a result of his accident.[26] Within a few days, Cochran began making stage appearances wearing the same costume. In a tragic accident, Cochran and Vincent were struck by a taxi in England in April 1960. While Vincent survived (though he further injured his leg), Cochran was thrown from the car while trying to protect his fiancée, Sharon Seeley. "Eddie and I," Vincent later stated, "were as close as two guys can get without being queer."[27] Both Cochran and Vincent were later inducted in the Rock and Roll Hall of Fame, and Vincent continued to record until his death from a ruptured ulcer resulting from his alcoholism. Their influence, however, was incredible. While their influence musically is well documented, their stylistic influence is less understood. Vincent's appearances in black leather were endlessly copied. For example, when Elvis Presley took the stage at the Grand Ole Opry in 1956, he wore a leather jacket and eye makeup. As Marjorie Garber discussed in her work *Vested Interests,* Presley was at once read as transgressing genders in his leather and makeup, and Opry manager Chet Atkins was quoted as comparing Presley's look to "guys kissin' in Key West."[28] Vincent played The Cavern Club in 1961 at the top of a bill that included The Beatles. Paul McCartney was wearing a leather shirt, the very brand of black leather shirt Cochran and Vincent wore. As one of the Cavern Club regulars recalled:

> Gene Vincent was top of the bill and knew our kid [Paul] was important. That is why he had his picture taken. He had full leathers and our kid had his full leathers, wow, and there is Gene the master, like Marlon Brando in *The Wild One,* he is on the Cavern stage and he is

going 'Be bop a lula, echo, echo, echo' and you can see the fans bored out of their heads. 'Gene Vincent? Excuse me. We're waiting for The Beatles.'[29]

When Larry Parnes died in 1989, having declined to manage the early Beatles and devoting himself to theater later in life, the man who was responsible for introducing black leather to rock and roll was remembered this way: "Parnes is said to have renamed some of his stars for their sexual potential, but though he undoubtedly adored the company of young men he was circumspect about mixing business with pleasure."[30]

While early rock drew its inspiration from Gestapo-turned-biker style, the gay men who had embraced black leather as a cultural symbol developed their own leather subculture. Drawing on the outlaw biker image in America and the style of British rockers, leathermen built a culture charged with sexuality, masculinity, and rebellion against sexuality itself. Leathermen were more than gay men in leather clothing. Rather, leathermen developed a subculture that was at once overtly homosexual, explicitly unassociated with the motorcycle, and increasingly connected with BDSM. Leathermen performed a dominating, aggressive hypermasculine machismo that transgressed the boundaries of heteronormativity connected to the outlaw biker image. The leatherman identity and style were also a denial of the cultural portrayal of gay men as effeminate, soft, and camp. "It presented a particular mode of decidedly masculine dress in a highly stylized form," wrote J. Stephen Edwards, "subverting the identity of masculine (and heterosexual) male biker and appearing more 'real man' than any heterosexual male might ever want to appear."[31]

Leathermen also embraced the criminalized portrayal of black leather, using its cultural power as a symbol of aggression. As John Preston wrote: "Leather was gay sexuality stripped of being nice."[32] By the time The Beatles were ditching their black leather for matching suits and a tour of America, leathermen had created a network of clubs, bars, and enclaves in major cities across America. But the black leather style of the leathermen was not as loose or soft as their rockabilly counterparts. The leathermen drew heavily on the biker image and, perhaps even more importantly, drew on Gestapo imagery to give leather a hard edge. One leader in this stylistic turn was Tom of Finland. Touko Valio Laaksonen was born in Finland in 1920. According to his biographers, Laaksonen slept with both Soviet and Nazi men when Finland was occupied during World War II.[33] According to his official biography, Laaksonen did not fulfill his desires for sex with men until he was drafted, and in his uniform, Laaksonen found the darkness of the streets and the soldiers, sailors, and SS men on motorcycles he lusted after.[34] Beginning in 1956, Laaksonen began publishing erotic drawings of gay men in Finnish and American muscle magazines under the name Tom. Laaksonen's imagery was often stark: policemen, soldiers, and sailors dominating other men, men in tight denim pants and jackboots with military caps on their heads, an exchange of power and violence encased in leather. Laaksonen's work became a hallmark of leather culture, published in the physique magazines that were often owned or edited by gay men in a growing leather scene. Gayle Rubin's work on the growth of leather culture in San Francisco is only one example. One of the most important centers of the leather world was Chicago. Historically home to an itinerant population of immigrant men, veterans, and workers, Chicago attracted thousands of gay and lesbian Americans in the years after World War II. One of those individuals was Chuck Renslow, who founded Kris Studio in 1954 as a publishing house for men's muscle magazines. Along with his lover Dom "Etienne" Orejudos (a muscle and leather artist influenced by Tom of Finland), Renslow opened the Gold Coast bar in 1958, the oldest leather bar in the United States.[35] The walls of the Gold Coast were adorned with large paintings of men in leather, denim, and uniforms in the style of Tom of Finland. Leather bars like the Gold Coast began holding leather pageants, displays of leathermen and their boys that harkened back to the pre-World War II queer world in urban jazz clubs. Bars had coded names: Eagle, taken from the symbol for a Harley, industrial and working-class names with a tongue-in-cheek double meaning such as The Manhole or San Francisco's Tool Box, versions of criminality such as Kansas City's Cell Block, or plays on the word "triangle" as a reminder of the pink triangle worn by homosexuals persecuted by the Nazi regime. As Victoria Steele explained in *Fetish*, the fetishized style and performance of leathermen were not just about sexuality, they were about power and perception.[36]

THE ORIGINS OF HEAVY METAL FASHION

Any discussion of the origins of heavy metal is bound by competing narratives. Metal fans and scholars themselves spend countless hours debating the first metal recording or the first metal band in an attempt to identify the roots of the sound, the scene, and the style. There is little doubt heavy metal as a sound emerged from industrial cities such as Birmingham and Walsall in northern England, Detroit and New York in America. Heavily influenced by the music of American blues and the clave rhythm Bo Diddley beat used by early American rock and rockabilly musicians including Eddie Cochran, heavy metal combined 1950s rhythms with the industrial and mechanized sounds that permeated the homes of the musicians. In 1968, Blue Cheer released its first album, *Vincentus Eruptum*, considered by some yo be the first heavy metal album. The first release was a cover of Eddie Cochran's hit "Summertime Blues." While English bands such as The Rolling Stones continued to record blues-based rock, Black Sabbath, Deep Purple, and Led Zeppelin produced the downtuned, industrial sounds of heavy metal. Iggy Pop and The Stooges, and later Fred "Sonic" Smith and the MC5, began infusing American rock with the industrial sounds of Detroit.

At the same time, heavy metal performers were beginning to create the style linked with the music: the heavy metal uniform. The examination of heavy metal style, however, has not made adequate connections to the leathermen of the 1960s and 1970s. In fact, the heavy metal style of studded leather jackets and motorcycle boots is typically connected only to biker culture in Britain and America and not to the quickly growing leather culture. For example, Deena Weinstein wrote: "elements of metal style are mainly derived from two late 1960s youth cultures: motorcycle culture (the bikers in Britain and the 'outlaw' gangs such as the Hell's Angels in the United States) and the hippies."[37] In truth, any examination of the images of early heavy metal reveal a style much more attuned to hippies than to bikers. Led Zeppelin's look consisted of flowing shirts, bell-bottom jeans, and floppy hats, their few leather items limited to long leather coats popular in the late 1960s and 1970s. Early Black Sabbath images show Ozzy Osbourne in a black leather jacket but not a motorcycle jacket: a double-breasted and belted jacket with butterfly collar, popular throughout the Western world at this time. These styles were the offshoots of Cochran and Vincent and the result of Elvis Presley's appearance on television in black leather in 1968. Even in Iggy Pop and The Stooges 1969 release "I Wanna Be Your Dog," whose lyrics were clearly related to BDSM practices, Iggy Pop writhed across the stage in gold lamé pants and eye makeup. Was this the hypermasculinity of outlaw bikers?

In actuality, the style of heavy metal that began with Cochran and Vincent in the early 1960s had burgeoned into a working-class rebellion against middle-class values. The hippie movement, its refusal to follow middle-class values, and the focus on ideals such as free love and communitarian economics did not apply very well to the children of working-class families. In industrial cities such as Birmingham (Black Sabbath), Walsall (Judas Priest), Detroit (Iggy Pop and Alice Cooper), New York (Blue Oyster Cult and Kiss), Boston (Aerosmith), and San Francisco (Blue Cheer), bands developed that rebelled against hippie ideals and middle-class values. Heavy metal sound and style reflected this: denim and boiled leather jackets, work boots, songs about hard work and harder playing. Another part of this perfect storm was a sudden nostalgia for the 1950s. *American Graffiti* (1973) and *Grease* (1978), along with the ten-year run of *Happy Days* (1974–1984) on American television renewed interest in jeans, white T-shirts, and black leather jackets.[38] The characters in these sources of inspiration, from the guys working in the shop in *Grease* to Arthur "The Fonz" Fonzarelli, were working-class guys with a gift for mechanics, women, and cool. Consider The Fonz, a character written as a high-school dropout abandoned by his family, able to fix anything mechanical simply by hitting it with his fist, snapping in the air for women to surround him. These characters were 1950s bikers, however, with pipe-leg jeans and motorcycle jackets, fast cars, and fast women, not the bullet belts and studded leathers of the BDSM world. Their look was an old story in rock, considered old news, a look even Elvis

Presley had cast off by the 1970s. So while bikers and 1950s culture enjoyed a nostalgic revival, rock musicians were adhering to the evolution of rock style born of Woodstock.

The only exception to that post-Woodstock appearance was in the performances of a handful of female rock musicians. From all its historical sources, leather was increasingly used by female rock musicians as a way to gain a foothold in the rock industry and perhaps as a way to announce the role of women in both popular music and in leather culture. There is little doubt that female rock musicians who sought to shake off the post-Woodstock image of the female musician moved into leather. According to one scholar, women in the British rock scene in the early 1970s used leather as a way to adopt a "more masculine, emancipated image."[39] Women from working-class backgrounds already had a long history of masculine dressing as a way of gaining access to patriarchal spaces, a phenomenon dating as far back as one can find. Certainly, young women who wanted to rock, who came from working-class backgrounds, and looked to early rock musicians for inspiration would be drawn to leather. As Amy Wilkins noted, negotiating the cultural pressure to conform to model that required women to be the caretakers of relationships also made it difficult for women to express their own desires.[40] But were female rock musicians displaying a masculine code alone or expressing themselves in a different way? How does a woman take pleasure in being the object of desire and fulfill her own desires where the threat of violence or the possibility of being completely ignored are always prevalent? "These contradictions," wrote Wilkins, "make it hard to pin down behaviors as either clearly subversive or clearly oppressive."[41] So were female rock musicians wearing leather to subvert the masculine rock code or not?

Throughout the 1970s, heavy metal was developing in the United States and Europe and leather culture was spreading just as rapidly. Women arrived on the hard rock and heavy metal scene at the same time. Though these women in rock were descended from the history of women in music, from the blues through the blues rock of Janis Joplin and the psychedelic rock of Grace Slick, a few women in rock took on a harder edge informed by the heavily masculine look of bikers, working-class heroes, and a rising feminist movement that questioned women's dress. Also informing this new movement was leather culture, which grew and developed its own women-centered organizations at the same time. While women were always part of the leather scenes in cities such as Chicago and San Francisco through bars and organizations already in existence, the lesbian and feminist movements in the 1970s informed leather culture as much as it did any other social structure of the time. The Society of Janus, a support organization for S/M folks, was formed in San Francisco in 1975. Samois, a group officially organized to support women who were S/M practitioners, was formed in 1978 in the same city, an outgrowth of meetings in leather bars and Society of Janus gatherings.[42]

Though not a heavy metal artist herself, Suzi Quatro continues to be an influence on women in heavy metal, whether performers or fans. Quatro emerged from the 1960s rock scene in working-class Detroit. A contemporary of Iggy Pop, Alice Cooper, and other emerging rock musicians from the upper Midwest, Quatro began as a bass player in a garage band in 1964. She was discovered by a British producer and had her first hit in 1973 with "Can the Can," a number one hit on the British charts. She continued to have a string of hits in the U.K. but never made the same impression on American charts. She appeared, and still appears, on stage in a leather catsuit that was the idea of Quatro's agent, Mickie Most, with a dog collar around her neck. She performed songs by male rock singers, recording covers of songs by rock and roll legends: Chuck Berry, The Rolling Stones, The Beatles, and Elvis Presley. She did not, however, change the pronouns in her recordings. As Philip Auslander has noted, Quattro sang "I Wanna Be Your Man" just as written, and appeared swathed in leather and without makeup.[43] She was a response to the glam and glitter of David Bowie and the post-Woodstock hippie rock of Janis Joplin and Grace Slick, a switcher of genders. Auslander suggests Quatro is the very definition of "cock rock" without the "cock," a powerfully potent combination of leather and the female form, with a low slung bass and a generation of young British boys at her feet.[44] Quatro is most famous in the U.S. as Leather Tuscadero, the character introduced in the television series *Happy Days*. She was introduced to the audience as the sister of Fonzie's girlfriend, Pinky Tuscadero, and first appeared in tight jeans, a leather jacket, and a Harley eagle T-shirt. In a July 2013 interview, Quatro told *The Telegraph* reporter Neil McCormick: "To this day, when I zip up, it just feels like I'm zipping on Suzi Quatro."[45] Though Quatro's style and gender-bending performance were highly influential, her use of S/M accoutrements such as the dog collar went unnoticed.

The question is this: how did heavy metal go from the striped bellbottoms and boiled brown leather coats of early Black Sabbath to the bondage-influenced style of Judas Priest and later bands? The answer lies in one man: Rob Halford. Halford was born in 1951 and raised in Walsall, England. In 1969 at the age of eighteen, Halford was introduced to the already formed band Judas Priest. Though the band had existed for a while as a blues-rock band, Halford's operatic singing style brought a different sound to the band. After releasing their single "Rocka Rolla" in 1974, the band began to grow in popularity. Their sound was increasingly industrial, featuring Halford's soaring falsetto paired with two lead guitars and a driven, down-tuned backbeat. In the 1970s, Judas Priest's members dressed much like their counterparts in Black Sabbath or Motorhead: denim, flowing shirts, boiled leather jackets. When Judas Priest arrived in American for their 1978 "Hell Bent for Leather" tour, all of that changed.

Though Halford was undoubtedly influenced by biker culture and blues-rock aesthetics, Halford took the stage in 1978 in the leathers and gear of a leatherman. This was not the first time leather style appeared on stage;

after all, Glenn Hughes appeared as Leatherman in the Village People from 1977–1979. The difference was the audience. Hughes's performances were part of the disco movement in America, one strongly associated with gay culture in America. Hughes himself was a gay cabaret singer, recruited along with his fellow performers in The Village People specifically to entertain in gay clubs and bathhouses. Halford's audience was different. The growing audience for hard rock and heavy metal was male, ostensibly straight, and strongly attached to a hypermasculine portrayal of hard work and hard sex. The audience was portrayed as a bastion of straight, young male behavior. Halford brought to metal a masculinity beyond hypermasculinity, the aggression and overt homosexuality of gay leathersex. Seeking an outlet for his sexual identity, he went to a leather shop in London and purchased a whip, military cap, studded leather jacket, and a Sam Brown belt (crosses the chest). He rode onto the stage on a Harley in 1978 in his leatherman gear and changed heavy metal permanently. When Halford publicly came out as a gay man in 1998, he explained the new look this way:

> So I said, 'OK, I'm a gay man and I'm into leather and that sexual side of the leather world and I'm gonna bring that on stage.' So I came onstage wearing the leather stuff and the motorcycle, and for the first time I felt like, 'God this feels so good. This feels so right.'[46]

Halford further discussed his use of leatherman clothing and gear in a *VH 1: Behind the Music* special on Judas Priest:

> Up until that moment, the look had not been completely tied in, as I felt, to the sound. So putting on this kind of stuff suddenly, you know, you look yourself in the mirror, you listen to the music, and it just connects. Let's face it, I was expressing myself every night when I went out in all that leather stuff. I was going out on stage every night, looking like Glenn from the Village People, and people weren't getting it.[47]

Within a year, other heavy metal bands began to copy Halford's leatherman look. Alice Cooper appeared in 1978 with leader singer Alice wearing all white, with one costume change into a Dracula tuxedo and cloak. One year later in 1979, Alice appeared onstage in bondage gear, straitjackets, carrying a riding crop. Soon every heavy metal group had to wear studs, jackets, military caps, and jackboots. Whips and crops became required. As a reporter for rock magazine *Creem* put it in September 1986, Judas Priest guitarist K.K. Downing "used to moan that he had to look twice at Iron Maiden to make sure Dave Murray wasn't really him."[48]

Far from the boiled leather jackets of England or the torn theatrical costumes of KISS, the leather Halford brought to metal was not just clothing but an aesthetic intended as a signal of marginalized sexuality. It was, and still is, an aesthetic signal that reads as motorcycle masculinity outside the queerscape, but inside the queerscape it is a signal of sexual subcultures and queer communities. This look was not unknown to mainstream popular culture as a signal of sexuality – after all, Glenn Hughes became Leatherman in the Village People in 1977 – but inside heavy metal the leatherman look was twisted into a sign post of heteronormative masculinity, despite its overt homoerotic aesthetic. Clearly, the leather look Halford introduced to metal came from the gay men's leather scenes of the 1960s and 1970s and continued to be reflected back in those leather scenes in the 1990s and beyond. For example, the logo for the International Mr. Leather competition in 1993 copied Halford's pose to near perfection. In essence, heavy metal's aesthetic was always a queer one. As a site of resistance, the heavy metal queerscape developed into what Deleuze and Guattari termed "uncertain desire-zones." Queer metal fans seek, in the spaces of heavy metal performance, the representation of their own desires. As a result, black leather operates within a series of performances, both reifying and challenging definitions of gender and sexuality in the heavy metal queerscape.

Figure 2.1 T-shirt from the 1993 International Mr. Leather competition, a competition for male-bodied members of the leather/BDSM community. The T-shirt image is based on the image of Rob Halford and demonstrates the crossover between the leather/BDSM and metal communities.

Another example of the queerscape is in its portrayal of leatherwomen. As Halford and Judas Priest continued to experiment with leather style and lyrics in their music, leatherwomen continued to develop a strongly political

movement. This movement was attacked by feminism as patriarchal posturing, and with its insistence on leaning towards straight male fans, heavy
metal portrayed leatherwomen as wanton, sexually available, visual spectacles. This was not excluded from leather culture, where leatherwomen
(regardless of the sex and gender of their sexual partners) could be masculine or feminine, submissive or dominant. The version that rose in heavy
metal, however, was the image of the feminine dominatrix, a revisioning
of S/M that positioned dominant women as there for a straight man's pain
and pleasure. No longer the gender bending of Leather Tuscadero, this new
image borrowed high femme leatherwomen and reimagined them outside
the leather culture that bore them. One example is The Runaways, a band
formed by promoter Kim Fowley specifically to create an all-female rock
band. The Runaways included Suzi Quatro fan Joan Jett and a young singer
named Cherrie Currie. Fowley dressed the girls in leather except for Currie,
who dressed in lingerie, corsets, stockings and garters, and stiletto heels. The
cock-rock woman was, in rock's imagination, temporarily moved to the back
so the corseted mistress could whip her male fans into shape. The success of
The Runaways in Japan and Europe led to more women in hard rock and
then heavy metal. Doro Pesch, a German power metal singer and member of
The Warlocks, burst onto the metal scene in 1980 in chaps and leather. In the
Sam Dunn film *Metal: A Headbanger's Journey*, Pesch described her clothing
and performance as specifically masculine, and explained she refused to bow
to promoter demands that she look more feminine.[49] Her album covers,
however, borrowed heavily from images of the feminine dominatrix.

The question that emerges is this: how did leather culture become the stereotypical image of heavy metal without being identified as such? Because
heavy metal is a queerscape, there was no need to identify anything. That
heterosexual critics, photographers, producers, and fans interpreted the
leather influence as straight is, in fact, proof the queerscape existed. In
her discussion of queerscape theory, scholar Helen Leung explained queerscapes challenge heteronormativity in the mainstream public space. As
Leung wrote:

> In the face of heteronormative ideology, queer desire has always
> demanded that its subjects negotiate in a world that refuses to legiti-
> mize their intimate relations and forge connections that often remain
> unintelligible in mainstream discourses.[50]

Heavy metal, in essence, became that queerscape, that space and place
where queer fans found intelligible signs. That Halford's leathers were not
resoundingly refused by the heteronormative world of rock music is not
surprising because they attracted attention, press, and dollars from a generation of people for whom the post-Woodstock world did not translate. Heavy
metal was always a place of queer connections, rendered unintelligible to
the heteronormative world.

Halford's introduction of BDSM to heavy metal remains a primary force in the genre's sounds, visuals, and style. No longer in the long hair and T-shirts of mainstream rock, Halford had closely cut hair and was shirtless beneath his leathers. As metal continued to grow in the 1980s, Halford's close-cropped hair and boots were rejoined with Nazi-esque imagery. Doc Martens, the classic English shoe preferred by bikers and rockers since 1913, became the preferred shoe of heavy metal fans, Riot Grrl followers, and homocore fans. Queer punk fans, who saw themselves as outsiders in punk scenes, adopted the homocore style as an indication of both their punkness and their queer identities. In his queer zine *J.D.'s*, queer punk and artist Bruce LaBruce combined heavy metal, punk fandom, and leather culture as specific signposts of queerness in musical scenes.[51] For example, *J.D.'s* Issue #1 featured a cartoon reminiscent of Tom of Finland's drawings of leathered police officers dominating civilian men against trees, except the *J.D.'s* cartoon had a gender-bending twist: the characters were all women. In LaBruce's zine, the threatening leathersex was from, by, and for women, a theme further explored in Issue #3 with its pictorial use of women on motorcycles, in leathers, and with whips.[52] Goth and industrial metal fans embraced bondage gear, leather, and Doc Martens as part of their uniform. Eventually, Doc Martens, denim and leather jackets, and short hair became synonymous with the 1980s queer movement.[53] The goth and industrial movements, with their roots in both heavy metal and alternative sexuality, found homes in the leather bars of Europe and America. "There were a number of gay men who were what I suppose would now be described as Goths, who really wanted the best of both of these two worlds," wrote Healy in *Gay Skins*. "The funny thing was that the gay pub in town did attract a lot of Goths: it was somewhere that they could go and not be thrown out for the way they looked."[54] Another example of this connection between goth and industrial heavy metal and BDSM sexual style is in the development of BDSM explicit goth and industrial metal in the 1990s. Led by bands such as Rammstein, Marilyn Manson, and Nine Inch Nails, goth and industrial metal delved deeply into the BDSM foundation of Halford's stylistic charge. Rammstein was founded in Berlin in 1994, and combined industrial sounds with heavy metal riffs and German classical music. Their album covers and stage shows have led to constant questioning about the band members and their sexuality, including assertions they might be closeted gay Nazis.[55] As part of their stage show since 1997, Rammstein's lead singer Till Lindemann rides a gigantic phallus during the song "Buch Dich," spurting milk all over the crowd.[56] During their 2012 tour of the United States, Rammstein entered the arena via a raised catwalk, with Lindemann leading four band members in on leashes and Sam Brown harnesses. The lyrics for "Buck Dich," from their album *Sennsucht,* translated as *Bend Over,* paint an S&M scene of a submissive disappointing their master: "Bend over, I command you/turn your visage away from me."[57] For Christmas 2009, Rammstein issued a special box set that contained one CD, a pair of handcuffs, a bottle of lubricant, and silicon dildoes modeled from each of the six band members. Earlier that year, the band's newest release, "Ich tu dir weh," was banned in Germany because it spread BDSM to minors. The video showed band guitarist Richard Kruspe with a naked woman in an S&M mask over his knee, preparing to strike her, to the lyrics "It does you good/Hear how it screams."[58] Rammstein was also banned in Russia and Belarus in 2012 for promoting homosexuality and pedophilia and for spanking each other on stage.

Marilyn Manson, founded in Florida in 1990 by Brian "Marilyn Manson" Warner, became a catalyst for a great deal of debate about gender, sexuality, and heavy metal in the 1990s. Marilyn Manson shows and videos featured Warner and bandmates dressed in corsets, straightjackets, bloody post-surgical bandages, and Nazi-esque uniforms with the band's logo in place of a swastika.[59] Marilyn Manson's song titles and lyrics make frequent use of BDSM imagery or at least the conception of such imagery. Songs such as "Cake and Sodomy" (1994) and "Everlasting Cocksucker" (1995) are a few examples. The link between Halford's introduction of BDSM and Marilyn Manson's use of BDSM explicitly in lyrics is perhaps best illustrated by the 2012 song "Pistol Whipped" from the album *Born Villain*: "When I undo my belt/you melt and you walk away."[60]

The best example of the continued importance of BDSM in heavy metal lies in the work of Trent Reznor. Reznor was the founder and remains the only original member of Nine Inch Nails, which he founded in San Francisco in 1988. He is also surrounded by rumors about his own identity, a topic about which he remains silent. Nine Inch Nails (NIN) is considered a cornerstone of industrial metal, combining screaming vocals with industrial noise, and lyrics focused on despair, resignation, and power exchange. NIN's 1992 album *Broken* featured the song "Happiness is Slavery," the video for which was banned on its release. "Happiness is Slavery" is a title taken from the preface of the bondage novel *Story of O*, and the video featuring S&M performance artist Bob Flanagan showed Flanagan submitting to domination by a machine. Reznor's lyrics were strictly S&M: "Slave screams he hears but doesn't want to listen/Slave screams he's being beat into submission."[61] In the video, Reznor sits locked in a small cage. In a separate room Flanagan enters, lights a candle, and ceremoniously strips, folds his clothes, and washes himself before lying in the machine. The machine then engages in a variety of S&M practices, including piercing, cock and ball torture, and cutting. At the end Flanagan is ground by the machine and used to feed the garden below. Once Flanagan is gone, Reznor walks in, lights the candle, and prepares to begin the ceremony again.[62] Here the industrial machine is not only the soundtrack, it is the sexual process itself. Reznor was again censored with the release of NIN's best-known song, "Closer." Titled "Closer to God" when it was released as a single, the song is about sexual obsession. The video for "Closer" is shot on grainy film, recalling underground pornography or homemade films. Reznor appears several times: hanging from shackles in an S&M hood, seated against a wall with a ball gag in his mouth, all in a medical scene surrounded by diagrams of genitalia and various animals suspended or preserved in the scene. Reznor's lyrics: "You let me violate you, you let me desecrate you/You let me penetrate you, you let me complicate you."[63]

Perhaps the greatest example of the queerscape crossing of masculinized heavy metal and BDSM sexuality is in Reznor's work as a producer. Reznor has produced albums for NIN and Marilyn Manson, among others, but his most important queerscape project is a single album by the band 2wo. 2wo was founded by Rob Halford after he publicly came out in 1998 and after he left Judas Priest to strike out on his own. 2wo was a major departure from Priest's driving heavy metal. Instead, on the album titled *Voyeurs*, Halford moved into the industrial metal of NIN and Rammstein with an album that was entirely about BDSM. Song titles on *Voyeurs* included "I Am A Pig," "Leave Me Alone," and "Gimp." The only single from the 2wo album was "I Am A Pig." The video opened in what appears to be a basement sex club with various scenes of bondage, cross-dressing and drag, leathersex and stripping. The song features Halford's soaring voice and the last shot is Halford himself: head shaved, goatee blackened, wrapped in furs and looking towards the sky. The liner notes feature the same image of Halford, this time with a subway car in the background, and when folded out the liner notes include several scenes of bondage and domination through the windows of the passing subway.[64] This album was nothing like Judas Priest and did not resemble Halford's later work with other bands. Was this album Halford's coming out as a BDSM leatherman? In his interview for *Behind the Music*, Halford spoke about using the whip on stage:

> If I'd be on stage and I'd see someone getting into the whip ... you like this do you? Some more [motions whipping]. ... You start wailing on their ass. ... It's amazing how people will, you know ... [chuckles] ... get into a good thrashing [clears throat and looks serious]. We all need a good thrashing now and again.[65]

In the lyrics for 2wo's "I Am A Pig," Halford makes a potential allusion to his years in Judas Priest: "Don't be stupid everybody knows/I was only straightening my clothes."[66]

In her essay on the famous BDSM club The Catacombs, Gayle Rubin discussed the importance of the soundtrack to BDSM sexuality. In the first issue of *Brat Attack*, a zine for S/M lesbian women published in San Francisco in the 1990s, writers published a "Kinky Music Hall of Fame" featuring songs recommended for BDSM scenes. No longer the disco soundtrack of the 1970s, this list features two industrial metal songs: "Head Like A Hole" and "Pretty Hate Machine," both by Nine Inch Nails.[67] Presentation notes titled "Music in Your Toybag" cite Metallica's *Black Album* and the heavily industrial metal soundtrack to the film *The*

Matrix as preferred music for triggering "tempos of whipping, spanking, etc. lyrics talk for top/dom (mouthing along)."[68] A 1998 pamphlet entitled "Music in the Scene" is an A to Z listing of music appropriate to BDSM play, and among the goth and ambient selections are all three Nine Inch Nails albums, two Marilyn Manson albums, and the industrial metal band Front Line Assembly. Metal's pre-Halford imagery of death, graveyards, and upside-down crosses began to appear in leather culture after Halford came out. Biblical and religious imagery, an old staple of heavy metal borrowed largely from the Spanish Inquisition and later from Norse and Viking history, also crossed into leather culture in distinctly heavy metal ways. One example is the poster "Jesus Is Coming," promoting a leather party in San Francisco in the 1990s. The poster image is taken from a Black Sabbath album cover but the demons are revisioned as BDSM practitioners in leather, latex, and masks. T-shirts became popular in leather culture as advertisements, a move taken entirely from heavy metal's use of the T-shirt as its primary method of marketing and its primary use as a show of solidarity among fans. A 2003 BDSM fundraiser for AIDS charities was titled "Back in Black," the title of an influential hard rock/heavy metal album by the band AC/DC used in a poster that made triple entendres of blackness, leather, and bisexuality. The best example of the conversation between leather culture and metal culture, however, is the patched vest. Bike clubs, beginning in the 1950s, offered patches for its members to wear on the backs of their jackets or on a denim vest that could be worn alone or over the jacket. Heavy metal took the denim vest from its working-class roots, where the jacket often came as part of a blue-collar uniform and its first patch was likely the employee's name. Heavy metal bands quickly began producing patches as a cheap way to promote themselves and help fans identify themselves as metalheads. By the 1980s, a denim jacket with patches was part of the metal uniform and that style continues today. Metal bands still sell patches and heavy metal fans adorn both denim and black vests with the patches of their favorite bands. Leather biker clubs offered large back patches to their members as well, but in the 1970s and 1980s leather clubs, bars, and gatherings also offered patches. Many people who identified with leather and BDSM began sporting patch-covered vests over their leather jackets. The 1999 patch for the leather/BDSM organization FIST shows a hand and arm sheathed in studded leather reminiscent of Halford's defiant 1970s poses, and in the fist is a single red rose with a falling drop of blood. The title chosen for the 1998 New Mexico leather gathering was Heavy Metal and its commemorative pin shows a pair of handcuffs. When Rob Halford came out, he opened a door that swung both ways. "You know, for years I never understood why I was called to an early teenage world of heavy metal, what purpose it had in making me who I am today," wrote Ken Kinakin in his essay "Rob and Me." "Now it is in focus; it all seems so clear. ... Heavy metal made me gay and I am proud."[69]

Figure 2.2 Motorcycle jacket and vest of a gay leatherman, with patches and pins from motorcycle runs and leather/BDSM clubs across America. From the collections of and permission from Leather Archives and Museum, Chicago, Illinois.

Figure 2.3 Closeup of gay leatherman's vest showing patches and pins. From the collections of and permission from Leather Archives and Museum, Chicago, Illinois.

Figure 2.4 Image of metal fan's vest, also known as battle vest or armor. Rather than patches from motorcycle runs and clubs, this metal vest has patches from metal bands, tours, and concerts. Vest and image courtesy of Joseph Bauer.

Figure 2.5 Studded jacket of the author. Permission from the author.

In her discussion of homocore, scholar Ashley Dawson suggests that even the most overtly heterosexual masculinity carries a strongly homosexual eroticism. "Homocore's subcultural stylists denaturalize the hegemonic discourse of gender by appropriating the elements of this discourse and rearticulating them," wrote Dawson, "thereby offering up an alternate reality."[70] Studies of heavy metal have, however, relied on heterosexual masculinity as the only way to conceptualize performance. Heavy metal's heterosexual masculinity, territorialized as part of a queerscape where signposts could be clearly read, were accepted as hypermasculine unreal solutions to queering sexuality by the straight, white listeners, critics, and scholars. While this queerscape may appear ephemeral, ghettoized, and even reduced by its connections to heavy metal, the two are not incongruous. Rather, a queerscape is a social and cultural space regardless of its status in queer politics, popular music, leather culture, biker history, or any other hierarchical valuation. According to Gordon Brett Ingram, queerscapes build provisional alliances to remain in the public sphere, visible and readable to all who seek them.[71] This is where heavy metal sits, as a queerscape in clear public view, open to anyone who enters, the steady thumping bass line on which hypermasculinity has based its performance. That some of heavy metal may not be empathetic is, in a word, expected. Queer fans, performers, writers, and musicians all live in a world where some hatred of queer identities, and leather identities, is expected. Acceptance is neither expected nor required, a belief heavy metal fans share when talking about their own culture. Sam Dunn stated at the end of his film *Metal: A Headbanger's Journey* that if the viewer did not get it, that was OK because heavy metal fans do not need to be understood. The queerscape mirrors, or rather authored, that very sentiment. As Gordon Brett Ingram put it more elegantly:

> The queerscape embodies divergent and sometimes competing and even conflicting strategies to make contact, to survive homophobia, and to make room for a diverse set of social and arbitrary experiences often grouped under the rubric of 'community.'[72]

To paraphrase Sam Dunn's conclusion in *Metal: A Headbanger's Journey*, if heterosexual, heteronormative, and masculinist heavy metal folk do not get that, it is OK. The queer fans of heavy metal have Halford and they do not need you: you need them.

NOTES

1. Mick Farren, *The Black Leather Jacket* (New York: Abbeville Press, 1985): 12.
2. Joan Jett, *Fetish*, Polygram, ASIN B00000J7QA, released June 8, 1999, compact disc.

3. Farren, *The Black Leather Jacket*, 12.

4. John Gill, *Queer Noises: Male and Female Homosexuality in Twentieth Century Music* (Minneapolis: University of Minnesota Press, 1995).

5. D. Robert DeChaine, "Mapping Subversion: Queercore Music's Playful Discourse of Resistance," *Popular Music and Society* 21, No. 4 (1997): 9.

6. Walser, *Running with the Devil*, 133–134.

7. L. and M. Cuirmale, "Gay Leather Fetish History." Accessed June 24, 2014. http://www.cuirmale.nl/index.htm.

8. William L. Dulaney, "A Brief History of 'Outlaw' Motorcycle Clubs." *International Journal of Motorcycle Studies* 1, No. 3 (November 2005), http://ijms.nova.edu/November2005/IJMS._Artcl.Dulaney.html.

9. Geoffrey J. Giles, "The Denial of Homosexuality: Same-Sex Incidents in Himmler's SS and Police," *Journal of the History of Sexuality* 11, No. 1 (2002): 256–290.

10. Marilyn DeLong, Kelly Sage, Juyeon Park, and Monica Sklar, "From Renegade to Regular Joe: The Black Leather Jacket's Value for Bikers," *International Journal of Motorcycle Studies* 2, No. 2 (Fall 2010), http://ijms.nova.edu/Fall2010/IJMS_Artcl.DeLongetal.html.

11. Mark E. Gardiner, "The Real 'Wild Ones': The 1947 Hollister Motorcycle Riot." Accessed August 14, 2014, http://www.salinasramblersmc.org/History/Classic_Bike_Article.htm.

12. Dulaney, "A Brieft History of 'Outlaw'Motorcycle Clubs."

13. There is a great deal of controversy around the Hollister photograph. Research by several historians have some doubt about the image and whether it was staged by Barney Petersen. For more information see the article by Jerry Smith, "The Hollister Invasion: The Shot Seen 'Round the World," http://cycleguidemagazine.blogspot.com/2010/07/hollister-invasion-shot-seen-round.html.

14. Peter Hennen, *Faeries, Bears and Leathermen: Men in Community Queering the Masculine* (Chicago: University of Chicago Press, 2008): 139.

15. John Preston, "Introduction," in *The Leatherman's Handbook: The Original*. New York: LT Publications, 1994: 27–28.

16. Gayle Rubin, "The Miracle Mile: South of Market and Gay Male Leather 1962–1997," in *Reclaiming San Francisco: History, Politics, Culture,* edited by James Brook, Chris Carllson, and Nancy J. Peters (San Francisco: City Lights, 1998): 253.

17. Hennen, *Faeries, Bears and Leathermen*, 140.

18. DeLong et. al., "From Renegade to Regular Joe."

19. Rubin, "The Miracle Mile," 254.

20. Thompson, *Leather Folk*, xix.

21. Ibid.

22. Cuirmale, "Gay Leather Fetish History."

23. Johnny Stuart, *Rockers!* (London: Plexus, 1987).

24. Ibid., 41.

25. Ibid.

26. Cuirmale, "Gay Leather Fetish History."

27. Ibid.

28. Marjorie Garber, *Vested Interests: Cross-Dressing and Cultural Anxiety* (New York: Harper Perennial, 1997): 367.

29. Yer Logos, "Live: Cavern Club, Liverpool (evening)," *The Beatles Bible*. Accessed June 24, 2014, http://www.beatlesbible.com/1962/07/01/live-cavern-club-liverpool-189/.

30. Steve Walker, "Obituary: Larry Parnes." Accessed June 20, 2014. http://www. rockabilly.nl/references/messages/larry_parnes.htm.

31. J. Stephen Edwards, "Motorcycle Leathers and the Construction of Masculine Identities Among Homosexual Men." Accessed July 1, 2013. http://www.some-graymatter.com/motorcycle.htm.

32. Victoria Steele, *Fetish: Fashion, Sex and Power* (New York: Oxford University Press, 1996): 157.

33. Berndt Arell and Kati Mustala, *Tom of Finland – Unforeseen* (Helsinki: Like, 2006): 23–24.

34. Valentine Hooven III, "Tom of Finland: A Short Biography." Accessed July 1, 2014. http://www.tomoffinlandfoundation.org/foundation/touko.html.

35. Owen Keehnen, *We're Here: We're Queer: The Gay 90s and Beyond* (Chicago: Prairie Avenue Productions, 2011): 343.

36. Steele, *Fetish*, 5.

37. Weinstein, *Heavy Metal*, 127.

38. Shawn Cole, *'Don We Now Our Gay Apparel': Gay Men's Dress in the Twentieth Century* (New York: Berg, 2000): 170.

39. Stuart, *Rockers*, 125.

40. Amy C. Wilkins, "'So Full of Myself as a Chick': Goth Women, Sexual Independence, and Gender Egalitarianism," *Gender and Society* 18, No. 3 (June 2004): 331–332.

41. Ibid., 332.

42. Pat Califa, "A Personal View of the History of the Lesbian S/M Community and Movement in San Francisco," in *Coming to Power: Writings and Graphics on Lesbian S/M*, edited by SAMOIS (Boston: Alyson Publications, 1981; 3d 1987).

43. Philip Auslander, "I Wanna Be Your Man: Suzi Quatro's Musical Androgyny," *Popular Music* 23, No. 1 (January 2004): 9.

44. Ibid., 3.

45. Neil McCormick, "Suzi Quatro interview: 'When I zip up, it just feels like me'," *The Telegraph*, July 27, 2013, http://www.telegraph.co.uk/culture/music/10191291/Suzi-Quatro-interview-When-I-zip-up-it-just-feels-like-me.html.

46. Judy Wieder, "Heavy Metal Rob Halford: Between a Rock and a Hard Place," *The Advocate*, May 12, 1998: 64.

47. *Behind the Music, Behind the Music Remastered: Judas Priest,* Episode 5, 15 July 2014, http://www.vh1.com/video/behind-the-music-remastered/full-episodes/behind-the-music-remastered-judas-priest/1631871/playlist.jhtml.

48. Robert Matheu and Brian Bowe, *Creem: America's Only Rock 'N' Roll Magazine* (New York: Harper Collins, 1988), 232.

49. Sam Dunn, *Metal: A Headbanger's Journey*, film, directed by Sam Dunn, Scott McFayden, and Jessica Joy Wise (Banger Productions, 2006).

50. Helen Hok-sze Leung, "Queerscapes in Contemporary Hong Kong Cinema," *Positions* 9, No. 2 (2001): 444.

51. Bruce LaBruce, *J.D.s #1, 1985*. Queer 'Zine Archive Project, accessed June 13, 2013, http://archive.qzap.org/index.php/Detail/Object/Show/object_id/308.

52. Bruce La Bruce, *J.D.s #3 1987*. Queer 'Zine Archive Project. Accessed June 13, 2013. http://archive.qzap.org/index.php/Detail/Object/Show/object_id/345.

53. Cole, *'Don We Now Our Gay Apparel,'* 175.

54. Murray Healy, *Gay Skins: Class, Masculinity and Queer Appropriation* (London: Cassel, 1996): 106.

55. Essi Berelian, *The Rough Guide to Heavy Metal*, Rough Guide Reference series, edited by Mark Ellingham (New York: Rough Guides, 2005): 299.
56. Ibid., 300.
57. Rammstein, *Sennsucht*, Slash Records, ASIN No. B0000057C5, released January 13, 1998, compact disc.
58. Rammstein, *Liebe ist fur alle da,* Universal Records, ASIN No. B002OOG6RQ, released October 20, 2009, compact disc.
59. Berelian, The Rough Guide to Heavy Metal, 212–213.
60. Marilyn Manson, *Born Villain*, Downtown Records, ASIN B007KIZ6IG, released May 1, 2012, compact disc.
61. Trent Reznor, "Happiness is Slavery." Directed by Jon Reiss, 1992, Vimeo video http://vimeo.com/3556108.
62. Ibid.
63. Trent Reznor, *The Downward Spiral*. Nothing/TVT/Innerscope Records, ASIN No. B000001Y5Z, released March 8, 1994, compact disc.
64. 2wo. *Voyeurs*, Innerscope Records, ASIN No. B0000061QC, released March 10, 1998, compact disc.
65. Behind the Music, *Behind the Music: Judas Priest.*
66. 2wo, *Voyeurs.*
67. "Kinky Music Hall of Fame." *Brat Attack* 1, No. 3 (n.d.): 41.
68. Jeremy, "Music in Your Toybag, " Unpublished, vertical file: Music-General, Leather Archives and Museum, Chicago, Illinois.
69. David Ciminelli and Ken Knox, *Homocore: The Loud and Raucous Rise of Queer Rock* (Los Angeles: Alyson Books, 2005): 13.
70. Ashley Dawson, "'Do Doc Martens Have A Special Smell?' Homocore, Skinhead Eroticism, and Queer Agency," in *Reading Rock and Roll: Authenticity, Appropriation, Aesthetics,* edited by Kevin J.H. Dettmar and William Richey (New York: Columbia University Press, 1999): 141.
71. Ingram, "Ten Arguments For a Theory of Queers in Space," 8.
72. Ingram, "Mapping the Shifting Queerscape," 11.

3   Outsider Togetherness

It just always spoke to me. Like I've tried listening to other music forms such as rap, country, r 'n' b and stuff of the sort but it all just gets commercial and unique. Plus a lot of artists in those genres don't even write their own music. Whenever one of those 'artists' are announced as a singer/songwriter (which is quite rare) everyone goes crazy as if it's this new phenomena and I'll be thinking, 'Aren't they all supposed to be singer/songwriters anyways?' Metal seems to be an art form that truly expresses one's inner self."
—Gay male fan from the United States

It evokes feelings of power and what I would call 'outsider togetherness.'
—Female bisexual fan from the United States

Resisting the call of gay normalization means refusing to write off the most vulnerable, the least presentable, and the dead.[1]

The logic of homosexual desire includes the potential for a loving identification with gay man's enemies.[2]

I think you're the only one.

At a conference, after I completed my presentation about the paucity of gender studies in heavy metal scholarship, a scholar asked to speak to me and gave me that comment. The commenter got my attention and I turned, expecting to see a smile following such a statement. This person was kidding, right? There was no such smile, and the look on my face went from humorous to dead serious. "Seriously," this person said, "you're the only one. There's nobody to study."

At that point I had already decided to survey queer fans of heavy metal because I knew my experiences were only one story. After this encounter, I resolved to work on understanding how queer fans of heavy metal thought about their lives as fans, their status in heavy metal scenes, and their love of heavy metal music. Heavy metal scholarship about fans has tended to focus on one of three topics: fans in non-Western locations (Baulch, Wallach, Hecker), fans as reified sex stereotypes (as discussed in Chapter 1), and fans as illustrations of adolescent rebellion and psychological diagnoses (Arnett).[3] These studies leave behind an oversimplified view of fans as heterosexual teenagers, perhaps with psychological problems or addictions to drugs and alcohol but united in their fandom, regardless of borders. I did not fit these narrow portrayals of heavy metal fans, nor did all of the fellow fans I knew and associated with.

The title of the chapter is drawn from a quote by a survey participant, who described his position as a queer fan of heavy metal as a "feeling of outsider togetherness." In this chapter, I will present an in-depth analysis of the stories, beliefs, and experiences of queer heavy metal fans in heavy metal scenes as presented in my qualitative study. A focus of this chapter will be the many ways in which queer fans believe their overlapping identities (queer individual and heavy metal fan) perform with each other and against each other. I will also explore queer fans' affect in the metal world and how they consume heavy metal music and its productions. This chapter focuses on the fans themselves, how they identify as both queer individuals and heavy metal fans, and what those identities mean in relation to the sounds and performances of heavy metal.

The core of this discussion of outsider togetherness is the survey "Queer Fans of Heavy Metal." Active from January 2009 through January 2013, this online survey was designed to collect information from self-identified queer fans of heavy metal anywhere in the world.[4] When the survey closed, there were 548 respondents from thirty-nine countries in the Americas, Europe, Southeast Asia, Africa, Australia, and the Middle East. Respondents were asked a short series of quantitative census questions, followed by a battery of open-ended, qualitative questions about their experiences in heavy metal scenes. Originally, the survey was posted on a queer metal fan discussion board and further snowball sampling proceeded as the link was cross-posted on web pages and fan discussion boards around the world.

The census questions in the survey were designed to ascertain four things: the gender identity and sex of the respondent, their age range, their home country and place of residence, and the age when they first started listening to heavy metal. In the survey, respondents were allowed to select as many sexes and gender identities as they saw fit. For example, under "Sex," respondents indicated the following sexes: Male (59.8%, n=326), Female (31.7%, n=173), Male-to-Female trans* (3.9%, n=21), Female-to-Male trans* (3.5%, n=19), and Intersex (1.5%, n=5).[5] Possible selections from "Gender Identity" were more numerous, and respondents were allowed to select any/all of the choices available. In addition, respondent's choices were recorded in the order of selection.[6] For example, of the 142 respondents who identified themselves as bisexual, only 97 identified as bisexual alone. Ten identified as bisexual and femme, ten more identified as bisexual and leather/BDSM, six identified as bisexual and masculine, and thirty identified as bisexual and queer or genderqueer. One bisexual respondent, who listed herself as a female living in Australia, gave her gender identity as "bisexual, masculine, effeminate, queer or genderqueer, leather/BDSM."[7] Of the thirty respondents who identified as femme, five of them selected femme as their only gender identity. One hundred and thirty-nine respondents identified as gay and eighty of those respondents selected gay as their only gender identity. Gay followed by bisexual was selected by only eight respondents, while seven selected gay and leather/BDSM. Three female-to-male trans* individuals selected gay followed by queer or genderqueer (two from Canada and one from Israel), and an intersex respondent from the United States identified as "gay, queer or genderqueer, effeminate, leather/BDSM."[8] Nine individuals identified as leather/BDSM alone, representing the United States (three females), one female from Bulgaria and Puerto Rico respectively, and one male from each of the following: Netherlands, Germany, Sudan, and Poland. Taken individually, 46 respondents identified as lesbian, 139 as gay, 32 as trans*, 94 as queer or genderqueer, 25 as butch, 30 as femme, 76 as masculine, 18 as effeminate, and 48 as leather/BDSM. The average age of becoming a metal fan was 15 but respondent fans listed ages in a range from eight to fifty. The youngest self-identified queer heavy metal fan was thirteen and the oldest was seventy. In terms of locality, 351 of the respondents resided in cities or urban areas, 120 resided in suburban areas, 46 in small towns or villages, and 20 responded they resided in a rural area. Queer fans of heavy metal are extremely diverse.

Table 3.1 Gender identity of respondents

This chart indicates total number of respondents who selected each identity, and does not indicate respondents who selected more than one identity.

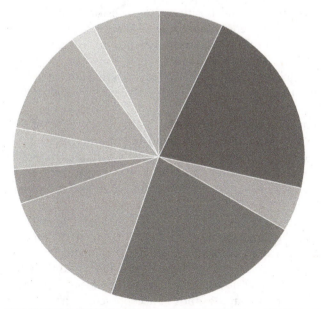

- Lesbian (n=46)
- Gay (n=139)
- Trans (n=32)
- Bisexual (n=142)
- Queer (n=94)
- Butch (n=25)
- Femme (n=30)
- Masculine (n=76)
- Feminine (n=18)
- Leather/BDSM (n=48)

Table 3.2 Sex of respondents

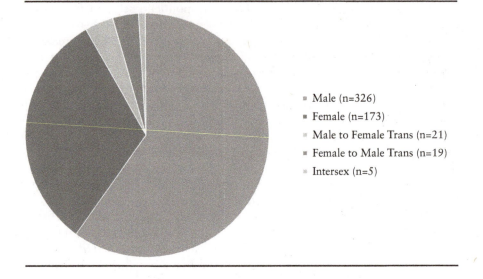

- Male (n=326)
- Female (n=173)
- Male to Female Trans (n=21)
- Female to Male Trans (n=19)
- Intersex (n=5)

While the diversity of queer fans is important, more important is their experiences in, with, and connected to their love of heavy metal. In order to explore those experiences, this chapter will utilize Kath Weston's street theorizing as a way to understand the queerscape. According to Weston, street theorizing is the use of everyday discourse, streetwise wisdom, as the best way to discuss lived experience. It is juxtaposed with straight wisdom, the wisdom of academic theory, and positioned by Weston as a way "to reconfigure the field" of queer theory. According to Weston, street theorizing "is easy to remember and easy to mobilize, whether to tease, describe, disparage, or philosophize."[9] Heavy metal fandom, like any other dedicated fandom, has a language all its own. On one website providing advice to first-time attendees to international heavy metal festivals, one blogger wrote:

> Metalheads invent their own slang words. Nothing is ever 'cool'; it's 'kreig' or 'kvlt' or 'nekro.' If a metal band is particularly admired, they're considered 'tr00' or 'epic' or even 'epically brutal.' And whenever you greet someone you must – and this is very important – string together an impressive set of adjectives: 'Most grymm and metal hails to you!'[10]

Heavy metal fans speak the language of metal fandom, and street theorizing provides an academic way to connect the language of metal fans with academic concepts about queerscape, identificatory practices, and the ethos of queer fans. The survey of queer heavy metal fans revealed four important themes: the mythos of homophobia, the ethos of acceptance, living between two worlds, and affective audiotopia.

MACHO CUNTS, DICKHEADS, AND THE MYTHOS
OF HOMOPHOBIA

One of the ways in which the queer fans devise a heavy metal queerscape is in the discussion of homophobia in heavy metal. Heavy metal is often stereotyped as extremely homophobic and therefore dangerous for queer fans. In my experience, which certainly resonates with my ethnographic discoveries, straight friends who do not listen to metal always question how wise it is for me to be a metal fan. Am I not concerned about my safety? Within my survey, I asked several questions about homophobia in heavy metal from the queer fans' perspective, including questions about safety, incidences of hateful speech or actions, and recollections of homophobic performances my informants witnessed. Fans have seldom been party to hate speech or violence. In fact, less than one percent of my informants have ever witnessed violence based on gender identity or sexuality. Metal's hypermasculine façade projects rampant homophobia but inside the metal queerscape it appears non-existent. How does this outsider togetherness operate behind such a façade? The assumption that heavy metal is a bastion of homophobic action is also inextricably linked to the belief there are few to no queer fans – or performers for that matter. The seeming perpetual use of this assumption is based entirely on heavy metal's masculinity. Heavy metal is so masculine, the story goes, there is no room for queer fans in that milieu. In their article on women in heavy metal scholarship, Hickam and Wallach wrote about this assumption: "While heavy metal music and subculture have continually evolved in myriad ways over the past five decades, the majority of musicians and fans have been, and continues to be, male."[11] In another example, heavy metal scholar Marcus Erbe discussed gay metal act Maris the Great as "violating the genre's predominately heterosexual code."[12] Perhaps the best example of this mythos of homophobia in heavy metal comes from Bashe's book *Heavy Metal Thunder*:

> Headbangers are notoriously homophobic and generally regard any act that does not go in for metal's mucho-macho posturing as beneath contempt. As with the membership of any gang, individuality may be encouraged, but only as it is defined by the gang itself.[13]

This myth, it seems, is a major part of the masculininst canon of heavy metal scholarship.

Important to this discussion of the mythos of homophobia is the street talk of "macho cunts" and "dickheads." According to Urban Dictionary, a website intended to gather street theory, a dickhead is "usually male person who 'thinks with his dick.' A person whose actions seem motivated by sexual desire at the expense of common sense or intelligence. … An excessively macho individual." This is the usage in heavy metal, typically used to describe ubermasculine posturing. It is always used when someone knocks into you, approaches you sexually without an invitation, or other unwritten rules of the heavy metal floor. This is typically juxtaposed with "dude," and is roughly interchangeable with "asshole" or "asswipe." A dude is part of the scene, acts appropriately according to the scene, is generous to his friends, and loves the music. Be a dude, goes the heavy metal street theory, don't be a dick/asshole/asswipe. Queer fans of heavy metal use this term for the stereo-typed metal fan who fit Bashe's homophobic mythos: uneducated, working class, drunk, and disorderly. "Macho cunts" is a bit different. Cunt is an old word, stemming from Middle English, and has served as a slang term for female genitalia for generations. A macho cunt, however, is not a descriptor for women. Macho cunts are hypermasculine men who mistreat women, see others as sexual objects, and do everything in excess: big cars, big muscles, big attitudes. As one blogger stated, macho cunts are "genuinely frightened of homosexual men, as though sexual orientation is contagious."[14] In a queerscape twist, however, macho cunts are hypermasculine men who are actually looking for gay sex, according to heavy metal fans. Interestingly, the term is also used in online pornography and queer male sex sites where macho cunts are alpha male tops who have sex with effeminate male bot-toms ("pussy bottom boys") as dominants. It is these two types, the dick-head/asshole/asswipe and the macho cunt, that queer heavy metal fans often discussed as related to the mythos of homophobia in heavy metal scenes.

The survey included a series of questions about homophobia in heavy metal. Respondents were asked if they were the victims of verbal harass-ment and/or physical harassment and, if so, were asked to describe that experience as far as they were able. Survey respondents were also asked about instances of homophobia they saw or were aware of among bands and performers, including homophobic comments in interviews, homopho-bic speech or simulated violence on stage, and anecdotes about performers taking part in homophobic actions or gestures. When asked if metal is homo-phobic, only a small percentage said "yes," but always with a caveat. "Some bands have homophobic lyrics, but only a select few really mean it," wrote one gay male fan from the Netherlands. "In general I believe the community isn't homophobic at all. In fact, heavy metal has always been a refuge for 'different' people. Somehow, queer metalheads aren't really a big part of it, but that doesn't mean they aren't welcome."[15] Fans often wrote that metal was no more homophobic than any other genre of music, or responded that the amount of homophobia depended on the genre of heavy metal. In the entire pool of respondents only a handful stated they had been physically abused or harassed. "Not explicitly so, but I do find sometimes that in the mosh pit I have been ganged up upon," wrote a MTF trans* lesbian from the United States, "and specifically moshed against and roughed up, more often now that I look androgynous/feminine than when I was presenting as a male."[16] A male lesbian from a rural part of the United States wrote: "Not me personally but I have had to fight guys in the parking lot pre-show tail-gating because they were starting shit with my gay friend."[17] Less than two percent of the survey respondents selected "yes" in response to the question,

"Have you ever been physically abused in a heavy metal space?" Queer fans simply do not experience that violence, that mythic homophobia so ingrained in our understanding of heavy metal scenes and sounds. For those who responded yes, the stories were largely about attacks on female-bodied fans. In all, four female fans from the United States and Sweden wrote they were groped and "ass grabbed" at concerts, while another female bisexual wrote she was raped at three shows in her lifetime. Other fans noted transphobia was a growing problem, especially for female-bodied trans* folks. One MTF trans* butch lesbian from the United States explained:

> Lots of the musicians from older legacy metal bands from like the thrash era and stuff say misogynist, homophobic, and transphobic things to try to assert their heteronormative masculinity. I can't really give you a list because they all are like that.[18]

Other queer fans mentioned avoiding harassment by seeking assistance from other fans. "No when I have a problem I have friends or random people in the audience stick up for me," explained a female leather-identified American in her late thirties, "or I grab a girl and honestly get aggressively sexual with her consent and it sends the ass wipe moving." A MTF trans* femme lesbian fan from American wrote: "Once or twice I've gotten a little bit of hassle, but other fans attending stepped in to set things right."[19] Perhaps the best illustration of the lack of homophobia among fans is this quote from a butch lesbian female from Canada:

> No. If anything, it's been comments about women rather than queers. Everybody knows I'm gay, and if there's some New Person who makes a homophobic comment, both me and my friends are quick to jump in with some 'Hey, you know she's queer, right? What do you say now?' type of thing. More out of embarrassing someone else for a self-righteous kick than actually making a social/political statement, though, of course. It's kind of hilarious and sweet in that cheesy, metal way.

When asked if they were ever the target of homophobic verbal harassment or assault, less than one percent answered "Almost Always" or "Frequently," while ninety-five percent of respondents answered "Hardly Ever" or "No." Many fans who selected "Hardly Ever" suggested the other fans who were using homophobic language were, in fact, closeted queers. Recent turns in queer theory have focused on shame, mockery, and other ways of feeling queer. As Heather Love explained, feelings of loss and shame, the "costs of homophobia," are central to the very identity we call queer.[20] I suggest the street theory that homophobic individuals are just deeply closeted is a way of reflecting shame back on agents of its delivery. Rather than feeling backward, it is as though we hold up a lens and focus a beam of homophobic shame directly on that moment's agent of shame. Leo Bersani, in his influential essay "Is the Rectum a Grave?", wrote gay-macho produces two reactions: mockery and sexual excitement.[21] If we replace gay-macho with macho cunt, what becomes of these reactions? Queer fans are certainly mocking the macho cunt and his excess but is there sexual excitement in that moment of mockery and disgust? And in that moment, we see both reflection and remembrance, a feeling backward and an aggressive laser pointing forward. "It can be because macho cunts want to act out their frustration and aggression but most of those guys will be the first to flop out their cock and ask you to suck it when they find you are a Pansexual like myself," wrote one male fan from Australia. "I guess they are afraid of what they know about themselves but are too afraid to admit."[22]

Where is the mythic homophobia if the queer fans are not victimized by it? While fans did not overwhelmingly identify homophobic verbal or physical abuse among fans, they identified several instances of homophobic talk and behavior among certain heavy metal performers. Older fans recalled an infamous 1989 action by Sebastian Bach, then lead singer of the band Skid Row, who appeared in a T-shirt reading "AIDS Kills Fags Dead." Younger fans mentioned comments against gay marriage by Megadeth leader Dave Mustaine, homophobia in some Norwegian black metal songs, and anecdotal stories taken from online discussion boards, newspaper articles, and interviews. There were, however, some common patterns among the respondents about the most homophobic acts in heavy metal. Survey respondents identified three primary examples of homophobic heavy metal acts: an album titled "Smashing Rainbows," hate crimes among black metal bands (see Chapter 4), and Kerry King of the band Slayer.

In 2008, the album "Smashing Rainbows: Rock Against Homosexuality" was released by Fetch the Rope records. Though not well known in the mainstream rock world, this album was a collection of heavy metal songs advocating violence against queer folks and racial minorities, featuring slurs and threats. The album's producers categorized the songs featured as hardcore, black, and death metal. Created by supporters of the White Power movement in the United States, "Smashing Rainbows" remains for sale through White Power online sales. After protests from the GLBTQ community in the United States, the album was pulled from Amazon sales in September 2011. Songs on the album include People Haters' "Smear the Queer," The Raunchous Brothers' "Dying In Pain," and a song entitled "Kill the Faggots" by Evil Incarnate. This album also features the song "Ghosts of Flossenberg" by Arghoslent. Flossenberg, one of the most violent and horrific concentration camps of Nazi Germany, operated from 1938 to 1945. Nearly 100,000 people were imprisoned there and 30,000 were murdered at the camp. In this song by Arghoslent, the songwriters link Judaism with sodomy and homosexuality, and suggest the deaths at Flossenberg were just. "May homophobia outlive us all," is the last line of the song. According to a gay male bisexual respondent from the United States who self-identified as femme: "It's said before that some of the pioneers of Scandinavian black metal committed acts of violence and hate towards homosexuals. We all know it's just 'cause it helps them feel so trve and kvult though. Whatever, assholes are prevalent in every culture."[23]

A majority of the queer fans surveyed identified Kerry King of Slayer as the most homophobic performer they could identify. King, an influential guitarist and founder of one of the most important bands in metal, is perhaps best known inside the queerscape for his homophobic actions. In fact, many informants had stories they overheard or events they witnessed about King's homophobia. One informant stated King walked off stage when given a cup of ice at a show. The ice machine was broken, so the bar manager went next door to the gay dance club to borrow a cup of ice for King. He reacted by throwing the cup at the crowd and leaving the stage.[24] Others pointed out quotes by King in the press suggesting his homophobic attitudes. King has been photographed with a swastika on his guitar and has used gay slurs in interviews and on stage. Most recently, King discussed Slayer's search for a new drummer. It seems Adrian Erlandssen (formerly of At The Gates and Cradle of Filth) "hits like a fag." According to King, "This is Slayer; people expect more."[25]

What makes Kerry King's nearly unanimous appearance as *the* homophobic heavy metal performer (according to queer fans) most interesting is not the slurs themselves. What makes it important is the fact King is also the performer most surrounded by a "he must be gay" whisper campaign. In an extension of the shame-turned-spotlight move that queer metal fans already make, King is the homophobic metal master most often talked about as potentially queer by queer fans. Thousands of blogs, metal mag online comments, and chat room discussions have posted talk about the possibility King is a closeted gay man. In the online pop culture site Urban Dictionary, "bear" is defined as "A good example of what a typical bear looks like would be Kerry King of Slayer."[26] In a further sample sentence: *Dude, Kerry King is such a freakin' bear!* No doubt some of this discussion is meant to create a discourse that opposes King's homophobic stance. "Kerry King. I read an interview in Guitar World where he spent 1/2 of it ranting against gay people. In GUITAR World. He's such a dick," a masculine gay respondent from the United States said.[27] After all, what better way to chastise a homophobic public figure than loudly suggest the homophobic is nothing more than a closeted queer? Or as queer folks often suggest, you know the biggest homophobes are the biggest queers. Another way to think about this position is in the song "Hats Off To Halford," on the *Hair: Debatable* album of musician and performance artist Atom and His Package. In his ode to Rob Halford, Atom wrote: "Oh, I wish everyone in heavy metal would be homosexual, if not only to make those Nazi fuckin' pricks in Slayer, a little uncomfortable."[28] This kind of protest is political, one where queer metal fans suggest King is gay in order to upset his position as a king of metal and turn his homophobia around so it becomes a discursive weapon. This pseudo-outing of Kerry King could be something else though. What if, as we turn our understanding of metal subculture away from the heteronormative and consider the queer gaze, Kerry King becomes an object of desire? In what Foucault termed "scopophilia," queer fans obsessively look at Kerry King so he becomes not just a subject of derision but an object of desire. According to Foucault, such scopohilia was compelled by "an unacknowledged search for illicit pleasure and a desire which cannot be fulfilled."[29] Certainly no queer desire for Kerry King will be fulfilled. In fact, even to say so suggests one may seek pleasure from a subject that professes only hatred. But that, in effect, is scopophilia: the pleasure that is sought, gazed upon, even stared at in fascination (or disgust), and still desired. Consider, for example, a quote from Brian Cook, former bassist for the metal band Botch. In a 2006 article in *Decibel* magazine on queers in heavy metal, Cook puts this voyeuristic desire in Kerry King terms. "I definitely prefer the straight edge, shaved-head jock types," said Cook, "Then again, I do like the fat-dude-with-a-big-beard-and-tattoos look. Kerry King is totally hot. He'd probably kick my ass for saying that."[30] Perhaps queer fans of King feel the same way: both attracted and threatened but still watching. In this way, the homophobia of heavy metal is reterritorialized in the queerscape as a spin on homophobic violence that makes the homophobic act a sexualized one. "The logic of homosexual desire," wrote Leo Bersani, "includes the potential for a loving identification with the gay man's enemies."[31] Kerry King may be a dickhead, maybe even a macho cunt, but he's an attractive macho cunt.

I'M NOT CAMP: THE ETHOS OF ACCEPTANCE

According to heavy metal scholars Brian Hickam and Jeremy Wallach, heavy metal has an ethos of acceptance. This ethos depends on common themes, themes that reappear in music, style, corporeality, and performance, regardless of the genre of heavy metal under discussion. "Conversely, themes *common* to almost all subgenres of heavy music – 'fighting the world,' unity, and personal strength," wrote Hickam and Wallach, "may also be key to metal culture's ethos of acceptance, as they emphasize solidarity and steadfast resistance in the face of external adversity."[32] While this ethos of acceptance could be understood as an effect of masculinist brotherhood, understanding heavy metal as a queerscape gives those common themes a new and different meaning. The solidarity and resistance queer folks must undertake is different indeed, the personal strength and "fighting the world" required takes on a new meaning when seen through the lens of queer lives. In fact, the ethos of acceptance provides queer fans with an association, a belonging that comes from their operation in the heavy metal queerscape. This ethos of acceptance is a kinship, a queer family that draws from both existing routes of queer kin the trappings of the heavy metal brotherhood. Just as Elizabeth Freeman explained queer kinship as "ways of attaching to larger structures and thus belonging," queer fans constantly renew their kinship with heavy metal by framing it as a queerscape.[33] This ethos of acceptance is a queer acceptance, where resistance and determination for outcasts are rewarded with solidarity and kinship. Metal's ethos of acceptance is the ethos of the queerscape.

The queerscape's ethos of acceptance is predicated on two important ideas: the denial of a gendered performance marked as camp and the corporeality of metal's fictional kinship. The phrase "I'm not camp" and the denial of campness was a frequent occurrence in the survey of queer heavy metal fans. Camp represents something stripped of power, something to be made fun of, something strongly and stereotypically gay. Camp is also closely attached to the corporeality of metal kinship. Masculinity, the very veil that covers the queerscape, is required for metal kinship. For queer fans, that masculinity turns into a repudiation of camp in order to prove kinship with metal's masculinity. As Elizabeth Freeman explained, "Kinship marks out a certain terrain or corporeal dependency."[34] In the heavy metal queerscape, masculinity – or at least the repudiation of femininity – is that corporeal dependency. "I just love the music and I'm not camp or effeminate to start with!" wrote a gay male fan from the United Kingdom.[35] A gay male fan from Ireland, when asked if heavy metal made him feel more masculine, explained: "I'm horribly unfit and not masculine at all but I'm definitely not camp or "feminine."[36] "I would have to say it makes me feel more 'manly' than the stereotypical limp-wristed homos that flock to the current pop starlets," a male masculine fan from Canada replied.[37] In order to understand the corporeal kinship of "I'm not camp" and the ethos of metal acceptance, the survey included a variety of questions about masculinity, spatiality, and identity.

One question asked in the survey was: "Does metal make you feel more masculine or butch?" Respondents replied in one of two ways: either that metal did make them feel more masculine or that their masculinity or femininity was simply confirmed and comfortable in metal scenes and spaces. Queer fans who felt their identity confirmed in heavy metal, however, often expressed their feeling that metal provided a kinship where that acceptance was possible. "I don't think it makes me any more of a dude than I already am," wrote a FTM trans* bisexual fan from the United States.[38] "It definitely allows me to be who I am," a gay male, masculine-identified fan from the United States stated. "In gay spaces my masculine presentation is always considered suspicious. In metal I am allowed and encouraged to be a man."[39] Metal scenes did not make a bisexual, genderqueer, and butch-identified female from the United states feel more masculine, "but it is a place where I don't have to femme up to please others."[40] "It's about being part of a wider audience where sexuality doesn't matter," said a female lesbian from the United Kingdom.[41] "I feel like myself at a metal show," expressed the ethos of acceptance felt by a femme, leather-identified female from the United States.[42] A gay male leather/BDSM-identified fan from Brazil explained that acceptance:

> Although heavy metal has a 'butch image,' I don't think it makes someone 'feel' more masculine. I think it is the opposite causal relationship:

it is the only few places where one can be their natural and 'manly type' unapologetically.[43]

A FTM trans* fan who self-identified as bisexual, genderqueer, masculine, and leather/BDSM expressed both the ethos of acceptance as it is reflected in a uniquely queerscape experience:

> First, being part of something so heavily macho and dominated by straight cis guys makes me feel like 'part of the club.' Also, it makes me feel good, happy, powerful, and confident, so it alleviates my gender dysphoria.[44]

For some fans, the corporeal performance of masculinity was the very core of their experiences as queer fans of heavy metal. These fans felt heavy metal did give them a more masculine and/or butch identity, one that supported their own identity as a queer person. For example, a female genderqueer and butch fan from the United States expressed her identity in the heavy metal queerscape as a validation of her gender expression:

> It certainly validates my masculine performance while being femme-bodied. The general community of metal-heads are male, and seems to abide by a particular 'type' of hegemonic masculinity. Females are either butch/andro, or hyper-sexualized within the community. I have always chosen the butch presentation.[45]

Another view of gender expression in the heavy metal queerscape suggested heavy metal was inherently a space for queer expressions. A gay male fan from the United States stated:

> Metal as a genre of not just music but a lifestyle sorta encourages a very brawny masculinity. Which enturn [sic] encouraged a train of thought where men were encouraged to show their masculinity by expressing a kind of effeminacy to show how secure they were in being a man.[46]

Another way of examining the ethos of acceptance in heavy metal's queerscape is through the use of style. Heavy metal is dependent on its uniform as an identifier of membership: jeans, band T-shirts, black leather, boots or sneakers. It is this uniform that provides some homology, some internal orderliness, which Hebdidge identified as a subcultural practice.[47] Survey respondents were asked questions about their style, how they dressed when they went to heavy metal concerts, and interview subjects were asked to describe their typical use of space at a heavy metal concert. Very few respondents explained their typical dress was anything other than the heavy metal uniform and when they did, it was identified as queer clothing. A female, leather-identified bisexual from the United States explained:

> I personally wear what I think will be practical and comfortable but to an extent I do play up my sexuality a bit and the wardrobe is not my everyday wear. I wear combat boots, my bullet belt or my studded belt, tight black pants or shorts with stockings or ripped up tights in warmer weather, leather jacket, fitted band shirt (bonus points if there's a hint of cleavage) etc. ... I suppose I'd describe my personal show aesthetic as Sarah Connor meets femme fatale without showing too much skin. I won't wear heels, or an elaborate dominatrix-y outfit to a show because I'd rather not be stuck standing in the corner all night worrying if my makeup's okay or if I'll topple over in the crowd because I'm wearing ridiculous shoes.[48]

Clearly, the "dominatrix-y" and "ridiculous" are not part of the queerscape's corporeal homology. Other fans, however, found the acceptance in the kinship of heavy metal specifically because their queer style did not violate heavy metal homology. For example, a female lesbian from the United Kingdom who identified as masculine and genderqueer explained how heavy metal style was part of her identity development:

> When I was younger I was called butch/masculine by my parents because I wore a leather jacket, which I found problematic. I now consider myself a masculine woman and suppose that my interest in heavy metal is congruous with my masculinity.[49]

At play in this concept of heavy metal style and identity development is the corporeal aspects of queer kinship. In his study of gay skinheads in Great Britain, scholar Murray Healy explored the role of the skinhead "uniform" as an erotic code, one that signaled queer community and erotic possibilities that would be read differently by heterosexual viewers. As Healy wrote:

> The skinhead image operates as an erotic code within gay subculture, but as a street style, unlike clone (or cowboy or leather) codes, it can be worn safely beyond the physical confines of the subcultural leisure environment: in the street, gay skinheads will pass as straight to the heterosexual imperative while advertising an erotic interest in masculinity to informed readers (other gay men).[50]

The idea is that reading as butch in heavy metal is part of the uniform. And this uniform, while it may be read as straight metal fan to the heterosexual imperative, in fact is read as a signal to erotic desires on the part of queer fans. It is a uniform that, while it may have separate meanings outside the queerscape of heavy metal, can be closely linked to queer codes in heavy metal.

When closely linked, those queer codes embrace work to deny camp-coded behavior in an effort to highlight heavy metal kinship. Or, as Ingram explained in his discussion of the queerscape: "A queerscape is essentially a sum total of subjectivities, some more closely linked, for a time, than others."[51] DBT, a fifty-seven-year-old Native American pre-operative transsexual who identified as a lesbian, explained the linking of subjectivities this way:

> OK ... I don't hang with many TGs [transgender folks] ... I don't like labels. ... I just recently discovered that about me ... that I don't like labels. To me, the stereotypical Trans woman likes to dress up a lot ... big heels ... you know the type, I'm sure. A lot of them like to do drag, even though they are not really drag queens. They walk and talk a certain way, typically. I'm not judging ... I'm just saying ... it seems to be how I view them. Hardly any of them are into metal ... they're more into rap or Lady Gaga type of crap. Well, I'm not. I'm a metal chic! And I like to dress like a normal chic that you see walking down the street who seems to have a non-traditional lifestyle. For me, I wear skinny jeans and rock tee shirts and hi top sneakers. So for me, metal definitely has an impact on my identity because I basically live it 24/7. Its just my way.[52]

"It's a cliché, but a metal gig has always been something of a family," explained an eighteen-year-old gay metal fan from the United Kingdom. "Doesn't matter your race, creed, religion, sexuality, gender, you're just there to have a good time with each other."[53]

QUEER BY NATURE: AUTHENTICITY BETWEEN TWO WORLDS

Writing about heavy metal fans in Navajo and Ute youth communities in the 1980s, scholar Donna Dehyle discussed the role heavy metal played in allowing those youths to resist domination and mainstream hegemony. She also explained Navajo and Ute youth who identified as metal fans faced rejection from both aspects of their identity.

> Within the intersections of these two idealized worlds, the heavy metalers were seen as bad Indians by their Anglo and Indian peers. Bad Indians need to be controlled or made invisible by the disapproving majority of Indian youth and Anglo students, teacher, and administrators. This was done by attacking the visible symbols and physical appearances of the heavy metalers.[54]

The queerscape of heavy metal mirrors the problematizied intersection as well. Just as the Navajo and Ute youths identified by Dehyle were considered less than authentic Indians, queer heavy metal fans are sometimes considered less than authentic metal fans. In his 1996 work on heavy metal youth, Jeffrey Arnett explained: "From the mouths of metalheads comes a cry of alienation."[55] At the same time, being a queer heavy metal fan can, and does, lead queer fans and their peers to question how authentic their queer identity truly is. Gordon Brett Ingram wrote: "Sometimes being a queer feels like being an alien."[56] In this intersection between two authenticities, the authentically queer and the authentically metal, where do queer metal fans occupy a territory? In this interstitial space between two subjectivities, can there be an authentically queer metal fan?

According to a gay male and genderqueer fan from the United States, "Metal is queer by nature."[57] This is a complex bit of street theory. Does metal have a nature? Does queer have a nature? And where do continued political debates about nature versus nurture, and the naturalness of homosexuality, fit in this discussion? Using the idea of metal as queer by nature, how do queer metal fans conceive of the naturalness of their queerscape? In order to explore these questions, the survey included several questions about relationships with people both inside and outside the metal world, as well as questions about why queer fans participate in metal scenes. Along with these questions, queer metal fans were asked to respond to questions about the metal scene and their place in it. In his exploration of scenes in rock music, Mark Olson looked at the idea of scenes as authenticity machines. "The rock formation is always producing mobility, always trying to differentiate itself from the logics of everyday life, to claim or reclaim authenticity," wrote Olson, "where authenticity marks difference from the commodified existence that perpetually encroaches."[58] The heavy metal queerscape is also claiming authenticity, an authenticity that counters both the hegemonic veil of heterosexual masculinity in heavy metal and the stereotypical view of queer life that claims pride and community as its hallmarks.

Authenticity is a major concern in heavy metal, both in the academic discourse around heavy metal and in the talk amongst fans about authenticity: authenticity versus "sellouts," "authentic" musicians and their performance, "real metal" and the lack of authentic integrity associated with other genres of music. I argue the authenticity of metal, indeed the authenticity of queer metal, is defined by the queerscape itself. Grossberg explained a scene is less defined by sound than by "social style, relationships, and allegiances."[59] Rather than see authenticity in heavy metal as generic, it can be reframed as an aspect of style and allegiances within heavy metal. When you add the concept of queerscape, then authenticity can be seen as a way in which queer fans territorialize heavy metal and refashion it as authentically queer as well. Being authentically a queer metalhead means you set aside isolated aspects of queer and metal separately, and build allegiances within the interstitial space they occupy together. This is more than putting on the metal uniform; it is a feeling of authentic allegiance to a queer metal nature, even when those two seem mutually exclusive. Healy noticed much the same role of authenticity in his study of Britain's gay skinheads. According to Healy:

> If being a skinhead is about being authentic, then it has to be more than just dressing up, because fashion is only skin-deep. So this tangible shallowness of the skinhead's surface appearance is counteracted by abstract, deep concepts sites at a mythologized interior. ... Genuine skinhead identity is the expression of something unseen and internal: a sense of real commitment to the essense of skinheadism, rather than the mere donning of a fake, surface fashion. In gay subculture, this requires a commitment to a public, full-time, social street identity as opposed to a private, part-time, sexual leisure identity.[60]

Perhaps the most important aspect of the authenticity of heavy metal's queerscape is that it in fact works against alienation. The queerscape takes people alienated by others and brings them together in a move that is essentially de-alienation. In her application of Bakhtin's concept of the carnival to heavy metal, scholar Karen Halnon concluded that for her informants, heavy metal was far from alienating. Halnon discovered heavy metal was a point of rebellion against the mark of civilization and "metal is a dis-alienating, liminal utopia of human freedom, creativity, and egalitarianism."[61]

Survey respondents' thoughts about metal's queer nature illustrate the dis-alienating role the metal queerscape plays for queer fans. Metal "just makes me feel like less of a stereotype," explained a gay male fan from the United States. Another gay male fan from the United States suggested he dealt with his gender frustrations through metal:

> When I listen to metal, it gets me in touch with certain aspects of my character that are bound up in my masculinity. I think a lot of my favorite bands tap into a very specific kind of frustration that comes with being socialized as male in this culture. That said, the way I experience masculinity is probably very different than the way some others experience it.[62]

A gay male leather-identified fan from Equatorial Guinea linked his dis-alienation in the metal queerscape with masculinity in his home village:

> [Metal makes me feel] more manly because I am real effeminate and when I bang my head I feel like a man. The village I was born in – all men bang their head to drums during ritual dances so I bang my head to metal music.[63]

Another fan, a genderqueer and pansexual nineteen-year-old from the United States, suggested the dis-alienation of the heavy metal queerscape gives him comfort. He wrote:

> The energy, the heaviness, the speed, in a few cases the lyrics, more often than not I don't pay attention to them, and I guess the feeling

that you are participating in a culture outside the mainstream is comforting to me because I consider myself a misfit in a lot of ways.[64]

Questions about metal bands and performers the fans identified as queer revealed one important piece of the queer nature of metal: queer metal fans claim as authentically "queer" a variety of metal bands, performers, genres, and stylistic cues that might not be read as queer by anyone else. For example, an American gay male, who also identified as bisexual and effeminate, wrote, "Mainstream deathcore/metalcore bands are pretty queer!"[65] While fans identified Rob Halford overwhelmingly ("I could see a leather daddy coming from a mile away," explained an American bisexual female fan), and commonly identified Gaahl from the band Gorgoroth, their thoughts on queer performers ranged wildly beyond those two.[66] "Joan Jett, Rob Halford, Paul Stanley," wrote a lesbian, genderqueer and leather-identified female from Canada, "they give off an energy of queer that I see in my day-to-day queer friends/family as opposed to stereotypical queer labeling done by public opinion."[67] "Glam bands had a sort of queerness to them by default, because they challenged notions of masculinity," explained a gay male and genderqueer fan from Canada.[68] "Metal is such a male oriented, homosocial space," a lesbian female fan from the United States explained, "that with the exception of dudes like Gene Simmons and Lemmy, they all seem a wee bit queer to me."[69] One fan, a genderqueer male from America, suggested avant-garde metal was queer: "Many avant-garde bands like Sigh, Enslaved, Maudlin of the Well, have a kind of genre-queerness in the way they approach their sound and music as a whole."[70] "Bands such as Charon, HIM, For My Pain and other Finnish 'love metal' bands do look a bit more queer to me," wrote a masculine gay male from Russia and living in the United Kingdom. "Same applies to the vast majority of the female led symphonic bands."[71]

In addition to identifying genres and bands as queer, surveyed fans formulated a list of performers they assumed, suggested, or even wished were queer. In this twist on the idea of queer nature and authenticity, fans read some performers as authentically queer based on their natural instincts as queer individuals. This is more than a reference to the infamous gaydar; it is an appropriation of metal performers as potentially queer, an appropriation of performers due to the appearance of a queer substance. In a harkening to Judith Butler's discussion of gender performativity, claiming metal performers as potentially queer by nature reveals the queerscape by destabilizing gender and sexuality in the temporality of metal performance.[72] "Dan Briggs of Between the Buried and Me. I've always had a feeling about him. I have no proof one way or the other (nor does it really matter to me)," a gay male fan from the United States suggested.[73] A female genderqueer lesbian, who also identified as butch and masculine, replied, "I believe Trent Reznor is out as a bisexual."[74] "I PRAY Herman Li's gay!!!!" wrote a gay male fan from the United States of one of the lead guitarists from the band Dragonforce.[75]

Charlie Benate, drummer and songwriter for thrash band Anthrax, was the subject of longing for a gay male and masculine fan from the United States: "I WISH Charlie Benate (since he's gorgeous)."[76] "I'm pretty sure the lead singer from Bullet for My Valentine loves the shaft but that's just because the way he moves around on stage is kinda fruity," explained a lesbian-identified male from the United States.[77]

Another aspect of these queer claims to authenticity are, in fact, pointed towards potentially threatening subjects. As Heather Love detailed in her monograph *Feeling Backward*, central to gay identity is a link to impossibility.[78] Much like the scopophilia surrounding Kerry King, queer fans of heavy metal identify as authentically queer not only performers who are not out but performers who have engaged in homophobic speech. That they are queer is not only conjecture, it may indeed be impossibility. At the same time, such an impossibility reveals Love's "feeling backward" as it pertains to the costs of homophobia for queer metal fans. An intersex and gender-queer respondent from the United States best illustrated this link between queer nature, the fans, and authenticity:

> I keep getting this feeling that someone in Slipknot might be, but I honestly don't know who any of them are as people, besides Paul, the bassist that just passed away (RIP) and the singer, Corey. I think Mike Patton, if he counts as a metal musician, might be bi. In truth, I always kinda wished that Tom Araya was queer. Chino Moreno might be queer as well.[79]

Araya, the lead singer for Slayer, told a 2004 Ozzfest press conference they would not play any "gay metal" with Rob Halford seated on stage. Slipknot, an American metal band formed in Iowa in 1995, has members performing in masks, their identities (and their desires) subsumed under a costume. What better links to impossibility than the lead singer of a band who often suggests homophobic opinions and a band of members hidden in masks? What could be more authentically queer, and authentically metal, than desiring men in metal drag?

THE MUSIC MAKES ME WANT TO FUCK: QUEERSCAPE AS AFFECTIVE AUDIOTOPIA

Heavy metal fans like fucking. Not the sexual act necessarily but the word: fucking. Good music is "fucking awesome," great music is "fucking epic." Heavier sounds are "fucking heavy," while harder beats are "fucking hard." A singer calls out someone in the mosh pit for bad behavior, it could be "fucking harsh" or "fucking cool." An overcrowded show might elicit calls of "Fucking hell!" or "Fucking nuts!" Your favorite performer's first appearance on stage turns fucking into an excited phrase: "It's fucking Halford!"

The line to the ticket window or the bathroom is "fucking long," you might be "fucking screwed." Bad opening bands get a "fuck this" or even calls of "get off the fucking stage" or "fuck you." Encyclopedia Metallum, the web's largest and most complete guide to heavy metal bands, lists thirty-three bands whose names begin with fuck, including Fucktory-X from Italy, Fuckhammer from Ireland, Fuck-Ushima from Finland, and simply Fuck from the United States.

For queer fans, fucking may take on a different meaning. Queer fans are already fucking with gender, fucking with space and place, fucking with stereotypes about heavy metal and queerness. At the same time, self-identifying as queer also means taking on the stereotype of sexual deviance, of fucking with family, marriage, and so-called traditional values. For the queer metal fan, fucking represents the double-edged sword of their alterity, both a "fucking metalhead" and a "fucking queer" and at once not entirely accepted (or acceptable) in either. The street discourse on fucking is a way to understand that dual alterity by hailing queer fans of metal. As Judith Peraino detailed in her monograph _Listening to Sirens_, hailing can apply to music. In essence, music goads individuals into questioning their own identities and allows them to use the sonic gestures of music to negotiate their identitites.[80] According to Biddle and Jarman-Ivens:

> Sonic gestures become codified, having gendered meanings ascribed to them over a period of time and generated through discursive networks, and those meanings are mutable according to the cultural, historical and musical context of those gestures, and the subsequent contexts into which they are constantly reinscribed.[81]

The problem, however, is this alterity is one of affect because music's sonic gestures are not always legible. For queer fans, the lyrics and sounds take on meanings not necessarily intended, meanings subsumed in the queerscape rather than legible to the heteronormative mainstream. As Peraino stated:

> Music is notoriously resistant to legibility; and although cultural, feminist, and queer theorists within musicology have worked hard to reveal the signatures of subjectivity and ideology in musical sounds, it is arguably music's resistance to legibility that allows for the use of music as a strategy for negotiating queer identity within dominant heterosexual culture.[82]

"I think that is because I am more aggressive, the music makes me want to fuck. ... I don't care who," explained a female and leather-identified metal fan from the United States.[83] Heavy metal community is both public and private. While concerts and shows, listening to music with friends, even walking the streets in a band T-shirt are public acts, the acts of listening, feeling, and identifying with lyrics and performers is private. Other scholars have noted the importance of sonic gestures in subcultural life. For example, Christopher Small suggested sonic gestures like music were an activity that included listening and understanding the meanings of particular music.[84] In *Queer Voices*, Freya Jarman-Ivens explained the voice, as a sonic gesture, was a site for the emergence of queer individuals and queer spaces.[85] R.J. Warren identified the sonic gestures of pop music as "a thing of intimacy and surprising faith."[86] In his work on music and identity, Simon Frith wrote that imagined forms of desire are enacted in the bodily matters of musical activites.[87] "Music," explained Frith, "gives us a real experience of what the ideal could be."[88]

The sonic gestures present in the heavy metal queerscape are most evident in their role as an affective audiotopia. Affect, most commonly thought of as a Deleuzian concept, was originally applied to the study of the power of bodies to affect other bodies in space.[89] Josh Kun, however, revised the concept of affect to address the problem of bodies affecting bodies in musical spaces. According to Kun, audiotopias are the spaces where music operates as a spatially affective practice, one in which listeners occupy both real and imaginary sonic space. Audiotopias are produced by sonic gestures and provide a way for oppressed and minority listeners to cope with their world in a reimagined sonic world. According to Kun, audiotopias are "spaces of affective utopian longings where several sites normally deemed incompatible are brought together, not only in the space of a particular piece of music itself, but in the production of social space and the mapping of geographical space that music makes possible as well."[90] Through the lens of audiotopia, it is easy to see the queerscape of heavy metal in the ways that queer fans think, talk, and feel about heavy metal's sonic gestures.

Queer fans of heavy metal provided myriad statements about heavy metal as an affective audiotopia. Fans talked about metal's rhythm, its loudness, its heaviness, and other sonic gestures. They also talked about lyrics, songs that were important or meaningful, and the affective role metal music plays in their lives as queer folks. Two questions were particularly important: a survey question that asked why respondents began listening to heavy metal, and an interview question about a respondent's favorite song. Their responses to these two questions revealed the queerscape's audiotopia in three themes: as an outlet for anger, as a path of individualism, and as a validation of their existence as queer people.

According to Hickam and Wallach, heavy metal serves as an outlet for anger. While many social scientists have written about heavy metal as music for disaffected youth to channel their antisocial anger, this is not inclusive of heavy metal scenes or communities. Audiotopia requires looking at music for its spatial aspects, not only its sonic ones. The queerscape of heavy metal, where queerness and heavy metal overlap, is an audiotopia where the queer fans express frustration, rage, and anger with the cultural systems that brand them. "Heavy metal is not an outlet for antisocial rage," wrote Hickam and Wallach. "It encourages the expression of healthy, *even justified*, anger."[91] Consider, for example, this exerpt from an interview by

Larissa Glasser with Randi Elise B., a roadie for metal bands such as Black Sabbath who later came out as trans*:

> Although heavy metal is still perceived in many circles as misogynist and homophobic, there is a power in this music and outlaw identity that harnesses a commonality with queer and trans culture. Occasionally, you may even run into someone who embodies that. When you first meet Randi Elise B., you know you've got someone with stories. I was aghast to find that someone in the community was once a roadie for Black Sabbath, Motorhead, and The Ramones. These were seminal bands I grew up with, sitting in my room alone and wondering what the **** was going on with my body: the music provided the extremity of expression I was seeking. Slayer had just as much influence on me as did The Bangles.[92]

The justified anger of queer fans is not just about their cultural status or a political consciousness. It is anger about one's body, one's desires, one's unfulfilled needs. Queer fans of heavy metal expressed their corporeal anger and frustration as connected to the sonic gestures of heavy metal. "It took me a while," wrote a gay male fan from the United States, "to start finding something to appreciate in the brutality, but when I finally learned to accept that, I threw myself head first into metal."[93] A genderqueer female fan from Sweden explained why she listened to heavy metal: "Because it makes me disappear from the regular world, and it makes me happy. To listen to music you really like is to be elevated from your regular thoughts and to enter a state of mind that is 'now'."[94] An American gay male fan from a rural area explained: "I connect with the music emotionally. It is intense, describes feelings or experiences that I have, let's me get my anger/depression out."[95] "It's great music that dares to be different," suggested a bisexual male fan from Australia, "and sometimes it just feels good to listen to a song that is angry and hard because you might be in the mood."[96] A genderqueer and butch female from the United States described her reasons for listening to metal in clearly audiotopian terms:

> I grew up listening to heavy metal, so it is a firm connection to my childhood. The anger and aggression often expressed in the subgenres is very cathartic. I consider going to live shows, moshing and thrashing about as a (relatively) safe method of releasing my own negative emotions. It is particularly wonderful to listen to politically/socially conscientious metal, as I think it is the perfect sound for my disappointment and frustration with society in general.[97]

For queer fans, the audiotopian aspects of the heavy metal queerscape echo their affective experiences, be they rage, or anger, or confusion. Or, as a bisexual female fan from the United States described: "It is dark and brutal and filled with rage, but at the same time it can be painfully beautiful."[98] In essence, heavy metal's sonic gestures, its audiotopia, provide queer fans with a way of coping with their changing affective status. A MTF trans* lesbian from New Zealand explained this best:

> It is my escape from the world and is my way of dealing with issues day-to-day. It is an outlet for much of any excessive emotion and it calms me. It makes me feel whole and it feels like the music itself can understand and relate to how I feel sometimes, so much so like it is an extra companion.[99]

The queerscape's audiotopia is also evident in queer fans' discussions of individualism. In his article on masculinity and metal lyrics, Adam Rafalovich discussed the facets of individualism in heavy metal music. "The narrative of the dominant self," explained Rafalovich, "depicts the destruction of, or victory over, perceived forces of repression."[100] Rafalovich, himself a fan and heavy metal musician, further explained these agents or perceived repression might be internal or external. For queer fans, the victory may be over external forces (family, culture, society) or internal (doubts, fears, identity). A genderqueer and leather-identified American female described why she listened to metal as a victory of individualism:

> It [metal music] resonates with me in a way that other forms of music don't. When I was a teenager it was more emotional, because I was very angsty. As an adult it's more about empowerment, individualism, strength, challenging the mainstream, being transgressive.[101]

Queer fans of heavy metal also identified heavy metal as a vehicle for opposing marginalization. A genderqueer American female wrote: "As I became more aware of queer identity, metal offered lyrics that spoke to my experiences of trauma, oppression and marginalization."[102] A gay male American fan explained how heavy metal helped him forge an individualism separate from a difficult family background:

> I think that I got into heavy metal because of being raised in a very homophobic church and my father was a church Sunday school teacher and deacon. It gave me some stable ground when I was young to vent my anger over my mistreatment as a teenager.[103]

Other fans identified heavy metal's audiotopia as the space where their queerness was welcomed, despite whatever the mainstream might think of heavy metal. A gay male fan from America suggested the queerscape welcomed him as a marginalized individual. "The energy, the heaviness, the speed, in a few cases the lyrics, more often than not I don't pay attention to them," the fan explained, "and I guess the feeling that you are participating in a culture outside the mainstream is comforting to me because I consider myself a misfit in a lot of ways."[104] Still other queer fans explained their individualism, so attached to the audiotopia of the heavy metal queerscape, was equated with acceptance. "Metal is also philosophical ideology it ask you to question what social and norm are calling 'bad sound'," wrote a bisexual, leather-identified female from Israel, "and to choose what sound you love for yourself."[105] A female leather/BDSM-identified American respondent stated: "There is so much emotion in the music … there is rage and sadness but power of finding oneself."[106] "When I finally was introduced to extreme metal," a female femme bisexual from Denmark confided, "I had a feeling of coming home – it resonated with me and it was what I'd always been looking for in music."[107]

Finally, the audiotopia of the heavy metal queerscape gives queer fans a validation of their identity. Such validation may present a stumbling block for theorists who question the very existence of identity itself but in the embodied lives of queer fans, validating one's identity imbues those fans with feelings of power, control, and spirit that other aspects of their lives may deny or ignore. In his article on fans of the film *Velvet Goldmine*, scholar Chad Bennett called this "transformational shame," or the use of queer affect among fans to transform shame into pride, self-actualization, and a repudiation of the shame of the proverbial closet.[108] Interestingly, for many queer fans, transformational shame and the validation of one's identity apply not only to their queer identity but to their identity as metal fans as well. For example, one Canadian fan who self-identified as a female masculine butch provided this response:

> I'm usually to Token Queer in various circles of straight people; I don't have many gay friends. I am just as openly gay as I am openly a metalhead. If someone doesn't like me being a metalhead, or queer, or whatever else I may be, it's more their problem than mine. I'm at the point in my life where I see no reason whatsoever to be closeted about two blindingly overt aspects of my life.[109]

For that fan, queers and metalheads could be equally closeted or choose to be equally out. Another fan discussed the community – not queer but metal – as her home. According to that bisexual female from the United Kingdom:

> I feel happier, I'm listening to music that understands me and I understand it. I feel part of a community even though I'm not always physically in the community, you are when you listen to metal. I'm first a metalhead, second a bisexual.[110]

A female leather/BDSM-identified fan from Bulgaria explained how metal fulfilled her needs as a queer person:

> Because of the extreme sexual energy I feel and the chance to express/ share within the subculture. Of course, there are 'higher' layers as well, many bands appealing to my intellectual and spiritual needs. Many of my favourite artists combine emotional extremism with musical eloquence, complexity and intellectualism (Ihsahn, Enslaved etc.). I

generally find the artists of the genre more open than the mainstream in addressing the human condition in its entirety – particularly referring to artists of the black/post-black subdivision.[111]

"It's more than just a musical genre," wrote a genderqueer male from America, "it's a philosophy, expression of defiance against oppression, and a way of life."[112] For queer fans of heavy metal, it was never just about the sonic gestures, it was about the audiotopia that those gestures signaled.

DIFFERENT IS HARD

In interviews with queer fans, my last question was always the same: what is your favorite song and what do its lyrics mean to you? I gave no requirements: metal or not, any song was allowed. More than any other question, the informants who elected to answer this question illustrated the queerscape of heavy metal. Their choices are illustrative of the ability of queer fans to locate signposts of the queerscape no matter how difficult. One metal fan, a twenty-three-year-old bisexual female from Scotland, chose Metallica's "Escape" from their album *Ride the Lightning*. "When I think of it, I always smile to myself," she wrote. "It's a song full of pride and rebellion."[113] The lyrics she identified as most important were "No need to hear things that they say/Life's for my own to live my own way."[114] She further explained her choice of song this way:

> People who find it easy to fit in don't normally become part of the metal community. There's just something about it for people who aren't simple creatures. And don't like your normal everyday things. I always think metal is for people who don't mind confronting things that scare them or are the darkside of humanity or the mysterious side of the world.[115]

Another fan, twenty-one-year-old gay male from Canada, chose "Gallows" from *Congregation of the Damned* by the metal band Atreyu: "Don't think we don't see your scars/Are you afraid of who you are?"[116] "The song is about a person's insecurities about themselves and how others see them," "wrote the respondent, "and sometimes I am self-conscious of that."[117] Another informant, a fifty-one-year-old gay male fan from the American Midwest, selected "Voodoo" by Black Sabbath with no further comment: "Call me a liar, you knew/You were a fool, but that's cool, it's all right."[118] An eighteen-year-old gay male fan from the United Kingdom chose an instrumental song, "March Into the Sea," by the postmodern metal band Pelican. When asked why the song was important to him, the informant replied: "It means a lot to me because while I don't associate it with any particular moment, no matter how rough the times it always calms me down and I can just feel whatever it is that is bugging me melt away."[119] "Periscope" from the album *Chimera* by the band Andromeda was chosen by an eighteen-year-old male from Holland who identified as a man who likes other men. According to this respondent, the song illustrated how he lived his life: the first two verses were how he dealt with problems, the third verse told something about his past and future, and the final verse asked and partially answered questions he asked himself. "And then the realization at the end," he explained, "and a kick in the ass for me to work on it. The ending of the song with a fast paced double bass drum sort of wakes me up for that."[120] The lyrics at the end of "Periscope," by the Swedish progressive metal band Andromeda, served as part of his map: "Hanging on to my only hope/I'm looking through my periscope."[121]

While all of these selections illustrate heavy metal's queerscape, the selection that best shows how queer fans of heavy metal are able to build a queerscape was from a thirty-eight-year-old gay male Canadian. "There are a number of songs which I've loved the lyrics too but I think the one that's stuck with me my whole life," this informant replied, "… Different is hard."[122] The song, featured in a Pufnstuf film and sung by Cass Elliott, was recited by the informant: "I used to wonder what hex I was under/what did I do to be different!"[123] When I asked the informant to explain why this song held so much importance for him, he simply replied, "Different is hard."

In his essay on queer space, scholar Jean-Ulrich Deseret explained queer space, indeed a queerscape, was latent until consumed by its own contradictions. "A queer space is an activated zone," Deseret theorized, "made proprietary by the occupant or *flaneur,* the wanderer. It is at once public and private."[124] The queer fans of heavy metal occupy a heavy metal queerscape that is both public and private, activated by their wandering in and out of its scenes, styles, and lyrics. They are the explorers of the queerscape, drawing a map for others to follow and following the signals of those before them.

Many informants and respondents asked where they could find other queer fans of heavy metal. The answer I gave them still stands. We are everywhere, we are heavy metal, and without us, metal would not exist as it does today. In my work as an anthropologist, I embrace the idea that all contacts with informants should be exchanges, conversations where I offer as much information as I request. When asked what song was important to me, I answered with the lyrics for "United" by Judas Priest: "Make a stand/We're gonna win."[125]

NOTES

1. Heather Love, *Feeling Backward: Loss and the Politics of Queer History* (Cambridge: Harvard University Press, 2007), 30.
2. Bersani, "Is the Rectum A Grave?", 15.
3. See Emma Baulch, *Making Scenes: Reggae, Punk and Death Metal in 1990s Bali* (Durham: Duke University Press, 2007), Jeremy Wallach, *Modern Noise, Fluid Genres: Popular Music in Indonesia, 1997-2001* (Middletown: Wesleyan University, 2009), and Pierre Hecker, *Turkish Metal: Music, Meaning, and Morality in a Muslim Society* (London: Ashgate, 2012) for exemplary examples of work on local scenes in heavy metal. The most frequently cited work on heavy metal as a scene for adolescents

dealing with psychological issues is Jeffrey Arnett, *Metalheads: Heavy Metal Music And Adolescent Alienation* (New York: Westview Press, 1996). For a discussion of the development of heavy metal music studies, see Andy Brown, "Heavy Genealogy: Mapping the Currents, Contraflows and Conflicts of the Emergent Field of Metal Studies, 1978-2010." *Journal for Cultural Research* 15, No. 3 (2011): 213–242.

4. The use of an asterisk is increasingly used as a way to denote the wide variety of non-heteronormative gender and sexual identities. It will be used in the text whenever a survey respondent identified themselves as "trans" without further comment. For more information see Hugh Ryan's January 2014 Slate. com Outward blog post "What Does Trans* Mean, and Where Did It Come From?" http://www.slate.com/blogs/outward/2014/01/10/trans_what_does_it_mean_and_where_did_it_come_from.html

5. The survey "Queer Fans of Heavy Metal Music" was approved by the Human Subjects Review Committee of the University of Central Missouri, the IRB of that institution, in January 2009 (#700117228). Survey respondents were anonymous, so in the text respondents are identified by the randomized five or six digit number assigned to the respondent by the online survey system. No identifying information was collected unless volunteered by respondent. The complete survey is in the Appendix.

6. While understood among queer fans, terms of sexual and gender identity may not be widely understood. Gay, lesbian, and bisexual are in general use as identifiers. Queer/genderqueer is a term preferred for those who elect to identify outside the traditional binary and can include those who identify as pansexual. Butch and femme, terms hotly debated in feminist and lesbian circles in the 1980s and 1990s, are used as a way to identify with a masculine gender presentation (butch) or a feminine gender presentation (femme). Intersex individuals are those born with the genitalia of both biological sexes. Trans*, which includes both individuals who have undergone sexual reassignment procedures or not, denotes those who see themselves as crossing the gender binary. For further discussion on this and other terms of gender and sexuality, see *LGBTQ Encyclopedia Today: An Encyclopedia*, edited by John C. Hawley (Westport: Greenwood Press, 2009).

7. "Queer Fans of Heavy Metal," respondent no. 289574.
8. "Queer Fans of Heavy Metal," respondent no. 14455.
9. Kath Weston, "Theory, Theory, Who's Got The Theory?" *GLQ* 2 (1995): 348.
10. F*cking C*nts, "10 ways to recognize a macho cunt (no, you're not 'men')." Accessed July 1, 2014, http://f-ckingc-nts.com/people/10-ways-to-recognize-a-macho-cunt-no-youre-not-men/.
11. Brian Hickam and Jeremy Wallach, "Female Authority and Dominion: Discourse and Distinctions of Heavy Metal Scholarship," *Journal for Cultural Research* 15, No. 3 (2011): 255.
12. Marcus Erbe, "'This Isn't Over Till I Say It's Over': Narratives of Male Frustration in Deathcore and Beyond," paper presented at the International Congress on Heavy Metal and Gender, Cologne, Germany, October 2009.
13. Bashe, *Heavy Metal Thunder*, 7.
14. F*cking C*nts. "10 ways to recognize a macho cunt."
15. "Queer Fans of Heavy Metal" respondent No. 25394.
16. "Queer Fans of Heavy Metal," respondent No. 26061.
17. "Queer Fans of Heavy Metal," respondent No. 28579.
18. "Queer Fans of Heavy Metal," respondent No. 144431.
19. "Queer Fans of Heavy Metal," respondent No. 26093.

20. Love, *Feeling Backward*, 4.
21. Bersani, "Is the Rectum A Grave?", 14.
22. "Queer Fans of Heavy Metal," respondent No. 289574.
23. "Queer Fans of Heavy Metal," respondent No. 144705.
24. PS, interview with the author, July 8, 2010, Skype interview.
25. "Kerry King: Ex-Soulfly Drummer Joe Nunez's Mother Wouldn't Let Him Play In Slayer!" *Blabbermouth,* June 10, 2002, http://www.blabbermouth.net/news/kerry-king-ex-soulfly-drummer-joe-nunez-s-mother-wouldn-t-let-him-play-in-slayer/#QXe2FeSy7eBm18AT.99.
26. "Bear" is a term used to describe large, hairy, male-identified individuals in queer communities. It likely originated with a 1979 essay by George Mazzei in *The Advocate* entitled "Who's Who In the Zoo?" Bears are often included in the constellation of sexual identities included in the leather community.
27. "Queer Fans of Heavy Metal," respondent No. 25400.
28. Atom and His Package, *Hair: Debatable,* Hopeless Records, ASIN No. B0001JXP6Q, released April 6, 2004, compact disc.
29. Stuart Hall, "The Spectacle of the 'Other'," in *Representation: Cultural Representations and Signifying Practices*, edited by Stuart Hall (London: Sage, 1997): 223–268.
30. Bartkewicz, "A Rainbow In The Dark," 68.
31. Bersani, "Is the Rectum A Grave?", 14.
32. Hickam and Wallach, "Female Authority and Dominion," 260.
33. Elizabeth Freeman, "Queer Belongings: Kinship Theory and Queer Theory," in *A Companion to Lesbian, Gay, Transgender, and Queer Studies*, edited by George E. Haggerty and Molly McGarry (London: Blackwell, 2007): 310.
34. Ibid., 298.
35. "Queer Fans of Heavy Metal," respondent No. 28539.
36. "Queer Fans of Heavy Metal," respondent No. 25904.
37. "Queer Fans of Heavy Metal," respondent No. 278285.
38. "Queer Fans of Heavy Metal," respondent No. 149456.
39. "Queer Fans of Heavy Metal," respondent No. 25480.
40. "Queer Fans of Heavy Metal," respondent No. 25852.
41. "Queer Fans of Heavy Metal," respondent No. 25899.
42. "Queer Fans of Heavy Metal," respondent No. 289356.
43. "Queer Fans of Heavy Metal," respondent No. 144514.
44. "Queer Fans of Heavy Metal," respondent No. 280017.
45. "Queer Fans of Heavy Metal," respondent No. 170758.
46. "Queer Fans of Heavy Metal," respondent No. 25430.
47. Hebdidge, "Style as Homology and Signifying Practice," 56.
48. "Queer Fans of Heavy Metal," respondent No. 60750.
49. "Queer Fans of Heavy Metal," respondent No. 26255.
50. Healy, *Gay Skins*, 60.
51. Gordon Brent Ingram, "Marginality and the Landscapes of Erotic Alien(n)ations." In *Queers In Space: Communities, Public Places, Sites of Resistance*, edited by Yolanda Retter, Anne-Marie Bouthillette, and Gordon Brent Ingram (New York: Bay Press 1997): 43.
52. DT, interview with the author, September 15, 2010, Skype interview.
53. CW, interview with the author, January 5, 2011, Skype interview.
54. Donna Dehyle, "From Break Dancing to Heavy Metal," *Youth and Society* 30, No. 1 (September 1998): 12.

55. Jeffrey Arnett, *Metalheads: Heavy Metal Music and Adolescent Alienation* (New York: Westview Press, 1996): 18.
56. Ingram, "Marginality and the Landscapes of Erotic Alien(n)ations," 32.
57. "Queer Fans of Heavy Metal," respondent No. 34976.
58. Olson, "Everybody Likes 'Our Town'," 280.
59. Grossberg, "Reflections of a Disappointed Music Scholar," 49.
60. Healy, *Gay Skins*, 130.
61. Karen Bettez Halnon, "Metal Carnival and Dis-alienation: The Politics of Grotesque Realism." *Symbolic Interaction* 29, No. 1 (Winter 2006): 35.
62. "Queer Fans of Heavy Metal," respondent No. 29618.
63. "Queer Fans of Heavy Metal," respondent No. 43279.
64. MB, interview with the author, August 1, 2010, Skype interview.
65. "Queer Fans of Heavy Metal," respondent No. 40899.
66. "Queer Fans of Heavy Metal," respondent No. 60750.
67. "Queer Fans of Heavy Metal," respondent No. 32102.
68. "Queer Fans of Heavy Metal," respondent No. 30675.
69. "Queer Fans of Heavy Metal," respondent No. 166600.
70. "Queer Fans of Heavy Metal," respondent No. 29791.
71. "Queer Fans of Heavy Metal," respondent No. 31833.
72. Judith Butler, *Gender Trouble: Feminism and the Subversion of Identity* (New York: Routledge, 1999): 179.
73. "Queer Fans of Heavy Metal," respondent No. 144549.
74. "Queer Fans of Heavy Metal," respondent No. 133698.
75. "Queer Fans of Heavy Metal," respondent No. 25430.
76. "Queer Fans of Heavy Metal," respondent No. 25400.
77. "Queer Fans of Heavy Metal," respondent No. 28579.
78. Love, *Feeling Backward*, 23.
79. "Queer Fans of Heavy Metal," respondent No. 26198.
80. Judith A. Peraino, *Listening to Sirens: Musical Technologies of Queer Identity from Homer to Hedwig* (Berkeley: University of California Press, 2006): 3.
81. Ian Biddle and Freya Jarman-Ivens, "Introduction," in *Oh Boy! Making Masculinity in Popular Music* (New York: Routledge, 2007): 10.
82. Peraino, *Listening to Sirens*, 7.
83. "Queer Fans of Heavy Metal," respondent No. 242656.
84. Christopher Small, *Musicking: The Meanings of Performing and Listening* (Connecticut: Wesleyan University Press, 1998): 2–3.
85. Freya Jarman-Ivens, *Queer Voices: Technologies, Vocalities, and the Musical Flow*, Palgrave Macmillan Critical Studies in Gender, Sexuality, and Culture series, edited by Patricia T. Clough and R. Danielle Egan (New York: Palgrave Macmillan, 2011): vii.
86. R.J. Warren Zanes, "Too Much Mead? Under the Influence (Of Participant Observation)," in *Reading Rock and Roll: Authenticity, Appropriation, Aesthetics*, edited by Kevin J.H Dettmat and William Richey (New York: Columbia University Press, 1999): 40.
87. Simon Frith, "Music and Identity," in *Questions of Cultural Identity*, edited by Stuart Hall and Paul du Gay (New York: Sage, 1996): 123.
88. Ibid.
89. Jason Lim, "Queer Critique and the Politics of Affect," in *Geographies of Sexualities: Theory, Practices, and Politics*, edited by Kath Browne, Jason Lim, and Gavin Brown (London: Ashgate, 2007): 54.

90. Kun, *Audiotopia*, 23.
91. Hickam and Wallach, "Female Authority and Dominion," 269.
92. Larissa Glasser, Interview: An Interview with Randi Elise B. In: *Transgender Tapestry*, 96, Winter 2001. http://www.ifge.org/index.php?name=News&file=articlesid=94&theme=Printer.
93. "Queer Fans of Heavy Metal," respondent No. 144549.
94. "Queer Fans of Heavy Metal," respondent No. 195118.
95. "Queer Fans of Heavy Metal," respondent No. 144508.
96. "Queer Fans of Heavy Metal," respondent No. 196676.
97. "Queer Fans of Heavy Metal," respondent No. 170758.
98. "Queer Fans of Heavy Metal," respondent No. 28527.
99. "Queer Fans of Heavy Metal," respondent No. 289363.
100. Adam Rafalovich, "Broken and Becoming God-Sized: Contemporary Metal Music and Masculine Individualism." In *Symbolic Interaction* 29, No. 1 (Winter 2006): 22.
101. "Queer Fans of Heavy Metal," respondent No. 251087.
102. "Queer Fans of Heavy Metal," respondent no. 256808.
103. "Queer Fans of Heavy Metal," respondent no. 262440.
104. LB, "interview with the author, September 1, 2010, Skype interview.
105. "Queer Fans of Heavy Metal," respondent No. 30744.
106. "Queer Fans of Heavy Metal," respondent No. 242656.
107. "Queer Fans of Heavy Metal," respondent No. 248705.
108. Chad Bennett, "Flaming the Fan: Shame and the Aesthetics of Queer Fandom in Todd Haynes' 'Velvet Goldmine'," *Cinema Journal* 49, No. 2 (Winter 2010).
109. "Queer Fans of Heavy Metal, respondent No. 36670.
110. "Queer Fans of Heavy Metal," respondent No. 25813.
111. "Queer Fans of Heavy Metal," respondent No. 26435.
112. "Queer Fans of Heavy Metal," respondent No. 144918.
113. CG, interview with the author, July 7, 2010, Skype interview.
114. Metallica. *Ride the Lightning*, Megaforce Records, ASIN No. B00EBDXSOW, released July 27, 1984, compact disc.
115. CG, interview with the author, July 7, 2010, Skype interview.
116. Atreyu, *Congregation of the Damned*, Hollywood Records, ASIN No. B002NPUCFS, released October 26, 2009, compact disc.
117. PM, interview with the author, July 7, 2010, Skype interview.
118. Black Sabbath, *Mob Rules*, Universal Japan, ASIN No. B005S1Y728, released December 27, 2011, compact disc.
119. JE, interview with the author, September 9, 2010, Skype interview.
120. DK, interview with the author, August 20, 2010, Skype interview.
121. Andromeda, *Chimera*, Massacre Records, ASIN No. B000DZIBSA, released January 21, 2006, compact disc.
122. JD, interview with the author, July 18, 2010, Skype interview.
123. Cass Elliott, *Dream A Little Dream*, MCA Records, ASIN No. B000002P3T, released February 11, 1997, compact disc.
124. Jean-Ulrick Deseret, "Queer Space." In *Queers in Space: Communities/Public Places/Sites of Resistance*, edited by Gordon Brett Ingram, Anne-Marie Bouthillette, and Yolanda Ritter (Seattle: Berg Press, 1997): 21.
125. Judas Priest, *British Steel*, Columbia Records, ASIN No. B0099139040, released April 14, 1980, vinyl.

4 Everybody Knows

The irony of heterosexual hegemony is that its very dominance means that many heterosexuals are ignorant of the changing homosexual landscape and have the arrogance not to think twice about the identities of 'straight-acting' individuals.[1]

When is the performance of gender purely a performance and when is it the discursively formed performance of gender? Can the two ever be separated? This study centers gender as a field of disruption in heavy metal but looks instead to the work of performance studies in order to understand the role that gendered performance plays in the heavy metal queerscape. Rather than seek to understand or define the gender and/or sexual identity of performers, I instead focus on the disruptive space between the performers and the fans. In this scheme, performers are not simply the vehicles for the representation of gender. They are, in fact, agents who use their bodies in performance as a way to trouble gender for the audience. In what scholar Daphne Brooks referred to as "opaque performances," performers use their work to challenge the acceptable categories of gender even if they appear to reify them. "Dense and spectacular, the opaque performances of marginalized cultural figures call attention to the skill of the performer who," wrote Brooks, "through gestures and speech as well as material props and visual technologies, is able to confound and disrupt conventional constructions of the racialized and gendered body."[2] In this chapter I will explore the ways in which selected performers and queer fans who perform heavy metal are subjectified to the regulatory and disruptive definitions of gender, and the methods those individuals use to disrupt and interrupt those definitions. The key to this focus on performance is the view of the fan. The performance of an on-stage persona is not necessarily congruous with an off-stage identity but in the world of metal, celebrity identity and persona are frequently conflated by fans. Therefore, the ethnographic work among queer fans is integral to understanding how these opaque performances are read and understood by the audience.

In *Running with the Devil*, Robert Walser discussed the role of gender politics in heavy metal music and performance. According to Walser, heavy metal is a space where hegemonic male power is reified and replicated, even if that means misogyny and exscription or the "total denial of gender anxieties through the articulation of fantastic worlds about women."[3] If heavy metal is considered as a queerscape, however, what happens to that modeled male power? Gay male heavy metal fans view male power, and the performance of masculinity, in a far different way than heterosexual male fans. Leather/BDSM-identified fans see desired subjects in the performance of heavy metal, and forge strong connections between their identity and heavy metal performance. For trans folks and masculine lesbians, male power may be distinctly avoided or reinterpreted as a specifically female-bodied act of identity and defiance of the very patriarchal system Walser suggests. At the same time, queer fans are consuming metal in new ways, across genre lines and typically not in the traditional power, thrash, and hair metal bands studied by Walser. In the queerscape, queer fans consume heavy metal sounds at a distance, often removed from a live performance. They model not the traditional masculinity proposed by Walser but rather a flexible understanding of gender reflected in the terrain of the queerscape. "Heavy metal is, as much as anything else, an arena of gender," wrote Walser in 1993, "where spectacular gladiators compete to register and affect ideas of masculinity, sexuality, and gender relations."[4] In the arena of heavy metal, however, those performances should be considered more operating theater, not a fight to the death. What if the gladiators are queer? What if the audience believes them to be queer? What is registered and affected then? In the queerscape of heavy metal, performances both real and imagined become lenses through which the gender and sexuality of heavy metal is dissected, reimagined, and presented to both audience and performer.

ROB HALFORD: THE METAL GOD

Rob Halford is perhaps the most famous heavy metal singer, queer or not, in the metal world. Among queer fans, he represents the penultimate: an out gay man, leader of arguably the most influential metal band (Judas Priest) in history, originator of the metal style, a man who metal fans, queer or not, emulate as both singer and performer. Though Halford is widely discussed, idolized, even sexualized in fan fiction, his band Judas Priest is still considered one of the most hypermasculine bands in metal's history. For queer fans, however, that history of performances and videos is rewritten as a queer history in which Halford was the victim of a homophobic scene he rehabilitated. In the queerscape, Halford's metal career is a hagiography, the story of a gay man who out-metalled the straightest members of metal scenes.

Much like the folktales surrounding the creation of other deities, the story of how Judas Priest got its name is a bit mythic. Influenced by the sinister-sounding band name Black Sabbath, possibly taken from a Bob Dylan song, the name Judas Priest was intended to connote both danger and solidarity.

"So I think the two words intermingle – the Judas and the Priest – the good and the bad, the light and the shade," explained Rob Halford in 1983. "We're not involved in Satanism. The name is just a name; it's been good to us."[5] Judas Priest is considered one of the most important heavy metal bands, indeed one of the most important rock bands, of all time. Referred to by fans as "the defenders of the faith," after their 1984 album of the same name, Judas Priest released their first album in 1974 and continues to record. Their latest album, *Redeemer of Souls*, was the band's first time in the Billboard Top Ten the week it was released. The band's lead singer, Rob Halford, secured a copyright for his nickname in 2009: Metal God.[6] Halford the Metal God leads Judas Priest, the defenders of the faith, in a mission queer fans have adopted as their own: staying faithful, to oneself and to heavy metal.

When asked what heavy metal performers were queer themselves, every queer fan surveyed answered Rob Halford, regardless of age, identity, country, or culture. While some of this fame among queer fans is no doubt because of Judas Priest, fans pointed to Halford's coming out in 1998, his style and costume, even his lyrics as signals to queer culture. Halford is revered, perhaps even worshipped, by queer metal fans. Even other queer performers point to Halford as a role model and icon. In fact, many queer fans think Rob Halford is the only queer metal performer. For example, lead singer Max from the Italian disco duo Hard Ton explained: "The lead singer of them [Judas Priest] is an icon to me as he's the only gay singer in the heavy metal scene."[7] In fact, for many queer fans Rob Halford is not only a heavy metal icon, he is their queer icon. He is the queer icon of heavy metal, an exhibition of queer-identified power. The fact that Halford's identity was a formative part of the uber-masculine heavy metal world only makes his legend greater in the eyes of queer fans. "With Halford coming out," explained one gay male fan from the United States, "I think a lot of attitudes were probably changed."[8] A lesbian female fan from Canada wrote: "When Rob Halford came out of the closet, I think this helped tear down the alienative effect often associated with metal."[9] The claims to the Metal God by queer fans were best expressed in the article "Rawk and a Hard Place" by Robin Ibbison:

> Priest hit big in the early 1980s as the interest in all things Metal took off, though, like [Freddie] Mercury, Halford initially made no outright comment on his sexuality, the fact he was living life offstage as an out gay man was plain to see in many aspects of his act. Halford's lyrical content would touch upon gay subject matter, often of a sexual (specifically gay SM) nature. He also made specific reference to gay culture in a manner rare beyond more obviously out performers, such as Divine or Rufus Wainwright. *Raw Deal*, for example, is an account of a night in a sexually-charged all-male bar, and after making specific mention of the 'denim dudes' of Fire Island, it pronounces: 'The true

free expression I demand is human rights.' That this song was released in 1977 – and that the band produced other similarly themed tracks around that time – makes Priest look stridently brave to a contemporary eye; and the fact that Halford hasn't been embraced by the gay community as one of its heroes, a glaring oversight.[10]

In his influential book on Michel Foucault, David Halperin wrote that Foucault was such a mythic figure in intellectual circles that he defied a rational explanation. "As far as I'm concerned," Halperin wrote of Foucault, "the guy was a fucking saint."[11] Halperin's gay hagiography of Foucault, a writing of the life of Halperin's saint, is instructive in the case of Rob Halford. In fact, Halford's hagiography crosses into euhemerism. Euhemerism, a concept from studies of religion and mythology, is the concept that myths can be interpreted as rational versions of historical fact. Stories of the Metal God, with whom the queer fans can have no rational relationship, are not only the stories of a saint. They tell a rationalized version of Halford's hagiography consistent with both queer fans' desires for an icon and heavy metal's need for an idol. The Metal God is defending the faith of the queerscape, the place where queers and heavy metal overlap.

Of the two stories that pervade Halford's hagiography, the biggest one is his coming-out story. Coming-out stories are practically required for queer-identified individuals. These stories are in effect origin stories of how one came to be queer and are confessional. As Foucault elucidated in *The History of Sexuality*, confession is essentially a move of discursive power. One confesses, admitting to faults and disruptions of biopower by discursively identifying as a subject to be enclosed. Fejes and Dahlstedt further proposed that, in the twenty-first century, the confession became a social norm wherein emotional problems could be enclosed by society as well.[12] Coming-out stories can be seen as a production of the modern confessional. One admits to disruption of the biopolitics of heteronormative society, describes it in emotional terms, and in doing so becomes enclosed as an openly queer person. Further, the coming-out story has become a trope in literature. Esther Saxey, author of *Homoplot: The Coming-Out Story and Gay, Lesbian, and Bisexual Identity*, wrote extensively on the coming-out story, its literary hallmarks and its politics. Saxey explained an individual's coming-out story as "a tale summing up their own journey to sexual identity and showing how their nature made itself known to them despite a hostile environment."[13] In essence, the coming-out story is a modern confessional trope in which an individual exposes and encloses themselves. Saxey further explains that coming-out stories typically detail one's victory over family and society and finding a relationship where one's desires are realized. "The coming-out story," explained Saxey, "is a pale shadow of the romance plot."[14] Halford's coming-out story, however, is quite different. Though it is indeed confessional, it reveals little to nothing about Halford's youth, or his coming of age as a gay man, or his romantic (or sexual) life.

Because Halford's hagiography is a production of the queerscape, its role as a confession must be metered with the role of fans in constructing the confession. Halford's coming-out story is more euhemerism as romance novel, a hagiographic tale constructed largely by fans instead of by Halford himself.

Halford first came out in an interview on *Superrock*, a short interview program on MTV, on February 4, 1998. He had at this point left Judas Priest and embarked on a solo career (he reunited with the band in 2003). His departure from Judas Priest was not without controversy, and rumors swirled about what led Halford to leave the band in 1992. He had suffered an injury while on stage the year before, he was having differences with both the band and their management, and Judas Priest had just completed a difficult lawsuit filed by the parents of a teenager who had committed suicide and saw Judas Priest songs as the cause of the young man's death. It was, needless to say, a turbulent time for the band. Upon leaving Judas Priest, Halford formed a new band, Fight, and released two albums in 1993 and 1995. Though the Fight albums were not critical or commercial successes in the heavy metal world, their reception in the queer metal world was much different. Fight was featured prominently in the newsletter of the Gay Metal Society in 1993 and 1995, and graced the cover of the June 1995 issue of the *GMS Headbanger*. The Gay Metal Society was a social organization of gay male metalheads formed in Chicago. Organizers of the GMS held parties and activities, and published a zine newsletter *Headbanger* that featured album reviews, concert reviews, cartoons and images of bands, a horoscope column and activities. They also ran a Gay Metal Society Hotline (780-0SIN) and provided a mail service for *Headbanger* subscribers who lived outside the area. In the June 1995 issue of *Headbanger*, the entire first page was devoted to Halford and Fight:

> Rob Halford, former frontman of the legendary Judas Priest, along with his band of amazing players, presents songs that pound like fists against the evils of AIDS, prejudice, the Holocaust, child abuse and domestic violence. They scream out for artistic freedom, an escape from a world of destruction, and love on a seemingly loveless planet. For Rob Halford, who influenced an entire generation while leading the legendary and often outlandish Judas Priest, the world could use a dose of reality. With his new band, Fight, no subject is off-limits – no matter how taboo.[15]

Written three years before Halford publicly outted himself, the devotion to Halford in *Headbanger* is palpable. While "they" may be screaming, the only vocalist is Halford, seemingly screaming about love and AIDS and subjects "no matter how taboo." In this way, the queer fans built the legend of Halford as a queer metal icon, more than just Judas Priest's Metal God but the saint and deity of the queerscape.

When Halford did come out in 1998, his announcement was simple, short, and in immediate heavy rotation on MTV. "I think that most people know that I've been a gay man all my life," Halford told MTV, "and it's only been in recent times that it's an issue that I feel comfortable to address."[16] When asked why he did not come out earlier, Halford expressed some concern about what coming out might have done to the band. Fifteen days later, on February 19, Judas Priest members Ian Hill and K.K. Downing gave a short interview to MTV about Halford's coming out. According to MTV news: "Guitarist K.K. Downing let out a mock yawn as bassist Ian Hill said, 'It must have been the worst kept secret in rock and roll'."[17] That May Halford did an interview and appeared on the cover of *The Advocate*, the most widely read gay and lesbian magazine in the United States. In the interview, Halford discussed his life in Judas Priest and revealed his peers in Judas Priest always knew about his sexuality. "Everybody in Priest always had an awareness that I was gay," Halford told interviewer Judy Wieder. "I have never experienced homophobia from anyone in Priest."[18] The cover image of Halford showed him in his full leather glory: bare-chested, handcuffs gleaming from his belt, with one arm grasping a microphone and raised in the air. The image of him inside the article, however, was much different. That photograph showed Halford sitting on stairs, his knees drawn, arms crossed in front of his chest. He was wearing all black and his eyes were cast downward. On the next two pages were four images with the tagline "The Macho Men of Metal" and featured four images of bare-chested metal bad boys of the 1980s: Eddie Van Halen, Tommy Lee of the L.A. glam metal band Mötley Crüe, lead singer of Metallica James Hetfield, and Axl Rose of Guns N' Roses. The juxtaposition was clear: these macho men, covered in sweat with long hair and growling lips, versus the demure man curled up on a lonesome staircase. The images seemed quite disconnected from Halford's interview. Halford discussed love, taking a boyfriend on the road with Judas Priest, the occasional gay male groupie, the evolution of his leather look and his love of heavy metal. "Obviously this is just a wonderful day for me," Halford stated at the close of the interview."[19] Halford's coming-out story was already under creation. The Metal God on the cover became the antithesis of macho metal men in one interview. In claiming Halford as a queer icon, his coming-out story became the confessional and he became the priest swathed in black, seeking absolution for his macho man sins.

The second story that stands as a pillar of the Halford hagiography is about revision. Like the euhemerism practiced by mythologists and religious specialists, Halford's coming out precipitated a revision of history in favor of a new myth: everyone always knew Halford was a gay man. Stemming perhaps from Hill's statement about the "worst kept secret" or from fans who were suddenly questioning their adoration of Judas Priest, suddenly everyone always knew. This construction of Halford's sexuality continues to this day. In a 2011 article for the heavy metal website Invisible Oranges, journalist Richard Street-Jammer wrote about Halford's coming out as a moot point to anyone who understood Judas Priest lyrics in the song "Raw Deal." "Look, my gaydar's not very well-tuned, but I knew exactly what Halford was talking about: he was in a gay club, doing what people of all sexual orientations and preference do during a night out on the town," he wrote.[20] The truth is, while Halford's bandmates and others who knew Halford personally were not surprised, the heterosexual audience for Halford was. "For decades, Halford performed in the most popular metal band in the world while wearing an increasingly ridiculous succession of leather-daddy outfits," wrote one journalist in 2009. "And metalheads were *still* shocked when he came out. What does that say about metal?"[21] Queer fans who were fans of Judas Priest, however, remembered identifying Halford as a gay man early on. "It's so funny whenever I watch the video to 'Don't' Go' where Rob has his leather master outfit on and the little moustache I just think 'How could they NOT know he's gay'!" wrote a gay male fan from Canada. Overwhelmingly, the revisionist hagiography of Halford's identity is based on lyrics of Judas Priest songs and Halford's S&M leather outfit. Though Halford did not discuss Judas Priest song lyrics in his 1998 interviews, he did discuss his leather style frequently. In his interview with *The Advocate*, Halford reminisced about buying his outfit, and about being "a gay man and I'm into leather and that sexual side of the leather world."[22] When asked about the aesthetic he created in heavy metal, Halford spoke specifically about queer fans:

> I guess that's true, because I met this guy recently, and he said, 'When I was 13, I used to watch MTV, and you would be walking around in your leather stuff, and I'd always get an erection.' A lot of men who are into leather are also into metal. They mayn't know they're gay until they see something that makes them feel hot.[23]

In fact, Halford cited S&M as the source of not only his style but his sexuality multiple times: in several press interviews, his interview for *The Advocate*, his coming out on MTV, even in his appearance in *Behind the Music: Judas Priest* (2001). This began to shift, however, in 2001. In September of 2001, Warner Brothers Pictures released the film *Rock Star*. The film was based on an article about Tim "Ripper" Owens, a Judas Priest fan and cover band singer who was hired to take Rob Halford's place in the band during his hiatus. In the film, actor Mark Wahlberg plays a young cover band musician, Chris Cole, who is suddenly hired to take over for the lead singer of the band he idolizes, Steel Dragon. The film then follows Cole as he becomes a debauched rock star before coming to his senses and returning home to his girlfriend and his cover band. There was no mistaking the film – it was an unauthorized and fictionalized biopic about the band's transition from Owens to Halford. The film, originally titled *Metal God*, was disavowed by Halford and the other members of Judas Priest. "This is the thing that's sort of not very good for us," guitarist Glenn Tipton told MTV News.

"Everybody still thinks it's the story of Ripper, but it isn't."[24] The key point of contention was one pivotal scene. When Halford left Judas Priest, it was a year before Owens was hired as the band's lead singer. In *Rock Star*, Chris Cole is called to an audition in the middle of a tour. He enters the recording booth and the fictional lead singer Bobby Beers storms into the recording studio in a kimono and pants. After yelling about leaving the band, Beers looks at guitarist character Kirk Cuddy and asks, "Is it because I'm gay?"

> CHRIS: You're gay?
> BOBBY: No, I got both my nipples pierced and bought a house in Morocco because I'm John fucking Wayne![25]

An argument ensues between Beers and Cuddy that ranges across the studio. Beers begins to shout at Cole about what it takes to be a metal star and compares himself to Elvis.

> CUDDY: Except Elvis was the king. (Snickering from the members of the band)
> BEERS: (pulls off a wig, revealing short hair under a stocking) And I'm just the queen. Very funny. Ha bloody ha. Bastards. You bastards.[26]

The members of Judas Priest threatened to sue Warner Brothers, and the film company quickly issued statements about the fictional nature of the film. "Ninety percent of the movie is based on pure rock star mythology," one of the film's marketing directors told MTV.[27] The question is, what mythology is under production in the film? Halford was clear that his "worst kept secret" was shared with the band from the beginning. In his coming-out interview with *The Advocate*, however, some of the roots of this myth become clear. Within the interview he mentioned traveling in Mykonos, as well as wearing his sister's clothes in early performances. These pieces of the interview were fleeting comments but within them lay a seed of the Bobby Beers mythology: Halford in a leather costume on stage but behind the scenes just a queen in a kimono. The same year *Rock Star* was released, Judas Priest released its second and last album featuring Tim Owens. "After a quarter of a century of defending the hard rock faith, Judas Priest are having fun and even laughing, the difficulties with ex-lead singers and lawsuits a thing of the past," a reporter for *Rolling Stone* wrote about the film and the new album in 2001. "That's a story even Hollywood couldn't come up with, but it's something people are paying to see."[28] When Halford rejoined the band two years later, Owens gave an interview to Neil Daniels for his unauthorized biography of Judas Priest entitled *The Story of Judas Priest: Defenders of the Faith*. Owens told Daniels he had no idea Halford was a gay man until he came out in 1998, despite his catalogic knowledge of the band, its songs, and Halford's stage persona.[29]

In a 2005 interview on NPR's *Fresh Air*, Halford was asked about his coming out. He told listeners he refrained from coming out earlier to protect the band. "I was always protecting Judas Priest."[30] When asked about his leathers, Halford told the interviewer he got them at his local S&M shop and the band "kind of stumbled upon it" as a look. The interviewer asked more direct questions about Halford and his own sexuality. "Subconsciously that was my way of saying, 'Look this is who I am'," explained Halford. "I'm not particularly attracted to that world [leather/BDSM]."[31] In the same interview Halford explained the look was created specifically to go with the Judas Priest song "Hell Bent for Leather." "Hell Bent for Leather" was a song featured on the fifth Judas Priest album *Killing Machine*, released in October 1978 in the United Kingdom and the following February in the United States. Halford premiered his leather look during the spring leg of the 1978 tour, which took place from March to July 7, 1978. Is this obfuscation on Halford's part or a refusal to admit to participation in the leather/BDSM subculture with which his style was identified? While it is impossible to know with certainty, when considered through the concept of an opaque performance the queerscape comes into focus. Halford, in signaling his own sexuality, whether subconsciously or not, used an image easily recognizable to queer audiences: the leather gay male. By claiming the costume as a link to a biker anthem like "Hell Bent for Leather," Halford keeps that performance an opaque signal. Was Halford a leatherman or did he wear a kimono and a wig? Did Judas Priest break up because of Halford's sexuality or because of other problems the band faced at that time? Like any hagiography, the story of a saint's life is mired with improbabilities, myths, miracles, and questions. His opaque performance, whether real or imagined for the stage, was the same signal to queer fans regardless of its origins. Halford's ability to continue to disrupt the enclosures around the Metal God reveals the masculinity of his performance as always in question, the most opaque of persona. Halford continued to confound in a 2010 interview with the *San Diego Gay and Lesbian News*:

> I just chose that kind of look because heavy metal for many, many years didn't really have the visual connections and their power connected to the music. So, I just kind of experimented and felt that particular image was more sensible and worked. So, that is something that is only an assumption. So, what I am trying to say is first that is the irony, and it is also a little bit disrespectful to look at somebody like that and there is an assumption that 'Oh they must be gay.' Personally I think it is disrespectful, not from you, but from people who are stating it that way. I think that that is all about stereotyping. And what we try to do consistently in the gay community is break away the stereotypical imagery of how we are perceived to be by straight culture. So it's kind of an irony tinged with stereotypical assumption. But there I was you know, and suddenly some straight people were saying, 'We should

have got that all along, because look at what he's dressed like.' I think that is very insulting and very narrow-minded. But that is all just part of the equation, of who I am and what I do.[32]

Or, as he told *The Guardian* in July 2014: "I've become the stately homo of heavy metal."[33]

GAAHL: HEAVY METAL'S QUEER TRICKSTER

Another performer queer fans identified as particularly important is Gaahl from the Norweigan metal bands Gorgoroth and Wardruna, among others. Kristian Espedal, whose stage name is Gaahl, performed with the band Gorgoroth and was an active part of the 1990s Norwegian black metal scene, a scene famous for church burnings and two metal performers who were convicted of murder. Gaahl was known to use racial and ethnic epithets on stage, telling interviewers he followed Adolf Hitler and the Roman emperor Nero. He served two jail terms: a six-month term in 2002 for assault and nine months in 2006 for assaulting and torturing a man at a party. In 2008, Gaahl came out as a gay man and won the Gay Person of the Year award at the Bergen Gay Galla in 2010. In a 2008 interview on Norwegian television, Gaahl was asked if being out would change the perception of him and his music. "I guess it will even out the score in a way," replied Gaahl.[34] To what score is Gaahl referring, and how does Gaahl's outing confound the queer fans' reading of his performances?

Gaahl's opaque performance, the one that attracts so many queer fans of heavy metal to Gaahl and the sounds of black metal, can easily be understood as the work of a trickster. The trickster is a common trope in fiction and in anthropology, descended from studies in mythology and the colonialism of Europeans. Tricksters are beings who disobey social rules and behaviors, are difficult to understand, and can elicit both laughter and fear. Though first discussed in the nineteenth century, the concept of the trickster as a cultural concept was solidified by anthropologist Victor Turner. Turner's theories on liminal and liminoid states of being drew on the work of Arnold van Genepp and others, and became an important influence on future theorists such as Foucault, Deleuze, and Guattari. According to Turner, rituals that denoted one's movement from one stage of life to the next were punctuated with liminal states, periods during which "a legitimized situation of freedom from cultural constraints and social classifications" existed.[35] "From this perspective, he [Turner] interpreted pilgrimages, popular riots, theater, student street protests, even revolutions, as liminal phenomena."[36] The trickster exists in that liminality and "only by breaking every taboo imaginable and becoming an outcast can he return to his element."[37] The trickster is a creature of myth, constantly engaged in an opaque performance because the trickster is always focused on disruption, despite any appearance otherwise. Black metal is highly performative and by Gaahl's own admission is purposefully inaccessible; some black metal bands do not even publish lyrics.[38] Gaahl occupies the queerscape, a self-identified gay man in what has historically been an overtly homophobic scene, and he does so as the trickster, constantly disrupting his image in order to remain in the liminal queerscape.

Gaahl's position as the queerscape trickster is visible in two ways: his position in black metal's history of violence and in the constant disruption of his own coming out. The violence in black metal, while largely isolated to a handful of events and individuals, is the master narrative of the genre. The key individuals in that master narrative are Varg Vikernes, Faust, and Gaahl. While Gaahl was identified by most queer fans as an out heavy metal performer, Varg Vikernes and Faust were agreed on as some of the most homophobic performers in heavy metal. Varg Vikernes, who performed in the Norwegian metal bands Mayhem and Burzum, was sentenced to prison in 1993 for the murder of fellow Mayhem member Euronymous and the destruction of four historic churches by arson. He's been discussed, criticized, vilified, and otherwise featured in several books (including the influential and controversial book *Lords of Chaos*). While Vikernes is well known for his outspokenness about the Christian church, he is not as well known for homophobic comments or actions. So why is Varg considered one of the most homophobic metal performers by queer fans? There appear to be two causes for this apparent confusion. First, from prison Vikernes suggested Euronymous was gay (and a Communist) and that was one of the reasons Vikernes killed him. As other scholars have pointed out, however, Norwegian black metal bands are dependent on their pose as ultra-right, eviler-than-thou performers.[39] Euronymous never came out or otherwise suggested he was gay. The only evidence seems to be Vikernes' word. In fact, several interviews and scholars have suggested the killing was more than likely over band decisions, power, fame, and income. But queer fans surveyed overwhelmingly identify Vikernes as someone who killed a gay man. Why? The fans are confusing Vikernes with Faust.

Bård Guldvik "Faust" Eithun was the drummer for Emperor, another formative Norwegian metal band. Faust was convicted in 1992 of the murder of Magne Andreassen, an openly gay man living in Lillehammer, Norway. According to documents, Andreassen approached Faust, asked him to go for a walk, and Andreassen never returned. Andreassen's body was discovered the next day with 37 stab wounds and massive head injuries from repeated kicking. Faust was sentenced to fourteen years and was released in 2003 after serving nine years of his sentence. He has since returned to the metal scene, working in various projects. As Keith Kahn-Harris has said, while Faust has discussed his time in prison, he has made few comments about his homophobic crime.

Why are Varg and Faust so easily confused? You could argue they share a genre, a sound, perhaps even a style and culture. But the confusion stems from the fact that neither man cares to deny or confirm information needed to clarify. Varg has no interest in clarifying why he killed Euronymous, and even further, there is no point in doing so. The aura of evil arsonist and murderer of closeted gay men is one that Varg would not deny because it feeds his fame and his pose. Faust, who has returned to metal and has offered very few statements exhibiting regret about his actions, also has no interest in giving some sort of confession/rebuke of Varg. Again, such a statement serves no purpose other than demystifying the pose of the uber-evil black metal musician who eschews social acceptability. "There is a threat of being excluded, attacked, and further marginalized in the [black metal] scene," explained scholar Sarah Kitteringham, "for calling attention to sexism, racism, and homophobia."[40] (101).

If one can be excluded from black metal for mentioning issues such as homophobia, where does that leave Gaahl? As a trickster, he never was completely inside the scene or completely outside. It is in the space where the disruption occurs, in the queerscape, that Gaahl sits. Interestingly, Gaahl has said very little about the crimes of his peers since he came out. It is not that he supports or refutes them but rather that his comments demonstrate his need to be betwixt and between as the queer metal trickster. When asked if he experienced a backlash from black metal colleagues after he came out, Gaahl's response was at the same time disturbing, ridiculous, and noncommittal.

> I think that when it comes to those murders it was only accidental that the victims were homosexuals. If people get too close to you and you don't like what's happening around you, a murder can happen! [laughs] I see it like this; Faust and me have a good relationship. It's just that when things come out in the media they paint this picture that shows an extreme anger against a certain group, but it's usually just an accidental fluke whether it was a black guy that got killed or a gay guy that got killed.[41]

Gaahl uses the same trickster disruptions, laughing at crimes that now might include you and painting hate crimes as flukes when referring to coming out. Gaahl's coming out occurred in an October 2008 interview with the German heavy metal magazine *Rock Hard*, and appeared online in English. When asked if he was worried about a backlash from right-wing black metallers, Gaahl told the interviewer: "My idea of art, and black metal especially, is the depiction of honesty without compromise. I really don't care how other people react to it or the feelings it might provoke."[42] When asked who he was, Gaahl replied "I'm an individualist." He subsequently appeared in a long interview on the Dutch television program *Face Culture*, where he explained he came out because his then lover, Dan DeVero, was saddened and a reporter asked. In a 2011 interview, Gaahl discussed a clothing line he was financing, having appeared at the line's runway premiere. When asked in the interview why he was so "happy" as opposed to his stage persona, Gaahl replied: "Ninety percent of my artistic expression is not perceptible to the world."[43] After further stating he planned to work in secrecy and had been on the earth "every 1,200 years," the interviewer asked Gaahl about his attraction boys.

> GAAHL: I guess I'm somewhat of an ephebophile. I don't really under-
> stand the physical contact. It's an element that's foreign to me.
> INTERVIEWER: You're saying you prefer boys in their mid- to late teens,
> aka ephebes.
> GAAHL: When it comes to the ephebe as a symbol, I'm more into the
> aesthetics of it all. Also, there's something about the gaze and the
> will. The will to discover the individual, to become something
> unique, that I think is very strongly present in the young man,
> prior to being colored by his surroundings – when you've exited
> the fantastic universe of childhood and are in the finishing stages
> of the hardest and most chaotic transitional period. I can't explain
> why, but I know that this is something I'm deeply captivated by.
> I love it: the unlimited will to be.[44]

If we consider Gaahl a trickster, then his opaque performance of masculinity is in question. In the black metal scene, one noted as the "most strident in its boundary patrolling," Gaahl admits to not only a queer sexuality but to a queer sexuality that could be considered disruptive or even criminal to some sectors of a queer community. He does not, however, provide a clear statement about any desire for a sexual relationship with the young "ephebes." In this way, the trickster confounds both black metal and queer sexuality, demanding of both that he remain liminal. His masculinity is a trickster performance that, in its opacity, reveals the interplay of black metal and sexuality in the queerscape. When asked if heavy metal was too macho, Gaahl replied: "Who's macho? I'm probably more macho than any of them! I've never seen metal as a macho culture. I think it's more about what people think has been a reality."[45]

BUTCH UNVISIBILITY: JETT, OTEP, AND FEMALE MASCULINITY

Throughout the heavy metal subculture, both inside and outside the queerscape, the common perception of female performers is the ubiquitous video vixen and the angry lesbian. The video vixen is hypervisible: on T-shirts, video music, album covers, and concert backdrops. The angry lesbian, the masculine woman just trying to look like one of the boys, is just as visible yet goes unnoticed or silenced as a bastardization of metal's male-bodied masculinity. According to Avery Gordon, hypervisibility leads to unvisibility: the presence of a true lack of the visible. It is this unvisible space that queer masculine women in heavy metal inhabit. Inside the queerscape, however, this unvisible aspect of masculine women collides with the opacity of their performances as read by queer fans. These performances become mirrors in which queer fans see themselves, still unvisible to the mainstream but hypervisible to the queer fan. Consider for example Joan Jett, a singer and guitarist considered one of the most important influences for women in rock. Though Jett does not always appear in histories of metal, among queer women in metal she is idolized as the godmother. Jett, who has quietly and sonically come out as both queer and a member of the leather community, is idolized both for her musical ability and her own brand of masculinity. One informant, a trans woman and metal guitarist, cited Jett as her model for "rocking out."

When I got my first listening equipment it was 1984, a turntable and double cassette player that was far improved from the portable cassette player I'd bought with green stamps. I came home from a garage sale with a handful of 1980s classics on 45 rpm records, such as Cheap Trick and Pat Benatar, but the real treasure was Joan Jett. "I Love Rock and Roll" was released just two years before and was a popular tune in my working-class neighborhood. I had even taped the video on *Friday Night Videos*, watched Joan lean against that record machine. Any Joan Jett record was, I surmised, a rocker. I did not even pay attention to the songs on the record, just snatched it up to bring it home. The record was a 1982 release from Boardwalk, side 2 "Oh Woe Is Me," side 1 "Crimson and Clover."[46] I had never heard either song.

It was 1984 and nobody thought Joan Jett was queer – at least nobody in my neighborhood. She was another leather-clad rock vixen, only she was singing and slinging an axe. In fact, in 1984 we said a lot of things in my neighborhood about what "gay" people looked like. I was told on more than one occasion that gay people wore the longer of their mismatched earrings in the left ear, while straight people wore their single dangling earrings in the right ear. I was ten and barely had an idea what gay even was. I just knew it was something we whispered about and it normally meant somebody was telling jokes about our female physical education teacher. But Joan did not teach physical education and I had no idea where she wore her dangly earring. The only other female rocker I listened to was Lita Ford, and she sang about getting into fights at a party. These were tough chicks, they got what they wanted when they wanted it. They didn't take anybody's shit. And they weren't these cute, perky pop stars who just didn't cover the way I felt a lot of the time. In my neighborhood cute girls got the boys but tough girls got to hang out with the boys. In the end, that's what I wanted, or so I thought at the time.

It was not until the next day that I put the Joan Jett record on and listened to the lyrics: "I don't really know her, but I think I could love her." I was stunned. I had never heard a woman sing about a girl before. I panicked and took the needle off the record. What did that mean? Joan thinks she loves a girl? After giving it some thought, I decided there must be a different answer. Joan liked boys, after all, I had seen her with a guy who must have been about 17. I knew how to play music and had indeed performed songs that were not written by me. I decided I knew the score. Someone else had written the song for her. None of that, however, stopped me from playing it incessantly. I knew every word by the end of the day and sang it loudly, even if I changed the lyric to "him." It was not just the lyrics, it was the emotion. The growling "sweet thing," the moaning "what a beautiful feeling": it was as though there were a mystery I was supposed to be able to solve.

About a month later I was housesitting for the family across the street – or, more specifically, watching their cable so I could see MTV, a channel we didn't get at home. It was 1984, so in heavy rotation were Van Halen's "Jump," "When Doves Cry" by Prince, and nearly the entire Cyndi Lauper debut album. Along with George Michael's "Careless Whisper" and the occasional *Ghostbusters* theme song, MTV didn't stray from the heavy rotation when I came over to water plants that summer. But on this day it was the video for "Crimson and Clover,"[47] sandwiched between "Call Me" and the Pointer Sisters. Who knows what individual was at the helm that afternoon? There was Joan in her black leather pants, shag haircut, and dark eyeliner. "I don't hardly know her, but I think I could love her." At first the video screen showed only Joan's lips mouthing the words to the song. "Like *Rocky Horror*," I thought. I had not seen the movie but knew about it and had no idea how transgressive the comparison was. Then she was smiling. Joan Jett, smiling? Tough girls do not smile, we snarl. Then she kept singing. "My my such a sweet thing," she sang as she stared into the camera with a snarl. "I wanna do everything" and her eyes widened like the proverbial kid in the candy store. I was absolutely entranced. Of course tough girls weren't sweet, but is that what she meant? What is everything? Do I want to do everything? She reclined on a couch and bit the heads off roses, those roses that sweet girls get. The bridge began with a knowing nod. The video was over before I realized I had not hit record on my *Friday Night Videos* VHS tape.

Then I could not stop thinking about Joan Jett. I do not necessarily mean sexual thoughts; when you are ten, thoughts are not that specific. I knew I wanted to know what "everything" was. I kept listening to the song, along with "I Love Rock and Roll," which I owned by then. What did she want from the guy dancing by the record machine? Which song did she really mean? And what do leather pants feel like? Possibilities began to open up, questions I was too scared to ask were simmering in my brain. I kept replaying the video in my head, and all the looks and gestures added up to one thing: I didn't know what was going on anymore. So I did the only thing I could think of: I started wearing my dangling earring in my left ear. I still do not know why or how I came up with that as a solution. Maybe I was just rebelling in my own way. Maybe I was sending a message to myself. Maybe I just wanted to start some trouble. I wanna do everything. …

It was ten years before I came out to anyone, when I was wearing Doc Martens and blasting Riot Grrl albums from my dorm room. I wrote WWJJD, "What Would Joan Jett Do," on my walls and played KRS records ordered from Olympia. My "Crimson and Clover" 45 was on the turntable for every crush I had, every secret date, for the girl who broke my heart. Then when I met my wife, I went home and played that well-worn 45. "I think I could love her." Joan Jett didn't make me queer, by any means. She kept me looking for everything, though, over and over.[48] In a way, Jett acted for me and other queer women in my generation like a one-way mirror. Those from the mainstream looking in could not make either of us out as long as Jett sang about boys standing by record machines and I sang along. But on the other side of that mirror, what is hypervisible to outsiders becomes an identificatory practice based on musical performance, gender, sexuality, and a pose of female masculinity that challenges the very structures that render it unvisible. The key to this unvisibility is female, even butch lesbian, masculinity.

In their introduction to *Oh Boy!*, scholars Dan Biddle and Freya Jarman-Ivens admitted their work, like so many others, did not examine "explicit expressions of non-male masculinity."[49] They did, however, briefly explain the role that such performances of gender play in popular music. As they explained:

> Sonic gestures become codified, having gendered meanings ascribed to them over a period of time and generated through discursive networks, and those meanings are mutable according to the cultural, historical and musical context of those gestures, and the subsequent contexts into which they are constantly reinscribed. Clearly, there are multiple ways in which genders are constructed, formed, performed, problematized, and negotiated within and between music genres, taking into consideration visual and aural, verbal and nonverbal coding of genders.[50]

The unvisible performance of female masculinity in heavy metal has multiple meanings in the queerscape of heavy metal. While the illusion of heterosexual male masculinity causes female masculinity to be coded as a defective copy of the male body, understanding male masculinity in heavy metal as an illusion covering the queerscape allows a different reading. This eventialization, or "disruptive bringing to light of that which is plain or clear to sight or understanding," is in direct challenge to the heteronormative readings of women in heavy metal.[51] By exposing the queerscape through the lens of female masculinity, the evidence used to ignore queers in heavy metal is ruptured.

Though Joan Jett was frequently mentioned by surveyed queer fans as an out, queer heavy music star, Joan Jett has in fact never publicly come out. Instead, both fans and performers have positioned Jett as queer through various media: song lyrics, performances, quotes from interviews, collaborations with specific artists, even the stickers on her guitar. "She might not identify as anything specific," declared journalist Trish Bendix, "but Joan is for all intents and purposes queer."[52] Jett has continuously refused to define a sexual orientation but has not shied away from the rampant sexuality in her songs or the blatant masculinity in her performance. As she explained to author Evelyn McDonnell:

> I'm not discussing personally who I'm doing anything with. As far as addressing sexuality, I'm singing to everyone and always have been since The Runaways. I think I'm pretty blatant. I think anybody who wants to know who I am, all they've got to do is listen to my music.[53]

Jett's career is nothing short of mythic. A guitarist and songwriter, she got her start in Los Angeles before helping found The Runaways in 1975. The Runaways were an all-female rock band, featuring future heavy metal great Lita Ford along with Jett on guitar. When the band broke up in 1979, Jett went solo. In collaboration with her long-time friend Kenny Laguna, she began recording solo records, formed Blackheart Records, and released her first album with the band The Blackhearts. In 1982 Joan Jett and The Blackhearts released their cover of The Arrows song "I Love Rock and Roll," which catapulted Jett and her band into fame and rock history. They continue to tour and record, releasing their newest album, "Unvarnished," in 2013. Jett's recording of "I Love Rock and Roll" was listed as #56 on the Billboard list of all-time greatest songs. She is called the Godmother of Riot Grrl, and has recorded with Bikini Kill's Kathleen Hanna, Dave Grohl of the Foo Fighters, and the recently transitioned singer for Against Me!, Laura Jane Grace. Though she may not be traditionally thought of as a heavy metal artist, in 2014 Jett was awarded a Golden God award, an award previously given to Rob Halford, Gene Simmons of KISS, and Alice Cooper. The Golden Gods are awarded to hard rock and heavy metal's best acts, and Jett is the only female ever to be named a Golden God.

How did Jett become an icon in the heavy metal queerscape? If heavy metal is inherently masculine and patriarchal, how did Jett rise to Golden God status? Her icon status boils down to the authenticity and masculinity of the heavy metal scene. Jett's music is inherently sexual, her guitar playing virtuosic, her charisma as a lead singer clear. In her work on Led Zeppelin, musicologist Susan Fast discussed the requirements of "cock rock" as blatant sexuality, lyrics and music combined with an overtly sexual image.[54] Jett meets all of these requirements but interestingly, her lack of a biological cock to rock is essentially ignored. In the queerscape, however, Jett's masculinity is loud, explicit, and understood as inherently queer. Steve Waksman wrote "it would be a mistake to conclude that … rock sexuality offers no satisfying outlet for female heterosexual desires."[55] Jett's position in the queerscape signals a different fact: rock sexuality offers an outlet for female homosexual desires as well. Jett is part of the heavy metal queerscape as the godmother of masculinity, the queer queen of cock rock.

Jett's status as the queen of cock rock is most evident in her lyrics. In her article on Jett's masculinity, historian Kathleen Kennedy presented Jett's songs as moving between a modern movement to include women in rock and a push against the sexual and gendered mores of American society. This oscillation, according to Kennedy, "makes Jett's music accessible not only to traditional rock audiences, specifically those adolescent and frustrated suburban males to whom rock is generally marketed, but also to queers and adolescent suburban heterosexual women."[56] As Jett admitted, her lyrics explain much about both her masculinity and her potential sexuality. In a 2011 interview, Jett identified "Bad Reputation" as the song she identifies with most. "I think the reason I have a bad reputation is because I'm a girl and dare to do these things that, you know, boys do," Jett explained.[57] This anthem, released as a solo recording in 1980, expressed Jett's intention to ignore gender boundaries: "A girl can do what she wants to do/and that's what I'm gonna do."[58]

What is most telling about Jett's lyrics, whether original or covered songs, is her positioning of masculinity at the forefront of her lyrics. For example, Jett's recording of the Gary Glitter song "Do You Wanna Touch Me (Oh Yeah)" exhibits female masculinity and queer sensibility. The song, an explicit request for sex, includes the lyrics "I'm a natural man, doing all I can/ My temperature is running high."[59] As Kennedy and others pointed out, Jett changed "natural man" to "natural ma'am." "Jett's substitution allows for the possibility that the ma'am is either Jett or her potential partner," wrote Kennedy, "lending ambiguity to Jett's gender and sexual performance."[60] For Jett, the ambiguity of the lyrics, combined with the masculine spectacle of her as the leader of the band, precipitates her status in the queerscape. As Jett told an interviewer in 2011: "Sex is always the theme in my songs."[61]

Along with her lyrics, Jett performs masculinity with her body. This aspect of female masculinity is central to Jett's performance. She performs in jumpsuits and sneakers, black leather jackets and punk rock T-shirts, never in what one might consider rock goddess style. Jett spoke to *Spin* magazine about her masculinity in 2013: "I could sit here and say, 'Hey, I'm in a girl's body.' But do I do girly things? Do I wear dresses and all that stuff? So I'm kind of like a boy too. Where do you really draw the line?"[62] Though there are several factors to her bodily performance, from her movement on stage to her low-slung guitar, a key aspect is Jett's identification with leather, both the fabric and the sexual identity. For example, the stickers on Jett's primary guitar are the subject of a great deal of attention among self-identified lesbian fans of Jett. According to a 2006 article on Jett from the GLBTQ newspaper *Southern Voice*:

While she declines to answer 'the question' [about her sexual identity], Jett's public image keeps fans guessing. Her white Gibson Melody

Maker guitar, covered in various stickers, at times has had "Gender Fucker," "Girls Kick Ass," as well as the black and blue Leather Pride flag plastered on it. ... According to the blogosphere, "Dykes Rule" and Tinky Winky stickers have also graced her guitar in the past. ... In recent concert photos and in Jett's new video for her song about a bisexual girl, "A.C.D.C.," a pink sticker bearing the iconic yet generic image of two women holding hands is located brazenly in the center of her guitar.[63]

Other fans have noted stickers with the phrases "tough titties" and the number "69" on Jett's guitar. Of particular note is the Leather Pride flag on Jett's guitar. Jett is singular in her tacit identification as leather/BDSM-identified among her peers in rock.

Jett recorded dozens of songs with content about black leather, sexual kink, and BDSM. For example, in her song "Black Leather," Jett sings about her black leather clothes and the power they give her. Briefly singing about how girls are made to wear clothing that makes them vulnerable, Jett sings about empowerment and being in charge of her own body: "My friends thought that I was a little angel/I couldn't help it if I felt like a beast."[64] In 1999, Jett released the album *Fetish*. It featured rereleases of Jett classics such as "Do You Wanna Touch Me (Oh Yeah)" along with new songs such as "Fetish" and "Baby Blue." Along with the new album, Jett featured a new look: she shaved off her iconic black shag haircut, dying her newly shorn hair blonde. As Kennedy explained:

She further accented her sexuality by performing in tight leather pants, latex tube tops, with whips, keys and chains hanging from her left hip. Her guitar has become a billboard for lesbian, feminist, and leather images and slogans, including a purple Teletubby, while her body sports several tattoos and various piercings.[65]

Fetish featured two versions of the title song, one marked XXX. The first version, marked without an X, is a blatantly sexual song about dominating a sexual partner. "Surprise, round and round the bed/Restrained while I find your head," Jett sings, "I'm gonna watch you come."[66] The XXX version is, however, even more explicit in its use of BDSM sexual themes: "find your head" becomes "fuck your head." Jett's 2006 album, *Sinner*, is the most explicit in its use of leather and BDSM-identified themes. *Sinner* includes songs such as "Fetish" and "Baby Blue" from the 1999 *Fetish* album, along with three explicitly gender-bending BDSM songs: "A.C.D.C.," "Everyone Knows," and "Androgynous." "A.C.D.C." is a queer slang term for bisexual and can also be used to describe someone who is engaged in polyamorous relationships. "A.C.D.C." is about a female lover of Jett, and the song is charged with sexuality as it describes a woman with "girls all over the world." In "A.C.D.C." Jett sings of wanting to see her lover's "ding-a-ling"

Figure 4.1 Artwork featuring Joan Jett's white Melody Maker guitar. The topic
of discussion among queer fans of heavy metal is the stickers on Jett's
guitar. Visible in this artwork are stickers including "Tough Titties,"
"69" (a slang term and symbol for mutual oral sex), a famous activist
image of two female symbols holding hands, and the official pride flag
for leather/BDSM-identified people: the black, blue, and white striped
flag with a red heart in the upper left corner. Permission and copyright
Karl Haglund, Fugitive Art.

and the lover "can't make up her mind." At one point the lyrics are "let's
be in it together," but Jett slurs the lyric to "lez-be-in."[67] "Androgynous" is
a disruptive retelling of the 1950s Dick and Jane stories, this time with the
couple as adults breaking the rules of gender, sexuality, and social mores on
dress. Dick "wears a skirt" and Jane "sports a chain" and Dick "might be
a father/but he sure ain't a Dad."[68] Jett sings of the famous fictional couple
as having the same hair and same body type, and reverting to the clothes
required by society tomorrow, eventually calling Dick and Jane "something."

"Everyone Knows" is an anthem of pride, a song for a lover about the spectacle of being queer in public. The song tells the story of Jett and her lover walking the streets and watching as viewers stare, talk about the couple, and react with fright and discomfort. "I see 'em stare at us /Whenever we're together/They haven't got the right/Just cuz we're wearin' leather."[69]

In her book *The Queer Art of Failure*, scholar Judith Halberstam explored the idea that queer culture developed along parallel lines, rather than on a pseudo-evolutionary model of "upward and onward."[70] One of the examples Halberstam uses is the butch lesbian, seen as both a failed woman and a failed queer. At the same time, Halberstam recognized queer women may identify with masculinist scenes precisely because of the attractiveness of explicit sexuality.[71] This tension between the cultural presupposition that female masculinity is a failure and it serves as a signal for queer women and girls is a tension Joan Jett occupies. "It's very brave. It's hard to be yourself," Jett explained in a 2013 interview.[72] Though decidedly masculine in inherently heavy metal, sexually aggressive, and physically dominating ways, Jett self-identifies as a girl in rock. At the same time, her recognition as a cock rock queen signals a clear understanding among fans that she's just as interested in the girls as any other cock rock performer. In the heavy metal queerscape, Jett's performances serve as signposts for female masculinity and reveal the mutability of masculinity in heavy metal, especially in the eyes of queer performers and fans. Though she may not be seen as a heavy metal musician by outsiders, inside heavy metal Jett is seen as a leader, a founder, a Golden God. When Jett was selected to win the Golden God award, the heavy metal equivalent of a lifetime achievement award, heavy metal magazine (and award sponsor) *Revolver* included a quote by heavy metal icon Alice Cooper. "No one deserves this award more than Joan Jett," said Cooper. "She's never compromised who she is – she's a rocker through and through. I wish some of the younger bands had the balls that Joan Jett does!"[73]

While Jett's sexuality and gender identity are tacit and embedded in her performance, the other female heavy metal performer that surveyed queer fans identified as out was Otep Shamaya. The leader singer of her namesake band, Otep, Shamaya is known for her overtly political lyrics, her poetry-based performances, and her identity as an out female lesbian. In a 2009 Internet list of the "Top 5 Gay Icons," Otep was the only female listed.[74] She arrived on the heavy metal scene in 2002 and was out from her first appearance as the singer for Otep. The band rose to prominence in the mid-1990s, appearing on the Ozzfest tour for four years. Otep Shamaya's brand of masculinity, however, is both parallel and divergent from Jett's. Shamaya's lyrics are deeply personal and frequently sexual in nature, and her role as the leader of her band is equally as firm as Jett's status as a band leader. They diverge, however, in terms of the overtness of both lyrics and sexual identity. Shamaya's work is political, focusing on everything from queer liberation to animal rights, misogyny and women's rights, and criticisms of American party politics. Her identity as a lesbian woman is as much part of her performance as her lyrics. She is arguably the most overtly queer performer in heavy metal. In fact, Otep makes frequent use of queer community slang in both lyrics and interviews. She is not signaling queerness, she is a beacon for queer fans. Otep made this statement regarding her fans in 2008:

> The people that support our music, they find a very inclusive environment. Most girls that I've talked to, they're either on the team or they're curious about the team. Some days they're on the team, some days they're not! [laughs] What's a lot more meaningful to me is when I see a lot of gay men coming to the shows. Sometimes these more aggressive shows can be very dangerous. You start to see a lot more people coming out, and if anything, our music and our messages inspire everyone to be comfortable with themselves and not judge other people, whether you're straight or bent or curved or whatever. You just accept people for who they are because we're all different and we're all unique.[75]

Who is "the team?" While that statement might require inference on the part of straight readers, for queer fans the meaning is quite clear. Shamaya communicates directly to her queer fans. "It's becoming a very inclusive tribe of people coming together behind the message," Shamaya stated of her fans in 2005.[76]

Though Shamaya's sexuality is central to her identity as an out lesbian heavy metal performer, the erotics of lesbian masculinity are not in her lyrical content. Her work is deeply political and aggressively in the face of her listeners. Shamaya is providing a response to the masculine male aggression identified with heavy metal and matching it with aggressive female masculinity. Otep's work not only touches on sexuality, it also deals with specific issues in the lives of women: rape, incest, abuse and violence, and misogyny. For example, the song "Menocide" from the album *Sevas Tra* (2002) was boycotted by the right-wing organization Fathers and Families, and Otep was awarded their fictional "psychopath of the year" award. "Menocide" is a jarring critique of patriarchy and abuse of women, and a call to action for women. Beginning with a scathing verbal assault on "prostate gods," the song builds into a cry to female deities and women of all cultures, ending with the chant "Kill your masters/MENOCIDE."[77] Otep's response to the award remained as solidly political as her lyrics. As she explained to the *South Bend Tribune*:

> 'It's not an anti-male song,' Shamaya maintains. 'I'm speaking out for women who are victimized. I've seen a man beat his woman, and when the police came out she was so afraid that she didn't let him go to jail.' By no means was Shamaya afraid to accept the men's group's prize. 'My reply to the psychopath award,' she says, 'was thank you very much.'[78]

Otep's 2009 album *Smash the Control Machine* was nominated for a Gay and Lesbian Alliance Against Defamation (GLAAD) Media Award in 2010. One of the two singles from that album, "Rise Rebel Resist," became a rallying cry at Otep concerts. The song indicts the mainstream, nuclear household as a site of hate crimes and homophobia, and calls on "the freaks, the faggots, the geeks" to rise up and refuse both abuse and normalization. "If I can't be loved/then I'll be hated," Otep sings, followed by the chant of the title. Otep's masculinity is aggressive in the face of heavy metal's traditional, heterosexual, masculine aggression. If heavy metal songs objectify women and suggest their subjugation, or promise two women together are hot and single women are there for sexual purposes, then Otep is the antithesis. "I was seduced by a music that was inclusive to *anyone* who ever felt outside the conformist paradigm of whatever popular culture considered 'normal,'" Otep told *Revolver* in 2006.[79] As Otep explained in a 2005 interview:

> Why should I hide anything. Why should I think along those terms? I don't feel like I'm something unique. So far I've only had a few people who seem to have a problem with me being here. Mostly because I'm a woman, and I guess I'm the antithesis of what they embrace as what a woman is. Like, you know, tits and ass. The sexuality of what I do is not even a part of it. If there is anything in there that people can see as erotic, it's not anything overt. Everyone needs an enemy, and all too often it's us.[80]

Though much of Otep's lyrics and works could be evidence of queerscape, one particular piece is of note. The American heavy metal magazine *Revolver* runs a special page in each issue entitled "The Hottest Chicks In Metal." Hottest Chicks commonly features the "bitch goddess" identified by Deena Weinstein: busty female musicians in black leather or white lace in sexualized poses. The page always features a quote from the Hottest Chick, usually the answer to some question about her backstage or tour bus antics. The women featured are typically intended for heterosexual male readers. In October 2009, however, the featured Hottest Chick was Otep Shamaya, wearing jeans and a sweatshirt and screaming toward the camera. The Hottest Chick question posed to Otep was: "What is the grossest thing you've ever eaten?" "The grossest thing I've ever eaten?" replied Otep. "I won't mention any names, but she is rather famous and well known in Hollywood. I adore her to death, but damn girl, tidy up the kitchen a little."[81] To whom was this quote referring? Heterosexual male fans could certainly understand the premise, but does a lesbian use those words with the same meaning as a straight man? The phrase "tidy up the kitchen" is a common piece of lesbian coded language, not in common usage at all. For whom was that intended? Otep's quote serves as a reminder that while the Hottest Chicks may be intended for a supposedly straight male audience, there are queer girls looking at the Hottest Chicks for the same reasons but with different sexual and gendered indentities. While they may seem to be marginalized by the stereotypical aspects of the heavy metal world, queer folks have created their own queerscape by following symbolic borders such as "tidy up the kitchen." This is where where queerness and heavy metal merge.

TRANS PERFORMERS IN HEAVY METAL

When Laura Jane Grace (formerly Tom Gabel) of the punk band Against Me! came out as transgendered and announced her intention to undergo transitional surgeries in a 2012 issue of *Rolling Stone*, the news was everywhere. Grace told Josh Eells of *Rolling Stone* that the masculinity of punk rock enabled her to explore her own identity. "With the band especially, I felt more and more like I was putting on an act," Grace stated, "like I was being shoved into this role of angry white man in a punk band."[82] There were reactions across the world of rock music, many of which suggested Grace was the first trans rock musician.[83] The truth, however, is that many heavy metal musicians had already come out as trans folks. Jade Starr, a well-known Australian drag queen and performer, began transitioning as an extreme metal singer in 2004. Starr described her attraction to heavy metal as a trans person:

> That culture of boys on the outside were aggressive and could come across as homophobic and violent but really those kinds of boys that listened to that music in a clan of quite lost or troubled people, they felt different so they could put out that person and blend in and nobody would question it. The clothing is like an armour, but there is an undercurrent of quite loving people who would do anything for each other.[84]

Annah Moore, the lead guitarist for Austin, Texas-based metal band Ignitor, documented her male-to-female transition in a 2005 Discovery Channel program, *seXchange: Him to Her*. In an interview for *Transgender Tapestry*, Moore stated: "Twenty years ago, I thought I was the only one like this, but then of course, you find out there's a few others, and then you get to 'Well, I'm the only one in METAL who's like this,' then you come meet more and more folks who have so much in common with you."[85] The Cliks is a Toronto-based metal band fronted by trans singer Lucas Silveira. "Journalists tend to see being trans as the new chic," Silveria told *Diva* magazine in 2008, "which I find really funny."[86] There are many other examples, far more than seem evident in other genres of popular music. Why is heavy metal, the supposedly monolithic genre of homophobia, the home of so many trans musicians and performers?

The queerscape, with its closely linked subjectivities, provides a platform where the extremity of individual experience can be enacted, displayed, and performed. Psychologist Michael Friedman wrote:

> People who like intense and rebellious music such as heavy metal actually demonstrate a high level of openness to new experiences and intelligence. They're also more likely to engage in civic activism. In fact, research suggests that heavy metal musicians and fans are 'gifted outsiders' with feelings of low self-esteem that develop from their sense of alienation. They turn to heavy metal for inspiration and support. This is perhaps one of the reasons that heavy metal musicians and fans are so dedicated.[87]

This alienation is required in a queerscape or, as Gordon Brett Ingram stated, a "landscape of erotic alienations, and alien(ated) nations."[88] In addition, heavy metal has a long history of interest in extremes of sound, lyrics, themes, and spectacles. Indeed, the acceptance of trans performers in heavy metal is an extension of what Keith Kahn-Harris identified as "bodily transgression" in heavy metal. While Kahn-Harris focused primarily on acts of bodily transgression among extreme metal performers, heavy metal as a genre is focused on such transgressions. Indeed, playing with gender in terms of costume and performance has been part of heavy metal consistently, from the gender-bending of 1980s hair metal to Rammstein's S&M gender play. A good example is Maris the Great, a gay metal musician described by scholar Marcus Erbe as "the impish zombie clown with a pink Mohawk and a giant plastic scrotum."[89] Whether these transgressions are in terms of using and abusing substances or the actions of a mosh pit (as Kahn-Harris explored) or in the bodily spectacles of costumes and instrumental virtuosity, heavy metal thrives on the transgressive body. The acceptance of trans performers, once considered as both a part of alienation and heavy metal's bodily transgression, is clearly part of the queerscape.

This queerscape alignment of alienation and bodily transgression is most obvious in the stories of Mina Caputo and Marissa Martinez. Mina Caputo was the lead singer of Life of Agony, a heavy metal band that saw tremendous success in Europe. She quit the band in 1996, became a solo performer, and underwent her transition. During a sudden flourish of press attention, details about Caputo's sexuality, gender, and genitalia became public in 2011, nearly a decade after she began transitioning.[90] Caputo told reporters she did not intend to have bottom surgery, she identified as a lesbian, and stated "just because I'm wearing a skirt doesn't mean I don't got big balls." Though Caputo explained she felt "boxed in" by heavy metal, the revelation that she identified as trans did not meet with a great deal of resistance in the heavy metal press. "I can't say I entirely understand what this all means for Keith's sexual orientation, but does it really matter?" wrote a reporter for the influential heavy metal website MetalSucks.com. "Transexual, gender reassignment, gay, straight, tall, short, skinny, fat ... we're just happy to see Keith expressing his true self."[91] Life of Agony reunited in 2014, and have played heavy metal festivals across Europe with Mina Caputo as their lead singer.

Marissa Martinez transitioned in 2007. The vocalist and guitarist for the extreme metal band Cretin, Martinez was the subject of an article in the extreme metal magazine *Decibel*. The reporter explained Martinez's story of transition, her previous life as Dan, and her work as the leader of Cretin with the tagline that Martinez was "changing the gender rules of extreme metal."[92] After discussing her journey to transition, Martinez explained what treatments were in her transition. The reporter elucidated Martinez's treatments as a primary example of transgression and extremity, just below a photograph of Marissa Martinez with her leather-gloved middle finger raised at the reader.

> Wanna talk about how extreme you are? Well, every night around 10 p.m., Marissa takes 15 pills at once, from five doses of Estradiol (i.e. estrogen) to six doses of Spironolactone, a testosterone-inhibitor. She affectionately refers to the transitional cocktail as 'sugar, spice and everything nice,' but there's no escaping how downright daunting the thing looks. *Decibel*'s Editor-in-Chief saw Marissa down it all in person at this year's Murderfest and says, 'Those things look like they could tranquilize a horse.'[93]

Clearly, in the heavy metal queerscape, bodily transgression and aggressive extremity demonstrate authenticity, and that is more important to belonging in heavy metal.

QUEER FUTURITY IN HEAVY METAL

In 2014, musician Drew Daniel released an album of black metal covers under the name of his electro-disco project Soft Pink Truth. Daniel was interviewed for the music website Pitchfork, and in the interview he discussed his love for black metal and his electronic dance music approach. Soft Pink Truth, an explicitly queer music project, focused on the "stream of sexual content within certain early black metal bands."[94] Daniel explained to Pitchfork's reporter that part of Soft Pink Truth's purpose was to "make a queer claim to take back" black metal from its homophobic associations with Varg Vikernes and Faust. As Daniel stated:

> So I went and saw [Faust's band] Emperor live, and they are fucking awesome. It was my birthday and I remember the drummer threw out a drumstick and I caught it. But the whole time I thought, 'I'm a kind of Uncle Tom motherfucker if I'm going to see Emperor and support

what they're about. They killed a gay man.' My record can't redress that kind of a crime, but it's part of a queer response to that sub-culture. I've also embroidered my Emperor shirt with 'Rest in Peace Magne Andreassen.' When I wear that, people are like, 'What does it mean?' Whatever. This is my self-important indie craft project.[95]

What does it mean to the future of heavy metal when a black metal fan lays claim to heavy metal music as reclaimed queer culture? How should we understand the ways in which queer fans and performers produce, consume, and identify with the supposedly uber-homophobic genre of heavy metal? "It seems that the only way we can love the other or the external world is to find ourselves somehow in it," wrote theorist Leo Bersani. "Only then might there be a nonviolent relation to the world that doesn't seek to exter-minate difference."[96] The heavy metal queerscape is, in this positioning of otherness, not the external world. It is the world of male-bodied masculinity that is external, while the queerscape of heavy metal is central. Masculinity finds itself in the queerscape of heavy metal, and in doing so does not seek the violent extermination of queerness at all. Queer performers built heavy metal, they continue to alter and expand its most rooted concepts, and they continue to challenge the mainstream, heteronormative conception of heavy metal as purely heterosexual in the first place.

NOTES

1. David Bell and John Binnie, "All Hyped Up and No Place To Go," *Gender, Place & Culture: A Journal of Feminist Geography* 1, No. 1 (1994): 13.
2. Daphne Brooks, *Bodies in Dissent: Spectacular Performances of Race and Free-dom, 1850–1910* (Durham: Duke University Press, 2006): 8.
3. Walser, *Running with the Devil*, 110.
4. Ibid., 111.
5. Jugulator, "The Judas Priest History." Accessed July 25, 2014, http://www.jugulator.net/judas_priest_history.htm.
6. Dana, "The Metal God, Rob Halford, Explains Why He Trademarked Name." Accessed July 21, 2011. http://eddietrunk.com/the-metal-god-rob-halford-explains-why-he-trademarked-name/.
7. "Get a Hard On For Hard Ton." *Boyz*, March 18, 2010: 12.
8. JB, interview with the author, August 24, 2010, Skype interview.
9. KC, interview with the author, August 24, 2010, Skype interview.
10. Robin Ibbison, "Rawk and a Hard Place," *Gay Times* (n.d.): 56.
11. David Halperin, *Saint Foucault: Towards A Gay Hagiography* (New York: Oxford University Press, 1995): 6.
12. Andreas Fejes and Magnus Dahlstedt, *The Confessing Society: Foucault, Confession, and Practices of Lifelong Learning* (New York: Routledge, 2013): 2.
13. Esther Saxey, *Homoplot: The Coming-Out Story and Gay, Lesbian and Bisexual Identity* (New York: Peter Lang, 2008): 2.
14. Ibid., 9.

15. Gay Metal Society, *GMS Headbanger*, Chicago, Illinois, June 1995, http://archive.qzap.org/index.php/Detail/Object/Show/object_id/84.
16. MTV, *Superrock*, YouTube video, 4:37, February 25, 1998, https://www.youtube.com/watch?v=UaOVLTmjUo0.
17. MTV News. "Judas Priest Speaks About Rob Halford's Sexual Openness."
18. Wieder, "Heavy Metal Rob Halford," 58.
19. Ibid., 69.
20. Richard Street-Jammer, "Rob Halford's Raw Deal," *Invisible Oranges*, November 8, 2011, http://www.invisibleoranges.com/2011/11/rob-halfords-raw-deal/.
21. Amanda Hess, "Top 5 Gay Metal Icons," *The Sexist*, August 26, 2008, www.washingtoncitypaper.com/blogs/sexist/2009/08/26/top-5-gay-metal-icons/.
22. Wieder, "Heavy Metal Rob Halford," 64.
23. Ibid., 66.
24. Jon Wiederhorn, "Judas Priest Turn Their Backs on 'Rock Star' Movie," *MTV News*, June 28, 2001, http://www.mtv.com/news/1444846/judas-priest-turn-their-backs-on-rock-star-movie/.
25. "Rock Star: Quotes," *Internet Movie Database*. Accessed August 17, 2014, http://www.imdb.com/title/tt0202470/quotes?ref_=tt_ql_3.
26. *Rock Star*, directed by Stephen Herek (Hollywood: Warners Brothers, 2001).
27. Jon Wiederhorn, "Judas Priest Turn Their Backs on 'Rock Star' Movie."
28. Steve Baltin, "Judas Priest's Real-Life Rock Star," *Rolling Stone*, September 20, 2001. http://www.rollingstone.com/music/news/judas-priests-real-life-rock-star-20010920#ixzz39jlD74bB.
29. Neil Daniels, *The Story of Judas Priest: Defenders of the Faith* (London: Omnibus, 2010): 74.
30. National Public Radio, "Judas Priest Lead Singer Rob Halford," *Fresh Air*, broadcast June 21, 2005, http://www.npr.org/templates/story/story.php?storyId=4712606.
31. Ibid.
32. Bianca Waxlax, "Q&A with Rob Halford: Heavy Metal Star Talks About Being Openly Gay, His New CD and His San Diego Gig," *San Diego Gay and Lesbian News*, December 14, 2010. http://www.sdgln.com/news/2010/12/14/qa-rob-halford-heavy-metal-star-talks-about-being-openly-gay-his-new-cd.
33. Alexis Petridis, "Judas Priest's Rob Halford: 'I've Become the Stately Homo of Heavy Metal," *The Guardian*, July 3, 2014, http://theguardian.com/music/2014/jul/03/judas-priest-rob-halford-quentin-crisp-interview-redeemer-of-souls/print.
34. Face Culture, "Interview Gaahl from Wardruna and Gorgoroth talks about being gay (part 7)," YouTube, 5:01, April 7, 2009, https://www.youtube.com/watch?v=2AZ2oIuxmYE&list=RD2AZ2oIuxmYE#t=6.
35. Victor Turner, "Liminality and Communitas." In *The Ritual Process: Structure and Anti-Structure* (Chicago: Aldine Publishing, 1969): 96.
36. Graham St. John, Graham, *Victor Turner and Contemporary Cultural Performance* (New York: Berghan Books, 2008): 198–199.
37. C. LaShure, "What Is Liminality?" *Liminality – The Space In Between*. Accessed July 19, 2014, http://www.liminality.org/about/whatisliminality.
38. Jon, "Unleashing Satan: An Evening with Gaahl." Accessed July 4, 2014, http://www.metalblast.net/interviews/unleashing-satan-an-evening-with-gaahl/.
39. Keith Kahn-Harris, *Extreme Metal: Metal and Culture on the Edge* (London: Berg Publishers, 2007).

40. Sarah Kitteringham, "Extreme Conditions Demand Extreme Responses: The Treatment of Women in Black Metal, Death Metal, Doom Metal, and Grindcore," MA thesis, University of Calgary, 2014.

41. Jon, "Unleashing Satan: An Evening with Gaahl."

42. "Gorgoroth Frontman Opens Up About His Sexual Orientation: I've Never Made Any Secret About It'," Blabbermouth.net, October 29, 2008, http// www.blabbermouth.net/news.gorgoroth-frontman-opens-up-about-his-sexual-orientation-ive-never-made-any-secret-about-it/.

43. Inma Varandela, "Gaahl Hates Your Sweatpants," *Vice United States*, February 28, 2011, http://www.vice.com/print.gaahl-hates-your-sweatpants-730-v18n3.

44. Ibid.

45. Jon, "Unleashing Satan: An Evening with Gaahl."

46. Joan Jett, "Oh Woe Is Me/Crimson and Clover," Boardwalk Records, 1982.

47. "Joan Jett and The Blackhearts: Crimson and Clover," YouTube video, 3:10, posted February 8, 2007, https://www.youtube.com/watch?v=hdhonK8NMm8.

48. Amber Clifford-Napoleone, "The First Time I Ever Heard: Over and Over," International Association for the Study of Popular Music blog IASPM-US.net (http://iaspm-us.net/the-first-time-i-ever-heard-amber-r-clifford-napoleone-over-and-over/). Accessed 1 April 2013.

49. Biddle and Jarman-Ivens, "Oh Boy!", 7.

50. Ibid., 10-11.

51. Lynne Huffer, *Mad For Foucault: Rethinking the Foundations of Queer Theory* (New York: Columbia University Press, 2010): xi.

52. Trish Bendix, "'Queens of Noise' Is The Most Queer Telling of The Runaways Story Yet," *After Ellen,* August 20, 2013, http://www.afterellen.com/queens-of-noise-is-the-most-queer-telling-of-the-runaways/08/2013/. Accessed August 8, 2014.

53. Ibid.

54. Susan Fast, "Rethinking Issues of Gender and Sexuality in Led Zeppelin: A Woman's View of Pleasure and Power in Hard Rock," *American Music* 17, No. 3 (Autumn 1999): 246.

55. Steve Waksman, *Instruments of Desire: The Electric Guitar and the Shaping of Musical Experience* (Harvard University Press, 1999): 18–19.

56. Kathleen Kennedy, "Results of a Misspent Youth: Joan Jett's Performance of Female Masculinity," *Women's History Review* 11, No. 1 (2002): 91.

57. "Interview: Joan Jett, Queen of Noise," *The Morton Report*, September 13, 2011, http://www.themortonreport.com/entertainment/music/interview-joan-jett-queen-of-noise/.

58. Joan Jett, "Bad Reputation/Jezebel," Boardwalk Records, 1981, vinyl.

59. Joan Jett, "Do You Wanna Touch Me (Oh Yeah)/Victim of Circumstance," Boardwalk Records, 1981, vinyl.

60. Kennedy, "Results of a Misspent Youth," 98.

61. "Interview: Joan Jett, Queen of Noise."

62. Kenny Herzog, "Joan Jett: 'I've Gotta Grow Up'," *Spin*, October 3, 2013, http:// www.spin.com/articles/joan-jett-unvarnished-new-album-interview.

63. Dyana Bagby, "Love the 'Sinner' Rocker Joan Jett back in spotlight with Warped Tour and her first CD in 10 years," *Southern Voice*, http://joanjettbadrep.com/ cgi-bin/fullStory.cgi?archive=200606&story=20060624-01southernvoice.htm, July 20, 2014.

64. Joan Jett, *Fetish,* Polygram, ASIN B00000J7QA, released June 8, 1999, compact disc.

65. Kennedy, "Results of a Misspent Youth," 105–106.
66. *Fetish*, Polygram, ASIN B00000J7QA, released June 8, 1999, compact disc.
67. Ibid.
68. Ibid.
69. Ibid.
70. Judith Halberstam, *The Queer Art of Failure* (Durham: Duke University Press, 2014): 73.
71. Judith Halberstam, *Female Masculinity* (Durham: Duke UP 1998): 323.
72. Evelyn McDonnell, "With Her New Album and L.A. Acclaim, Former Runaway Joan Jett Proves She Never Left," *Los Angeles Times,* October 26, 2013, http://articles.latimes.com/print/2013/oct/26/entertainment/la-et-ms-joan-jett-20131027.
73. "Revolver Golden Gods Turns 6!6!6!." *Revolver* 114 (April-May 2014): 16.
74. Hess, "Top 5 Gay Metal Icons."
75. Gregg Shapiro, "Otep Ascending: An Interview With Out Metal Goddess Otep," *Outlook Weekly*, April 10-April 16, 2008: 26.
76. Kris Scott Marti, "Interview with Otep Shamaya," *After Ellen*, January 31, 2005, http://www.afterellen.com/interview-with-otep-shamaya/01/2005/.
77. Otep, *Sevas Tra*, Capital Records, June 18, 2002, compact disc.
78. Jeff Harrell, "From Otep, with rage," South Bend Tribune, April 4, 2013, http://articles.southbendtribune.com/2013-04-04/entertainment/38287380_1_otep-shamaya-metal-band-band-members/2, 2.
79. Bartkewicz, "A Rainbow In The Dark," *Decibel* 23, 65.
80. Kris Scott Marti, "Interview with Otep Shamaya."
81. Revolver, "The Hottest Chicks In Metal: Otep Shamaya," *Revolver*, October 2009, 32.
82. Josh Eells, "The Secret Life of Transgender Rocker Tom Gabel," *Rolling Stone* May 31, 2012, http://www.rollingstone.com/music/news/the-secret-life-of-trans-gender-rocker-tom-gabel-20120531?page=5.
83. Matilda Battersby, "Man enough to be a woman and still rock 'n' rolling," *The Independent,* May 19, 2012, http://www.independent.co.uk/arts-entertainment/music/features/man-enough-to-be-a-woman-and-still-rocknrolling-7766426.html.
84. Annika Priest, "Gender Bender Divas Centrestage at Midsumma," *Melbourne Leader*, January 13, 2010, http://www.melbourne-leader,whereilive.com.au/lifestyle/story/gender-bender-divas/.
85. Larissa Glasser, "Interview: An Interview with Annah Moore," *Transgender Tapestry* 112 (Summer 2007): 35.
86. "The Cliks: Their *Snakehouse* Strikes Like A Viper," *Diva*, January 2008: 21.
87. Michael Friedman, "The Evolving Role of LGBT Musicians in Heavy Metal Music," *Psychology Today Online*, April 1, 2014, http://www.psychologytoday.com/blog/brick-brick/201404/the-evolving-role-lgbt-musicians-in-heavy-metal-music.
88. Ingram, "Ten Arguments for a Theory of Queers in Public Space," 10.
89. Erbe, "'This Isn't Over 'Til I Say It's Over'," 7.
90. Diane Anderson-Minshall, "Agony and Ecstasy," *The Advocate,* October 29, 2011, http://www.advocate.com/print-issue/advance/2011/10/19/heavy-metal-rocker-comes-out-transgender?page=0,0.
91. Vince Neilstein, "Keith Caputo Is Now A Woman … Sort Of," MetalSucks.net, July 15, 2011, http://www.metalsucks.net/2011/07/15/keith-caputo-is-now-a-woman-sort-of/.

92. Andrew Parks, "Daddy's Little Girl," *Decibel* 45, July 2008: 54.
93. Ibid., 55–56.
94. Brandon Stosuy, "Queer As Fuck: The Soft Pink Truth's Black Metal," *Pitchfork*, May 29, 2014, http://pitchfork.com/features/show-no-mercy/9417-soft-pink-truth/.
95. Ibid.
96. Leo Bersani, "Gay Betrayals," in *Is the Rectum A Grave? And Other Essays* (Chicago: University of Chicago Press, 2010): 43.

5   Eat Me Alive

Much of understanding queer identities in the twenty-first century is based in an understanding of consumption. The increasing pressure of queer commodification, something scholars including Urvashi Vaid have demonstrated had damaging effects on America's queer political and cultural movements, led to increased emphasis on commodity-based consumption as prerequisite for queer identity formation. In addition, queer individuals must contend not only with their consumption of popular music, media, and material culture, they must also deal with the consumption of queer lives, images, and cultural markers by the mainstream. "Under the intense pressures of globalizing capitalism," explained Ingram, "most of the freedom to live well and to construct a specific identity involving erotic expression has been closely linked to an individual's purchasing power."[1] Consequently, queer lives and queer communities are both defined and appropriated through consumption, and spaces where consumption occurs provide both a site for queer social practice and a place where queer identities are questioned. As Rosemary Hennessy wrote in her essay on queer consumption: "As social practice, sexuality includes lesbian, gay, and queer resistance movements that have built social and political networks, often by way of capitalist commercial venues."[2] For queer fans of heavy metal, indeed for queer-identified individuals, performances, or musicians in heavy metal, issues of consumption are vital for understanding the queerscape. The visibility of queerness in heavy metal concedes sexuality is part of its local and transnational scenes. At the same time, because queerness in heavy metal is inextricably linked to notions of power, discursive production, and style, it is bound to commodification and consumption. "We need a way of understanding visibility that acknowledges both the local situations in which sexuality is made intelligible," wrote Hennessey, "as well as the ties that bind knowledge and power to commodity production, consumption, and exchange."[3]

For heavy metal, as with any other genre of popular music, the role of consumption is not simply buying recordings. Consumption means the many ways in which music fans, performers, and gatekeepers produce, interpret, and commodify aspects of popular music. Therefore consumption can be understood as the ways consumers select offerings from a buffet of social media, video and audio recordings, stylistic cultural markers such as clothing and jewelry, lyrics, fandom, and the spaces of performance. As Will Straw explained in his essay "Music as Commodity and Material Culture," the willingness of many scholars to frame music as an almost ethereal art form, rather than as a commodity to be consumed, has created a gap in scholarship about popular music. Only understanding popular music as desire commodified and consumed clarifies the links between popular music, desire, space, and identity. In fact, consumption is the key to excavating the relationships between space, heavy metal, and the desires of heavy metal's queer fans. As Straw wrote: "From the perspective of the consumer, the musical commodity offers the possibility of repeating, at will, a prior experience already judged desirable."[4] Though Straw was writing more specifically about record collections and the act of collecting recordings, his supposition that commodities can be read as cultural texts where a desire can be read and reread by the consumer provides an interesting mode of interpreting the consumption of both heavy metal markers and queer-identified markers in the queerscape. What desires do queer fans of heavy metal read in a commodified cultural text such as a T-shirt, a concert floor, or a lyric? What desires are reenacted when a favorite album is played or a favorite band performs? How do such desires, encased in consumptive practices, act as markers of identity as both queer and heavy metal?

As important to a reexamination of consumption and queerness in heavy metal is existing stereotypes of metal fans as undereducated, underinformed, and in some cases mindless consumers of the music's sounds, styles, and trappings. For example, several existing studies of consumption using Bordieu's (1984) ideas about cultural consumption as a product of enculturation have focused on heavy metal fans.[5] One such study in 2008 on musical consumption and teenagers focused on a variety of groups, including one identified as "hard rockers." According to the authors, the musical tastes of studied individuals were "relatively autonomous effects of cultural capital."[6] The authors explained:

> Hard Rockers are competent students, though relatively unenthusiastic ones. They are not short of cultural capital, they are in university bound programmes, and neither their disdain for school nor their participation in peer group activity translates into serious underachievement. ... Hard Rockers are involved in a relationship of mutual disregard and that their respective musical tastes serve as a symbolic boundary between adolescent groups separated and divided by race, cultural capital, and school achievement.[7]

Bordieu's concept of musical tastes and consumption as tied to childhood predisposition is problematic in this sense. By examining consumption as a system of texts that reflect desires, scholars can better understand semiotic displays such as heavy metal as a factor in "group affiliation, emulation, and, even invidious distinction."[8] Consumption of such texts, specifically the ways in which the signs of heavy metal are consumed by queer fans, allows the fans to consume their desires in the public marketplace. In fact, since semiotics demands both a signifier (in this case the sounds and trappings of heavy metal) and the signified (the emotions that such signs engender), the link between the heavy metal queerscape and consumption crystallizes. The signifiers of heavy metal, from leather jackets to guttural lyrics, are commonly read by outsiders as lower class, uneducated, white, heterosexual, and male. For queer fans, those signifiers can be consumed because they seem disconnected from the queer body when viewed through the masculinized, heterosexual gaze. They do not look queer or seem queer so they must not be. Meanwhile, what metal music, style, and the bodies on which they are displayed become signified as queer by queer-identified fans. The very semiotic display that is marked as low brow and masculine by the mainstream becomes a veritable semiotic playground for queers whose use of heavy metal is signified as their own desires. Inside the semiotic display, queer fans have both the relative safety and explicit, exaggerated performances of their desires. "Music provides a particularly interesting example of modern relations between consumption and self-identity," popular culture scholar David Hasmondhalgh wrote. "Many people report that music plays a very important role in their lives. This role does not appear to have diminished with industrialization, commodification and the mass consumption of music: if anything, it has grown."[9]

How does the understanding of consumptive practices fit within the understanding of heavy metal as a queerscape? The theoretical writing on queerscape focuses mostly on architecture and on the need to have a queer public space that is differently eroticized and identified. Ingram, for example, wrote about a Vancouver beach as a site of interventional queerscape architecture.[10] Queerscape architecture, as Ingram explained, is a "systematic process of visibility through demanding adequate and equitable distribution of necessary resources like security, access, aesthetics and space."[11] The concept of queerscape, however, can best be understood as sites where queer expressions of desire take place. While the expression of desire might be more explicit in Halford's performance or in a fan's leather style, those same desires are most frequently expressed in the consumption of metal. Consumption happens in queerscapes, in those public spaces where desires are made visible. As Helen Leung explained in her study of Hong Kong films as queerscapes, the best way to conceptualize queerscape is by understanding it as a site of possibility, not an actual habitat.[12] I suggest the spatial aspects of queerscape theory can be pushed even further to include interior spaces of body and mind as the sites of possibility. When a queer fan of heavy metal buys music, cruises club shows, or reinterprets lyrics as queer, they are presenting their own consumptive practices as sites of possibility. Buying a concert ticket becomes a public act of desire in what is otherwise presented as a heterocentric, unwelcoming space, place, and scene. As Ingram wrote:

> How people view themselves as members of an erotic network of sexual minority, with prerequisite processes of coming out, of finding out where they can go and cannot go, has tremendous implications for personal as well as professional relationships, to respective communal environments. To a large extent, queerscape architecture responds to programmes based on certain historically rooted notions of desire, identities, acts, and the 'publicness of space.'[13]

Consumptive practices are desiring practices. These consumptive practices are absolutely central to understanding identities, the desires of queer fans of heavy metal (and, I would argue, any other category and genre of popular culture), and the importance of heavy metal as a queerscape. I endeavor to explore consumption as a desiring text of the queerscape in three modes: musical consumption, performance consumption, and corporeal consumption.

MUSICAL CONSUMPTION

In 2013, metal fans Howie Abrams and Sacha Jenkins published *The Merciless Book of Metal Lists*. Among the lists of best album covers and greatest metal drummers was "Rob Halford's Lyrics Re-examined," a list of Judas Priest songs the authors claimed to reinterpret given Halford's sexuality. The authors suggested Priest's classic songs were all about gay sex. "You've Got Another Thing Coming" was about Halford's sex acts, "Living After Midnight" the story of Halford visiting Amsterdam's "Red Light District in search of a Dutch stallion," and "Breaking the Law" was imagined as Halford boarding "a bus to San Francisco to get laid."[14] According to the authors, the list was a way to somehow right imagined wrongs.

> Imagine, if you will, being an awkward teenage boy screaming along to every single thing shrieked by Halford at a Priest show back in the day. … Fist in the air, chest puffed out, oblivious to the rest of the universe. Priest RULES, and you have become a slave to every riff, each delivered vocal, and all of the ill-advised choreography – only to find out "Hell Bent for Leather" doesn't mean exactly what you thought it did. Rob had PENIS on his mind, but no one was publicly aware of his love for the skin flute as of yet! So, we think it is wise to take a closer look at some of what Robbie boy had to say throughout the years and explore what he REALLY meant.[15]

Earlier in the book, Abrams and Jenkins refer to the lists as "universally accepted truths" and "any REAL Metalhead will agree with us."[16] For their

2014 tour in support of their latest album *Redeemer of Souls*, Judas Priest hired Steel Panther. Steel Panther is in many ways a 1980s hair/glam metal tribute band. They sing and perform original music but in the style and clothing of 1980s bands such as Def Leppard, Mötley Crüe, Poison, and Bon Jovi. Steel Panther is best known for songs that glorify sexual escapades, including "Community Property," "Asian Hooker," and "17 Girls In A Row." Among the songs on their 2014 setlist is "Glory Hole," the third release on the 2014 album *All You Can Eat*. The song focuses on a man's adventures seeking out glory holes, sites of public sex where a man inserts his penis through a hole in a wall, taking oral sex from unknown providers on the other side. "But you never really know who's sucking on the other side/Is it a boy or a girl, or a lady-man hermaphrodite?"[17] How do queer heavy metal fans consume the heavy metal Abrams and Jenkins consider "universally accepted?" Is "Glory Hole" part of that acceptance? What are the possibilities of a queerscape in the consumption of heavy metal beyond the simple gay people listen to gay music paradigm? How do queer fans consume heavy metal as a function of the queerscape?

In an exploration of music scenes in Brisbane, scholar Jodie Taylor concluded the city's queer scene operated as an alternative to what might be called the gay mainstream. The key, Taylor wrote, was music and the fact that musical consumption defined the anti-mainstream of the queer scene.

> The lack of genre-specific or codified musical tastes and performances within the queer scene correlates with queer's disidentificatory position. By defying collective sexual and musical classifications, the queer scene activates its resistance towards commodified aestheticism that is determined in the grounds of sexual identification. In opposition to the social limitations imposed upon expression of sexuality by the gay mainstream, as well as the gay scene's occupation with handbag music, Brisbane's queer scene encourages eclectic expression of sexual and musical play. It is through playing with multiple conventions and representations of gender and sexual norms, as well as musical norms, that queers activate a serious aesthetic challenge to gay cultural normativity. In doing so, they demonstrate the indeterminancy and elasticity that is characteristic of queer identity and queer cultural production in general.[18]

While Taylor's work focused on a particular scene, music operates with the same conventions in a larger queerscape such as heavy metal. The common image of gay men preferring musicals, for example, or the common link between lesbians and folk music serve a normative role. Queer fans of heavy metal, however, pose a serious challenge to that consumptive norm. In fact, queer fans of heavy metal defy the homophobic norm by consuming heavy metal music and further defy that norm by listening to the genres of heavy metal least expected by heavy metal's mainstream. Queer fans of heavy metal consume some of the most extreme genres of heavy metal produced.

The key to the musical consumption of heavy metal's queerscape is that music is more than just a constellation of sounds. As Christopher Small explained in his book *Musicking*, music is an activity.[19] The act of consuming music, of allowing the activity of music to inhabit your mind space, is crucial to understanding heavy metal itself. Heavy metal is understood by its fans as an activity intended for the mind and body, not simply for detached listening. For example, consider this description of heavy metal musicking:

> The emphasis in heavy metal music production is the enjoyment listeners get from the music itself; the physiological response of frustrated body rhythms, the process of tension and release, and the anticipation of such pleasure. Increased volume serves only to heighten this experience.[20]

Heavy metal music, regardless of its genre, was always seen as an activity, from the physiological responses of listening to head banging and concert mosh pits. In fact, the consumption of metal music can be understood as an indicator of the queerscape itself. "In musicking we have a tool by means of which our real concepts of ideal relationships can be articulated," wrote Small. "Those contradictions can be reconciled, and the integrity of the person affirmed, explored, and celebrated."[21] Queer fans of heavy metal, through the act of musical consumption, articulate their desires. Those desires are as varied and as multiple as the identities of queer fans and the genres of heavy metal.

Another part of the musical consumption of heavy metal among queer fans are the ways queer fans procure heavy metal. Much has been written about queer-identified folks and their links to consumerism and class respectability, even if such class mobility is not evident in practice. For example, Urvashi Vaid explained in her book *Virtually Unequal* that the published median income of LGBT people in 1995 was inflated by $50,000 because the statistic was based on subscribers to magazines intended for upper-class, white gay males.[22] At the same time, scholars of LGBT spatiality and community history have explored the links between consumption and a non-normative gender identity. For example, several studies have linked the development of queer communities to queer bars and neighborhood enclaves (Newton 1979; Chauncey 1995; Kennedy and Davies 1994).[23] But how do these competing narratives about queer people and their buying power work within the framework of heavy metal? First, heavy metal has consistently been described as working-class music, whatever its sex and race divisions. Second, while heavy metal provides a queerscape for queer-identified fans, it is not a queer place in and of itself. The lessons learned about queer culture, language, behavior, and relationships in Newton's Fire Island or Kennedy and Davies's lesbian bars are not part of the daily milieu of the heavy metal queerscape. In a move that clearly demonstrates the double-edged alterity of being a queer fan of heavy metal, queer fans consume heavy metal through traditional heavy metal networks at the same rate they engage with new technologies. When the queer-identified fans surveyed responded to questions about consumption of heavy metal music, sixty percent of the respondents got their music from websites (as might be predicted, given the music market of the twenty-first century) and sixty percent still purchased their heavy metal in the form of compact disc. Forty percent of surveyed fans used file sharing and/or swapping to get music, but forty percent of fans also indicated they still relied on concerts and music recommended by friends. Only fifteen percent of queer heavy metal fans used Facebook to consume their music but thirty percent still use heavy metal magazines.

Table 5.1 Methods of heavy metal consumption used by queer fans

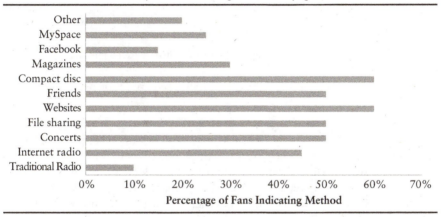

In his essay on queer consumptive practice, Peter Lugosi suggested consumer practices among queer groups could indicate a community because "community values and aspirations are implicitly and explicitly tied to consumption behavior."[24] The methods queer fans of heavy metal use to acquire heavy metal music indicate not a queer community but rather a heavy metal community that revolves around concerts, CD and file sharing, magazines, and contact with friends.

The double-edged alterity of queerness and a heavy metal identity is further evident in the genres of heavy metal that queer fans consume. Though surveyed queer fans of heavy metal expressed an interest in everything from classic heavy metal to pirate-themed metal bands, those surveyed overwhelmingly prefer the sounds of death and black metal. Ironically, these are two of the most controversial and extreme genres of heavy metal in production, and the genres are most frequently associated with homophobia, gender and other violence, sexism, and racism. At the same time, when the genres are examined according to gender identity and sexual orientation, the trends suggest interplay of queer identity and heavy metal fandom that is only possible in the queerscape.

Table 5.2 Preferred metal genres by selected gender and sexual identities

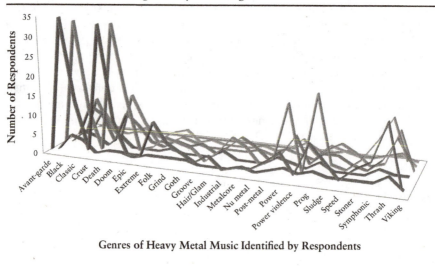

Genres of Heavy Metal Music Identified by Respondents

■ Bisexual ■ FTM ■ Gay ■ MTF ■ Lesbian ■ Queer ■ Trans* ■ Intersex

The two most popular genres of heavy metal among surveyed queer fans were death metal and black metal. Across gender and sexual identities, death and black metal were preferred genres regardless of age, locality, or nationality. The origins of death metal are, like much of heavy metal history, murky. According to one metal scholar, it began in San Francisco with the band Possessed, with additional influences from everyone from Bathory to Slayer in the mid-1980s.[25] The sound of death metal includes three important hallmarks: a bombardment of staccato drums known as blastbeats, a lyrical focus on death and gore, and the guttural vocals so often referred to as unintelligible by those outside metal scenes. While the sound may have had origins in California, Florida quickly became death metal ground zero, and metal record labels such as Relapse and Nuclear Blast became the vehicles for delivering death metal to the faithful. In addition, death metal was focused on extremity of sound: blastbeats faster than the band before, vocals more guttural than the previous release. Consequently, as death metal began to spin out subgenres around the world, the bands become more and more extreme. Black metal, a product of death metal and music by European extreme bands such as Venom, Bathory, and Celtic Frost, began to appear in the early 1990s. As the genre spread across Europe, it found a home and a stronghold in Scandinavia, especially in Norway, where black metal has an international reputation. The sound of black metal took aspects of death metal and pushed them to their limits. As Sharpe-Young wrote:

> Once this goal [singing about horror and attracting listeners] had been achieved, these bands could then apply themselves to perfecting

the art: the choking, mid-frequency guitars, the rasping, inhuman vocal style; bone-dry, blastbeating drums; and hugely distorted sound quality. What was previously lambasted as underproduction became the desired effect – anti-music.[26]

What is particularly interesting about the consumption of black and death metal among queer-identified fans is these same fans frequently identify black and death metal as homophobic, transphobic, and biphobic. Even more interesting is the fact the three groups who most often selected death and/or black metal as their favorite genre identified as gay male, bisexual, or queer. For example, a female bisexual fan from the United States explained homophobia was most prevalent in "most death metal – it's pretty easy to just avoid large swaths of metal, so I do."[27] At the same time, a gay male from the United Kingdom wrote: "This isn't a hard-and-fast rule, and I am grossly exaggerating, but the black metal and power metal scenes tend to be homophobic/transphobic, in my experience. Death metal dudes tend to be more laid back about such things."[28] When asked if heavy metal made fans feel more masculine, a female bisexual death metal singer from the United States stated: "The more death metal the band, the more butch."[29] Even more interesting is the fact that gay male and bisexual male fans often go to some length to describe black metal as androgynous in terms of sound. For example, one gay male fan from Sweden wrote he preferred the "androgynous vocals" of black metal.[30] A female bisexual fan from Denmark wrote: "I have the feeling that more of the Norwegian black metal musicians could be/are queer."[31] A female queer fan from the United States, when asked if she had queer friends who listened to metal, wrote: "Yes, I know a number of gay men who listen to black metal. Ironically, black metal is least tolerant toward gay people."[32]

Why are gay, bisexual, and queer fans embracing a music that is admittedly homophobic (see Chapter 3)? This is an aspect of musical consumption in the queerscape. Death and black metal are intended to push the envelope, to get increasingly more extreme. What could be more extreme than listening to music that objectifies and threatens you? Whether it is the professed Satanic beliefs of Norwegian black metallers or the gore-filled lyrics of brutal death metal, consuming heavy metal music means consuming not only the lyrics and sound but the physiological performance of listening within the heavy metal queerscape. The act of musicking with black or death metal requires an active avoidance of lyrics focused on anti-Semitism, racism, sexism, and homophobia, specifically because the music consumed is seen as so extreme that such challenges are simply artistic convention. On the jacket for his recent album covering black and death metal songs, Soft Pink Truth's solo performer Drew Daniel wrote:

> Black metal fandom all too often entails a tacit endorsement or strategic looking-the-other-way with regards to the racist, anti-Semitic,

> sexist and homophobic bullshit politics that (still) pervade the scene, on behalf of either escapist fantasy talk, shaky invocations of art as a crypto-religious path to transcendence, or – the oldest cop out in the book – the quietist [sic] declaration that 'I just like how it sounds.'[33]

Daniel knows this is the issue because as a self-identified queer and a metal fan, he understands the rules of consumption. If the music sounds good and if the music makes you feel power and release, then oppressive lyrics are simply consumed as the decorative garnish for the musical main dish.

After black and death metal, the genres most identified as preferred by gay men were power metal, progressive metal, and symphonic metal. Ironically, these genres are related as well. Power metal is often seen as one of the most sonically perfected forms of metal music. The genre is based largely on virtuosity: expert guitar playing, perfectly timed drums, technically challenging music, and fantasy-based lyrics sung at near operatic levels.[34] The fantasy-based lyrics lent themselves to fantastical appearances and epic concerts by bands such as Hammerfall, Anvil, Saxon, and Manowar. Progressive, or prog, took the technical proficiency of power to extremes, focusing on virtuosic instrumentation and musical complexity above all. Symphonic metal leaned more towards the fantastical themes of power metal, eventually including symphonic classical music and relying primarily on the soaring operatic vocals of female lead singers.

What draws gay male metal fans to the fantasy themes, technical proficiency, and operatic vocals of these genres? If musical consumption is based on a physiological feeling of escape, then surely no genre can offer as much escape from the mundane as power, prog, and symphonic metal. In addition, these genres are often vilified by followers of more extreme genres such as death, black, and doom metal. Power metal is frequently positioned as stereotypically gay in everything from blogs to scholarly work that suggests bands such as Manowar and Accept are sites of the gay male gaze.[35] Prog is often seen as too in-your-head, and symphonic metal is vilified by hypermasculine metal fans as pop music posing as metal. As a gay male fan from the United Kingdom explained, the "vast majority of the female led symphonic metal bands" seemed queer.[36] The key to understanding the appeal is the concept of camp. While many scholars and writers have discussed the theatricality of camp, it is best understood as embracing excessive theatricality and exaggeration. First explored by author Susan Sontag and anthropologist Esther Newton, camp is an artifice that likely has a subversive purpose: to provide a counterpoint to staid concepts of gender by exaggerating the very stereotypes they appear to embrace. In his 1997 book *The Death of Gay Culture*, cultural critic Richard Harris suggested camp and its requisite exaggerated female performance served as a template for identity formation among gay men. As Harris wrote:

Because of our fiercely fetishistic involvement with diva worship, the star even in a sense traded places with her gay audience, who used her as a naked projection of their frustrated romantic desires, of their inability to express their sexual impulses openly in a homophobic society, and to seduce and manipulate the elusive heterosexual men for whom many homosexuals once nursed bitterly unrequited passions. In the process of this transference, the diva was voided of both her gender and her femininity and became the homosexual's proxy, a transvestite figure, a vampish surrogate through whom gay men lived out unattainable longings to ensnare such dashing heartthrobs as Clark Gable, Humphrey Bogart, and Gene Kelly.[37]

One gay male Canadian metal fan spent the majority of his interview discussing the female singers of symphonic bands. His interests ranged from V from the band Benedictum ("both the sexy and kick your ass happening") to power metal singer Doro Pesch ("I can see the virginal aspect") to out lesbian female metal performer Floor Jansen ("she's not shy"). When asked why he loved power and symphonic metal so much, the informant replied: "Gay men have their divas, opera, pop, musical theater. ... Mine are the metal ladies."[38] Perhaps camp and its exaggerated gender performance did not disappear with classic American cinema but lived on in the form of fantasy-themed Manowar and Doro Pesch performances and the gothic opera of symphonic bands such as Nightwish and their ex-lead singer Floor Jansen. In the sounds of power and symphonic metal, gay male fans find their desires bound up in the embellished performance of metal's fantasy genres. The consumption of power, prog, and symphonic metal provides gay men with camp culture within the heavy metal queerscape.

Though lesbian-identified queer fans also selected death and black metal among their favorite genres, the genre most preferred by lesbian fans was thrash. Thrash is a hypermasculine genre of heavy metal and a genre probably most readily identified as heavy metal by those outside metal scenes. Thrash is the genre of famous and historically popular bands such as Metallica, Megadeth, Anthrax, and Slayer, and was heavily influenced by classic heavy metal bands such as Judas Priest and Iron Maiden.[39] Thrash had its origins in San Francisco and Los Angeles before spreading to New York and New Jersey in the 1980s. Sonically and in terms of music theory, thrash represented a new technical turn. Precision riffing, typically accomplished by picking guitar strings, combined with intricate structures based on guitar changes and time signatures marked thrash as frenetic music driven by men with low-slung guitars. One MTF transgender fan from the United States wrote that thrash bands were oppressive. "Lots of the musicians from older legacy metal bands from like the thrash era and stuff say misogynist, homophobic, and transphobic things to try to assert their heteronormative masculinity," wrote the fan. "I can't really give you a list because they all are like that."[40]

Why do lesbian fans seemingly embrace one of the most hypermasculine genres of heavy metal? Metallica and Slayer were the two bands most often mentioned by lesbian fans as preferred, and they certainly have a history of homophobic comments and colloquial stories among fans about homophobic behaviors. Though Metallica's flirtation with homophobia may be less explicit than Slayer and their guitarist Kerry King, in an April 2001 interview for *Playboy*, Metallica drummer Lars Ulrich explained lead singer James Hetfield's homophobia had caused rifts in the band. "Let there be no question about that," Ulrich told *Playboy*. "I think homophobia is questioning your sexuality and not being comfortable with it."[41] Just as gay male fans find themselves reflected in genres such as symphonic metal, lesbian fans find themselves reflected in thrash. In her essay on viewing Led Zeppelin, scholar Susan Fast explained that female fans of the band found the music empowering specifically because it offered a different construction of gender divorced from the body.[42] "Actions that are perceived as belonging to a feminine identity, or actions that cannot so unproblematically be assigned to male or female identities," wrote Fast, "can be written onto this 'male' body."[43] For lesbian heavy metal fans, thrash offers particular outlets for musical consumption. First, thrash music is loud, brash, and boisterous, appealing to the physiological feeling of the sound. Second, thrash lyrics typically focus on anger, frustration, power and control, sociopolitical concerns such as warfare, and the struggles of being misunderstood. Songs such as Metallica's "Master of Puppets" ("Master of Puppets I'm pulling your strings/Twisting your mind and smashing your dreams"), a song about drug addiction, and Anthrax's "Caught in a Mosh" ("Talking in circles we'll never get it straight/Just you and me in our theatre of hate") provide fans with an aggressive, physical outlet for the frustrations of invisibility.[44] Consuming thrash metal means consuming the sounds and lyrics that express aggression, as well as the visual spectacle of musicians garnering the attentions of other women. It is the sound of desire for control, power, and sex. When disconnected from the male bodies making the music, these musical actions as consumed by lesbian fans take on deeper, more complex meaning. A twenty-five-year-old female bisexual fan who selected thrash as her preferred genre explained her favorite song of all time was "Reign in Blood" by Slayer. She identified the lyrics, such as "Fall into me, the sky's crimson tears/Abolish the rules made of stone," as particularly important. According to her, thrash provided a powerful sense of belonging and recognition:

> It doesn't speak to me on a literal level. I've read Walser's *Running with the Devil*. The lyrics aren't very important, it's the mood it creates in the person. It has a sense of aggression – not mindless but channeled. I play it when I'm in a rut in my life, because rage is a great motivator. It reminds me of seeing the band. I felt a great sense of community and solidarity there ... mutual appreciation, solidarity, and fun. My circumstances just didn't matter anymore.[45]

In her book on queer voices, Freya Jarman-Ivens positioned the voice as a technology for the emergence of queer space. She explained such emergence happened when the listener connected their listening self to others. According to Jarman-Ivens, the voice is genderless and the consumptive act of listening serves as an act of desire.[46] "The queer potential of the voice," wrote Jarman-Ivens, "is felt most intensively at those points where technologies become audible."[47] Through the consumption of heavy metal music, queer listeners do precisely that. Their desires are expressed in the voices they consume and through those connections, they create a queerscape.

PERFORMANCE CONSUMPTION

In his writings, Foucault identified four types of technology: production, sign systems, power, and the self.[48] Foucault saw the technology of the self as the ways in which an individual, alone or with others, alters themselves in order to achieve ethereal qualities such as happiness or wisdom. As scholar Irvin Schick explained, this concept has been extended to a variety of disciplines in order to understand social constructions as technologies. Among these extensions is deLauretis's technology of gender, or technologies of space and place.[49] In order to understand the consumption of heavy metal performance by queer fans, it is important to expand the understanding of Foucaultian technologies to include the technology of music. Using what sociologist Tia DeNora termed the "aesthetic reflexive" activities of musicking, it is possible to understand music as an aspect of the technology of self and the role musical performance plays in the production of self. "To speak of this process of self-knowledge and its constitution," wrote DeNora, "is to speak of how the expressive and stylistic parameters of self are established, maintained and changed."[50] Understanding music as a vehicle for the technology of self provides a way of understanding the cognitive maps of the queerscape and the ways in which queer fans of heavy metal constantly test, appropriate, and reframe heavy metal as a queer public space. As Gordon Brett Ingram wrote:

> My underlying argument is that a "queerscape" – larger than a community and smaller and more grounded with less pretentious than any sort of singular "Queer Nation" or planet – necessarily reconstructs itself and in this way links cognitive maps, that are often at the core of studies in human geography, with activistic design and planning through day-to-day mediation of both desire and homophobia.[51]

Though Ingram wrote about particular spaces, his theory of the queerscape as cognitive map of sexual aesthetics is applicable to the study of musical productions, including heavy metal. In order to understand the consumption of heavy metal performance as a hallmark of the queerscape, it will be examined through three aspects of the technology of the self: self-identity, self-regulation, and aesthetic reflexivity of self and others. The key to each of these aspects of the self is the consumption of heavy metal performance.

Heavy metal performance takes many forms. In terms of consumption, however, that performance is limited to the ways queer fans consume a heavy metal performance. The sound and lyrics become secondary, in consumption, to other facets such as performance spaces (clubs, concert halls, and arenas), the movement of bodies as a way to get closer to heavy metal performances, and the stories fans tell about their first experiences consuming heavy metal performance. In essence, these methods of technology of the self provide queer fans with the ability to identify themselves as both queer and metal despite the seeming incongruity. Through the consumption of performance, queer fans of heavy metal build the cognitive maps so necessary for the queerscape and engage in the aesthetic reflexivity required for their continued self-identity as queer and metal. As Foucault wrote about the technology of the self: "The task of testing oneself, examining oneself, monitoring oneself in a series of clearly defined exercises, makes the question of truth – the truth concerning what one is, what one does, and what one is capable of doing – central to the formation of the ethical subject."[52]

Self-regulation, or the testing of boundaries imposed by the self and others, is central to the queerscape. For queer fans of heavy metal, the testing of boundaries is most evident in the ways queer fans navigate the scenes and spaces of heavy metal. The unwritten rules about navigating a heavy metal performance space are complicated. One's distance from the stage, engagement in the mosh pit, who you attend performances with and when, all these function as self-regulating aspects of heavy metal identity. This map of a performance space quickly becomes a cognitive map, giving metal fans an identificatory map of the performance space that indicates shifts in age, engagement with performers, and their consumption of the performance itself. This consumption of heavy metal performance then becomes a series of self-imposed borders where the technology of the self is examined and defined according to the spatiality of that consumption. In other words, where you stand in a concert and with whom becomes a way to identify your place in the heavy metal queerscape.

One of those unwritten rules of performative consumption is where a fan occupies space at a heavy metal performance. For example, many queer heavy metal fans, especially masculine-identified fans, get close to the stage. "I like to be as close as possible," explained a forty-seven-year-old American metal fan who identified as gay and masculine, "preferably pressed up against the stage."[53] Another masculine gay fan, a thirty-one-year-old fan from Canada, explained he was always on the floor near the stage unless he didn't like the band very much.[54] Queer fans who still wrestled with their identities were more quick to be along the edges of a performance, away from the stage and along the walls and fences. For example, an eighteen-year-old Dutch man who identified as "gay I guess, though I don't like saying that ... I prefer a man who likes other men," explained his preferred location was along the edges of the performance space "close to the fence or something similar I can lean on."[55] A twenty-year-old British man who said he was "ever so slightly bicurious" explained he only goes to large concerts and even then, he stays in the back. "I do feel like I'm in the way a lot," he explained, "especially in packed crowds."[56]

Another aspect of the identificatory map of a performance space is connected with bands and moshing. Mosh pits are a staple of heavy metal performances but not well understood outside the scenes and spaces of heavy metal.[57] Perhaps the best way to explain the mosh pit is through a recent study of mosh pits performed by a physicist. According to physicist Jesse Silverberg, mosh pits have simple but clear rules like gas molecules in air. Bodies react to the impact of other bodies while dancers in the pit randomly crash into other bodies. Time spent in the pit will quickly teach you about walls (when the crowd of the mosh pit splits in half and prepares to crash into the other half) and waves (when the people in the pit suddenly change direction and you get caught in the physical undertow). Though heavy metal fans are associated with mosh pits in the public imagination, in truth only a certain percentage of heavy metal fans consume performance via the pit.

Table 5.3 Focus of queer fans during concerts

■ Drummer ■ Guitarist ■ Males in Audience ■ Moshpit ■ Other musicians ■ Singer

When asked about their object of focus during a heavy metal concert, only twenty-one percent of queer fans focused on the mosh pit. Of those, some queer fans expressed their interest in the mosh pit was only as a spectacle. "I'm not a mosher," explained one gay male fan from the United Kingdon, "happy to watch others smash themselves up, I'll be in the area between mosh pit and stand arounds – hearing is what is important to me."[58] Fans who participated in the mosh pit explained the pit experience was their introduction to the metal community, like an initiation. "It doesn't make me feel more manly or anything but it definitely has made me more manly by being thrown into mosh pits by my older brother when I was young and having to mosh my way out," a trans*, lesbian femme fan from the United States explained. A female bisexual fan from Australia wrote: "Occasionally, the sheer visceral quality and the tendency to sweat elicits that butch feel; also, the combination of camaraderie and physical collisions during a show has that effect."[59] For queer fans of heavy metal, the randomness of the mosh pit is a primary piece of performance consumption.

In fact, it seems queer fans of heavy metal are paying closest attention to the singer or the other males in the audience. Given the fact the majority of respondents to the queer fan survey identified as male, why are so many focusing on other males in the audience? According to Tia DeNora, understanding self-regulation as a form of technology of self, especially when applied to music, requires the application of music as the representation of an aspired state. Though DeNora applied this primarily to sound, it is just as easily applied to the self-regulation of the body in relation to a performance. DeNora posited: "music is an accomplice in attaining, enhancing and maintaining desired states of feeling and bodily energy; it is a vehicle they use to move out of dispreferred states. It is a resource for modulating and structuring the parameters of aesthetic agency – feeling, motivation, desire, comportment, action, style, energy."[60] Most of the queer fans surveyed, over ninety percent, expressed they had few if any queer friends who also listened to heavy metal, and few if any friends who listened to heavy metal who identified as queer. Closely watching the singers of heavy metal gives queer fans the opportunity to consume that performance as a way to modulate their desires and channel their bodily energy towards the object of consumption: the singer. This is also the reason behind watching males in the audience. They represent a spectacle, a consumable object of body and feeling where the music acts as an accomplice in fulfilling queer desires. The apex of this is the mosh pit, where the disorganized movements of sweaty, out-of-control bodies slamming into each other provides a way to consume bodies in physical action without being policed as a queer person in a heteronormative space. "Musical performances, then," wrote Suzanne Cusick, "are often the accompaniment of ideas performed *through* bodies by the performance *of* bodies."[61] Through the consumption of musical performances, queer fans of heavy metal build a queerscape not only of the performance space but of the desiring body and mind.

Another aspect of the consumption of performance is the self-identity of queer fans of heavy metal. As discussed in previous chapters, the coming-out story is considered a key trope in the lives of queer-identified people. For queer metal fans, however, the coming-out story is about when they became a metal fan, not when they had a sexual awakening. "Music can be used as a device for the reflexive process of remembering/constructing who one is," wrote DeNora, "a technology for spinning the apparently 'continuous' tale of who one 'is'."[62] Queer heavy metal fans consider their metal coming-out story as important as the story of their gendered and sexual identity, and

in some cases more important. Their consumption of heavy metal performance, the tipping point that brought them to their community of metallers,
becomes a key to their complex identities. Queer fans of heavy metal who
consented to interviews were asked three questions about self-identity and
coming out: when they first encountered heavy metal, if they had come out
as queer before or after becoming metal fans, and if being queer had any
effect on their identity as a heavy metal fan. Though there are some gen-
erational differences in technology, these heavy metal coming-out stories
indicate two common threads: their introduction to heavy metal was jarring
at first, and something about heavy metal just felt right. Consider this statement by a gay male from Finland about finding metal:

> I was 13 or 14 when I was searching through sites to download songs
> from, and downloaded Napalm Death's 'Twist the Knife' based purely
> on the name. It sounded like horrible noise at the time and I deleted it,
> but something stuck because about six months later I went and found
> the song again and this time it made a lot more sense. ... Napalm
> Death was really the one thing that really got me going.[63]

Compare that with the heavy metal coming-out story of bisexual female fan
in Scotland:

> When I was six, my sister started playing this Metallica mixtape on
> holiday. My ears caught onto it. I knew when I went into primary
> school, I considered myself a rocker/metaller but I didn't talk about it
> in primary school coz no one said they liked it so I just said to myself
> when I'm older, that's my identity.[64]

The similarities to the coming-out story trope are striking. Queer fans discovered something in the metal performances they consumed, something
that "got them going" or they "caught onto." It was secret, hidden, but nonetheless part of their identity. A Dutch gay man explained he found metal
"after finding Pestilence's The Consuming Impulse on [sic] my grandfather's
attic and trying it out ... although it scared the shit out of me at first (I was
10)."[65] Another fan who identified himself as a gay pansexual told his metal
coming-out story, beginning as a third-person narrative:

> There are a couple of points I could pick out, but it's best to start at the
> beginning. Young (name redacted) of only 5 years old, having started
> to learn piano, is exposed to a huge variety of music. ... When I started
> to learn guitar aged 13, I became heavily influenced by Pink Floyd, and
> became known in school as a bit of a guitarist. One guy asked me to be
> in a band with him. When I asked what kind of music he listed a few
> bands: My Chemical Romance and Bullet For My Valentine. Went on
> from there really.[66]

What purposes do these stories serve? For queer fans of heavy metal, coming into heavy metal represented coming into a community, one that was seen as oppositional to mainstream ethics of self. It meant making decisions that were scary, that had to be hidden. The parallels between queer fans' performance of self-identity and their perceptions of heavy metal performance as a force towards identity development are uncanny, if not staggering. The consumption of performance serves as a template for the outsider identity of heavy metal's queer fans, providing a trope of the queerscape. In the stories of self-identity, queer metal fans find the points where queer and heavy metal become analogous. As Jodie Taylor explained in her book *Playing It Queer*:

> The queer world is not made clear for us; rather, we come to feel it, find it and know it as selves that have already been shaped by other aspects of culture, style and taste, and we bring these with us into our queer worlds. The routes that we take to find queerness are often varied and unconventional, requiring us to traverse the cultural spaces that might otherwise contain us if we were not, as queers, seeking to inhabit a queer world.[67]

The last aspect of performance consumption is aesthetic reflexivity. According to sociologist Tia DeNora, aesthetic reflexivity is a strategy through which individuals preserve their self-identity in the midst of a crowded, modern existence. By reflecting on the aesthetic qualities of self-identity, individuals find a way to conserve themselves despite a rapidly changing and difficult world to navigate. "Heightened aesthetic reflexivity," DeNora suggested, "is thus conceived within current social theory as a function of the (often contradictory) demands made upon the self under advanced modernity."[68] The consumption of heavy metal in the queerscape is inherently about self-preservation in a seemingly hostile environment. In addition, the alterity of being both queer and heavy metal means the demands made on the self often lead to the subsumation of self-identity.

One way of locating aesthetic reflexivity in performance consumption is in slash fiction about heavy metal performers. Slash fiction is a form of fandom well known in online fan circles but woefully understudied in scholarly work on fandom. Fan fiction is an old practice, born no doubt from fans dreaming up possible lives, and futures, with their pop idols. As one group of scholars has elucidated, slash fiction is also ignored by queer theory and queer readings of popular culture, and to their detriment.[69] Essentially, slash fiction takes two figures from popular culture (fictional or real) and puts them in same-sex relationships. These online short stories, which sometimes extend over several chapters, range from innocent love stories between two popular figures to adults-only, overtly sexual stories about same-sex encounters. The authors range from anonymous to those with online biographies, and can have large followings online. There are thousands of slash fiction stories about heavy metal performers. Websites such as adultfanfiction.org and rockfic.com serve as hubs of fan fiction activity, including volumes of slash fiction written by heavy metal fans. This particular form of performance consumption illustrates an interesting potential for aesthetic reflexivity: when self-preservation becomes the creation of a fiction of one's desires. What better way to preserve the self than in an anonymous archive of desire, and what better consumptive map of the queerscape?

Though there are thousands, perhaps millions, of fan fiction slash stories about heavy metal performers, some of the stories that revolve around Rob Halford and Judas Priest are most revealing. This is not particularly surprising. As the most well-known out queer metal performer, Halford carries the desires of many fans. What is surprising, however, are the people paired with Halford and the men of Judas Priest in these stories: some of the most famous, and often controversial, performers in heavy metal. One story, entitled "Winding Road," makes a connection between Halford's hiatus from Priest, his coming out, and the hiatus that lead singer Bruce Dickinson took from Iron Maiden, another of the most important heavy metal bands. In the 1997 story, author Caroline suggests the two men had a relationship that led them to be on hiatus at the same time. In the story Halford has just given his infamous 1998 MTV interview, and Dickinson arrives at Halford's door to rekindle an old sexual relationship:

> His hair may be shorter but I can still wind my fingers through it just, and he tastes so fucking good, not quite like I remember; different but still the same. Bruce twists in my lap so he's sat astride me, one hand cupping the back of my head. The other hand has nails scratching over my scalp and down my neck. I press back into the touch. Seems I've found another kink, his nails digging into my scalp, but then again Bruce Dickinson always was my kink and my biggest weakness. What I forgot was he was my biggest strength, too.[70]

In another story, "Top, Bottom, or Versatile" by an author known as Funky Canuck, the queerscape is even more clear. In this story, Rob Halford and the members of Judas Priest run a hedonist resort where young men are educated in the ways of kinky sex. The pupils in this story are all famous members of the great heavy metal bands of the 1980s: Sebastian Bach fresh from his homophobic T-shirt spectacle, Bret Michaels of Poison, Megadeth lead singer Dave Mustaine, Mick Mars and Vince Neil of Mötley Crüe, Metallica's James Hetfield and Jason Newstead, and other members of bands. In a story that spreads over eighteen chapters, the men of Judas Priest take the assembled heavy metal performers through a myriad of sexual scenes with each other, all of which revolve around dominant/submissive sex between men. The only men who are off limits and only service the men of Judas Priest are the "assistants": Robin Zander of Cheap Trick and Cinderella's lead singer, Tom Kiefer.[71] Though Halford and Judas Priest are frequent subjects of slash fiction, they are far from the only ones. "Nemo," a story from 2011, pairs Metallica's drummer Lars Ulrich with Twiggy Ramirez, the bassist from Marilyn Manson.[72] "Perchance To Dream," a 2005 story written by the author known as Mad Andy about a relationship between Alice Cooper and Lemmy Klimster, leader of the classic metal band Motorhead, is not sexual at all. In this very short tale, Klimster and Cooper hold each other on a balcony before going to bed for the night:

> Lemmy hesitated and looked out over the dozing city – it never really slept, not really – and shook his head, trying to clear the mismatched miasma of old wonderings and new uncertainties from his mind. Alice tugged at his waist, and he snorted through his nose; his lover was right. It would all look better in the morning.[73]

Hundreds of metal bands are represented in slash fiction, from classic bands such as Motorhead to every genre on the metal map, and fem slash featuring female-female sexual encounters with solo performers such as Doro Pesch or female-fronted bands such as Arch Enemy and Nightwish. On adultfanfiction.org, there are 129 stories for Rammstein alone.

These stories range broadly from genre of heavy metal, to type of relationship, to the mix of performers in the slash fiction piece. Slash fiction preserves the aesthetics of heavy metal, presents the desires of queer fans, and offers a new and different way to understand how heavy metal performance is consumed. Rather than simply consume heavy metal performance through videos or music purchases, fans who write slash fiction consume heavy metal performance as a stage on which their desires are given voice. The aesthetics of those heavy metal performances become enshrined in slash fiction, whether in the image of Rob Halford providing kinky sex education or in Lemmy exhausted on a hotel balcony. Stories such as these consume heavy metal performance and amplify their queerness, turning up the volume on the very performance aspects queer fans seek, note, and perhaps secretly hope for. This queer world-making, this queerscape of slash fiction, operates on the knife edge of queer heavy metal and offers an alternative narrative of queer fans of heavy metal. As Jodie Taylor proposed: "In popular music and subcultural studies in particular, there is little recognition of the stylistically and musically promiscuous histories of queerness and minimal attempts to understand how, collectively, these constitute significant acts of queer world-making."[74]

While slash fiction provides an alternate way of understanding performance, consumption, and queerscape, the key to those concepts is the desires of queer fans themselves. As De Nora wrote, aesthetic reflexivity is also about the preservation of self-identity through feeling. As De Nora elucidated:

> Individual actors thus not only engage in self-monitoring and self-regulation; they also seek out such 'goods' as 'space,' 'relaxation,'

'pleasure,' and so forth. ... Under any historical conditions where an individual feels a tension between what s/he 'must' do and what she 'feels like' doing, or between how s/he 'feels' and how s/he 'wishes' to feel, the problem of self-regulation arises and with it, the matter of how individuals negotiate between the poles of necessity and preference, between how they think they 'ought' to feel and how they 'do' feel.[75]

If queer fans of heavy metal consume metal performance, how do they feel about heavy metal and their place in it? Does heavy metal give queer fans what they need? What do they feel, and does heavy metal change those feelings? According to the queer fans of heavy metal surveyed, the heavy metal queerscape provides myriad ways for aesthetic reflexivity through the consumption of heavy metal. A gay male fan from Canada consumes metal "for its dark emotional nature (especially doom metal and all its subgenres), which allowed (and allows) me some reassurance, comfort and an outlet when I feel troubled. When I'm not troubled, I enjoy the music and powerful emotional expression in it."[76] "I feel like as a kid before I came out (albeit young at age 11) I was really angry but coupled with that anger was a real mythology buff who really loved the whole wizards and guillotines aspects of the genre," explained a bisexual male American queer fan. "I've always loved the darkness of metal."[77] When asked if metal made him feel powerful, a masculine gay male from the United States stated: "No, it makes me feel equal. More free. It's gorgeous, gruesome, and bare-all. I always feel raw and inspired whenever I listen to heavy metal."[78] "I love the exultant or cathartic release that the music inspires. I feel that it's a more productive and less destructive way for me to release frustration. And I love the combination of power and intricacy inherent in many subgenres of metal," wrote a masculine gay male from Chile.[79] A male-to-female, lesbian- and butch-identified survey respondent said this about how metal provides self-preservation:

> This is an interesting subject that I had delved into a bit in art school, mostly because I felt very alone among queer feminists for liking metal and among metal fans for being a queer feminist. While I don't really listen to lyrical metal (it's usually incomprehensible screaming) I know that a lot of hair metal bands were all about an 'us vs them' mentality, that is, that you feel alone, you might not have any friends who like the same music, but when the band and fans come together then they are united.[80]

Other fans explained the heavy metal queerscape not only as a source of self-preservation but also as a site of identity. In that way, the consumption of heavy metal performance becomes a method through which queer fans gain an aesthetic perspective on their own experience. For example, a leather-identified bisexual male from the United States stated metal "makes me feel free, like I don't have anyone to answer to and I don't have to live up to anyone's expectations."[81] "I felt absolutely marginalized as a member of the masses. Metal, while it is still a male dominated arena, allowed me in enough to not feel outcast," explained a gay, queer-identified respondent from India. "Aside from that, it is the sound, the heavy, melodic guitar/bass, the lyrics, the voice of the singers. All of it makes me feel empowered."[82] "I feel like I have to [listen to metal]. I feel like it's the only kind of music that really speaks to the anger and frustration I feel with the way society is," stated a leather-identified gay male fan from the Netherlands.[83] Finally, a queer-identified bisexual male from Australia wrote: "It just makes me feel like less of a stereotype."[84] These few reflexive statements clearly demonstrate the power of performance consumption in the identities of queer heavy metal fans. Such consumption serves not as sign posts to queer spaces but as internal identity markers.

CORPOREAL CONSUMPTION

The final form of consumption that is vital to the heavy metal queerscape is corporeal consumption. The consumption of the corpus, the body, may seem an odd connection to make to heavy metal, a spectacle of performance. Heavy metal fans, however, are well aware of the role that consuming bodies can take in the sounds, lyrics, and performances of heavy metal. Extreme metal genres such as death, grind, and gore metal often have the breaking down of the body as a theme in horror-based lyrics and videos. Industrial and goth metal share themes about life and death, decay, and blood-letting. Even classic, thrash, and power metal songs concentrate on the body with allusions to the body as machine, the bodies of women as sexual objects, or the body as a site of power. This can be extended to metal performance, where fans consume the spectacle of bodies in performance as musicians, as celebrities, and as objects of desire. The action of listening itself is corporeal, and heavy metal activities such as the mosh pit and headbanging are inherently corporeal. As Keith Kahn-Harris explained in his book *Extreme Metal,* drug use, excessive drinking, and sexual appetites are also an inherent part of the corporeality of heavy metal.[85] The body, as a site of desires, a physical object moving in space, an interaction between fans, or as the subject of music and sound, is critical to the heavy metal ethos.

In this respect, heavy metal has much in common with the experience of queer identity. In fact, the body is at the core of the cultures, histories, even languages of queer-identified peoples. Queer bodies are a frequent subject of legal, cultural, and community discourse as well. Since Foucault's first studies of body and disciplinary power, there has been increasing scholarship on the evolution of not only the homosexual subject but the homosexual body as well. In her essay "Scientific Racism and the Invention of the Homosexual

Body," Siobham Somerville summarized the development of understanding homosexuals as corporeal. Somerville traced the development of corporeal homosexuality from nineteenth-century medical discourse on race and sexuality through legal and social systems to the modern understanding of homosexuality. Eventually, according to Somerville, sexuality and the queer-identified body became a disciplinary system "of particular bodies ... thus a production of that historical moment."[86] Since the nineteenth century, the bodies of queer people have been categorized, debated, rebiologized, dissected, and studied. While queer-identified people have fought to control those bodies, they have continued to be dealt with in medical and academic discourse. While some of these studies have focused on further subjectifying the queer body, many have also sought to examine the discourse surrounding queer bodies. Through this work, the work of queer theory and queer studies, the understanding of the body as a site of identity formation, disciplinary power, and cultural performance has become increasingly clear. In fact, such studies have led to the current state of understanding gender, sexuality, and the expression of those terms: no longer simply bodies but very complicated bodies.

These two unique formations, the queer body and the heavy metal corporeal ethos, come together in the body of the heavy metal fan. In this instance, however, the body is not theoretical or hypothetical but rather an actual, lived body one inhabits. The corporeal ethos of heavy metal requires a sort of grounded corporeality, one based in heavy metal's affinity for horror, transgression, and biological dissolution. It requires an idea that the human body can be broken down, beaten, shaken, pushed to the brink of all kinds of extremes, and perhaps even beyond. At the same time, the queer fans must negotiate their own bodies, subjectified and categorized by themselves and others, as a material body in an interstitital space. "Bodies have a weighty materiality and biology that is undeniable," explained geographers Lynda Johnston and Robyn Longhurst, "but fleshy bodies always exist within the realms of political, economic, cultural and social relations."[87] Where the two come together is in the dirt, the gore, the consumption of those fleshy bodies that metal fans and performers commit. In an example of what Julia Kristeva termed abjection, queer fans of heavy metal delve into the dirt: semen and saliva associated with queer sex, the desecrated bodies of extreme heavy metal, the fascination with humans submitting themselves to machinery in industrial metal, the queer-identified willingness to reassign the body, in the muscle, genitalia, blood, and gore. "Dirt," wrote theorist Elizabeth Grosz, "is that which is not in its proper place, that which upsets or befuddles the other."[88] It is this collection of dangerous deposit that "transgresses the borders of respectability and respectable places," wrote Johnston and Longhurst.[89] Mary Douglas, whose 1966 monograph *Purity and Danger* was the impetus for Kristeva's work on abjection, saw this dirt as key to understanding taboo systems: "Dirt, then, is never an isolated event. Where there is dirt there is system."[90] In the heavy metal queerscape, where fans sometimes call themselves dirtbags and sing along to "Glory Hole," corporeal consumption makes a big, dirty mess.

First, consumption of the body in the heavy metal queerscape is visible in the lyrics of heavy metal music. In the genres queer fans identify as preferred, such as death and black metal, the consumption of the body is a penultimate theme. It is also a central theme in the work of queer-identified heavy metal musicians, whose lyrics are frequently judged in retrospect once the performer has come out. A good example of corporeal consumption in lyrics and the ways in which they are reexamined is the song "Eat Me Alive" by Judas Priest. Released in 1984 on their album *Defenders of the Faith*, "Eat Me Alive" has a particular role in heavy metal history. The Parents Music Resource Center (PMRC), founded by Tipper Gore and Susan Baker in 1984, was an organization seeking to censor lyrics that focused on substance abuse, sexuality, violence, and the occult. "Eat Me Alive," a song Tipper Gore claimed was about oral sex at gun point, was number three on the PMRC's infamous Filthy Fifteen list of the most objectionable songs.[91] The lyrics certainly suggest a sexual escapade, which the PMRC quickly surmised: "Bound to deliver as you give and I collect/Squealing impassioned as the rod of steel injects/Lunge to the maximum spread eagled to the wall/You're well equipped to take it all."[92] Eventually the PMRC was able to convince the United States government to require warning labels on albums with suspect content and a rating system that persists today. The song was considered by the PMRC to be too sexual, potentially masochistic, and probably homoerotic. That the music and lyrics of the Judas Priest song were transgressive, that the song delved into something about sexual bodies, is the key problem. Rob Halford later stated the song was "a spoof caricature sexual song."[93] Whatever its meaning, the song is an excellent example of songs about corporeal consumption and the ways in which those songs create further consumption of the performer. When the PMRC hearings took place, Judas Priest was at the top of their fame as leaders of heavy metal. Even in later years, the common belief was that Judas Priest's "Eat Me Alive" was about a man forcing a woman to perform oral sex. Consider, for example, this comment about Rob Halford in Walser's 1993 *Running with the Devil*: "Gay fans celebrate metal musicians whom they believe to be gay, such as Judas Priest's Rob Halford, and confirm and contest each other's 'negotiated' readings of the texts."[94] The abject idea that gay metal fans might place themselves at Halford's feet, that the fans might be seeking to do the consuming, and consummation in "Eat Me Alive" was what made the song dirty, and it is what makes it so simple to consider a gay fan's reading of lyrics as "negotiated." Admittedly, Halford was not out in 1984, nor was he out in 1993 when Walser wrote. "Eat Me Alive," however, remains the song heterosexual metal fans point to as the point they knew about Halford.

Death metal, the most preferred by queer-identified metal fans, is rife with lyrics about corporeal consumption. In fact, as scholars have noted, the dissective examination of the body is so inherent to the genre of death metal, it lacks some transgressive quality for those inside the scene. Michelle Phillipov, for example, wrote extensively on death metal music criticism. She noted the transgression in heavy metal is aimed towards the mainstream audience for shock value, not towards the death metal fans whose scene does not revolve around abject transgression.[95] For death metal fans, pleasure is derived from the abject in lyrics, not fear or trepidation. As Phillipov stated:

> Combined with scene members' practices of reflexive anti-reflexivity, this results in fans who experience transgressive sonic and lyrical conventions as pleasurable, but who are simultaneously reluctant to embrace, or even acknowledge, death metal's full transgressive potential.[96]

Another view of the abject in death metal was suggested by Keith Kahn-Harris. Kahn-Harris focused on the abject and the idea that extreme metal musicians and fans were essentially reacting to perceptions of human weakness, the frailty of the body, and the more theatrical aspects of classic, power, and thrash heavy metal. For extreme metal musicians and fans, according to Kahn-Harris, the repetitive and explicit destruction of the abject, only to rebuild it and destroy it again, is the goal. Actions such as the involvement of metal performers in crimes (such as Varg Vikernes) or lyrics and album covers of bands such as Cannibal Corpse and Cradle of Filth all serve to consume the body, leaving behind the detritus of abjection. Extreme metallers, according to Kahn-Harris, "yearn for a deep engagement with the body; yet actively resist it as well."[97] Consider, for example, the lyrics for Meshuggah's "Marrow": "Tar-Black ejaculate/The seminal bile of conspiracy/The blood of those who died/Their innocence their marrow."[98] Meshuggah, a Swedish death metal fusion band, wrote the song as a political polemic about the war machine and its feeding on human bodies. The lyrics indicate how important abject images of body waste, a subject at the very core of the concept, are to death metal and other extreme genres. This corporeal consumption in lyrics lends itself to queerscape by normalizing the abject as inherent to the metal scene itself. That queer-identified fans attune themselves more closely to metal genres that embrace the abject should not be a surprise.

The penultimate example of corporeal consumption in lyrics is in the song "Mein Teil" by Rammstein. "Mein Teil," which translates literally as "my fate" or "my piece," is actually a slang term for "my penis." The song was written about the sensational murder case of Armin Meiwes, a German man convicted of murder and cannibalism in 2006. Meiwes's trial revealed a particularly abject and hidden sexual proclivity: vorarephilia, or eroticism and sexual release based on something being consumed. For Meiwes, the object to be consumed was another human being. Karley Adney's masterful paper on Meiwes provides the best overview of the Meiwes case and its abject features. Meiwes was a quiet man, cuckolded, isolated by his mother, and found himself unable to function after her death.[99] Meiwes's story then takes on aspects of Hitchcock's *Psycho* or Hannibal Lechter in *Silence of the Lambs* but no longer fiction. Meiwes entered a chat room for vorarephilia enthusiasts and posted an ad for a young man so he could "slaughter you and eat your delicious meat."[100] Bernd Jurgen Brandes answered the ad and the two met at Meiwes's home. The two had sex and then after some discussion, Meiwes agreed to bite off Brandes' penis. Meiwes ate the penis as Brandes exsanguinated, then ate some of Brandes's remains before storing the rest in his freezer.[101] Meiwas is often referred to in the press as the Master Butcher, and today remains in prison. Several films and television documentaries, books and essays, songs and novels were written after Meiwes's trial and imprisonment. By far the most famous, and perhaps the most controversial, was the song "Mein Teil" by Rammstein.

As Adney wrote in her paper, Rammstein's members were immediately fascinated by Meiwes's story. Rammstein was already well known for lyrical content that dealt with sadism, masochism, and other sexual behaviors that might be marked as deviant. The song, released in 2004, features the chorus "You are what you eat."[102] The video, which was immediately banned in several countries and relegated to late-night rotation on MTV, is filled with abject imagery. The video shows the band standing ankle-deep in sewage, the filth splashed on their legs and clothing. A man appears in tattered clothes and rotting teeth, spitting and screaming as he writhes on the floor. Till Lindemann, the band's lead singer, is shown sometimes with rotting teeth and a leather collar on his neck, sometimes with a woman in angel's wings performing oral sex. One band member, dressed as an older woman with a hat and gloves, occasionally appears to look disapprovingly on the scene. Another man, coated in white and wrapped only in a diaper, rocks on the floor in the rigid pose of a dead body. The penultimate moment of the video is when band member Richard Kruspe meets his own double and vascillates between fighting the double and intimately relating to the double, including licking the double's tongue.[103] "The performances by both Landers and Kruspe," wrote Adney, "capitalize on the mental torment of anyone wrestling with their identity." [104] The connections between the song "Mein Teil" and the queerscape are numerous. It draws on the story of a man who, depending on the interpretation, might be considered queer-identified. He is certainly non-normative in terms of his erotic and sexual desires. As Adney explained, the song also feeds on hegemonic stereotypes of gay men: standing in excrement, dressed as women, half-naked, with domineering mothers and deviant appetites.[105] In addition, the song and the video deal with transgressions of gender, sexuality, expression and desire, deviance and normalcy, and the very definition of abjection. Keith Kahn-Harris wrote: "While the inescapable *telos* of the most transgressive practices in the oblivion of death is not what most scene members want, it retains an overwhelming allure."[106] In "Mein Teil," heavy metal lyrics tap into the twenty-first-century debates about gender, sexuality, and the corporeal. In fact, it provides an abject avenue through which queer-identified heavy metal fans can reject the growing mainstream impulse in modern queer politics and instead find a home for deviance in the heavy metal queerscape's embracing of abjection and bodily transgression. "Resisting the call of gay normalization," Heather Love suggested, "means refusing to write off the most vulnerable, the least presentable, and all the dead."[107] In its march towards a telos of transgressive practice, heavy metal's queerscape has come to a point of contact with anti-assimilation, queer twenty-first-century politics, embracing the very abject cultural features that even the queer mainstream seeks to avoid.

There is one more way in which the heavy metal queerscape includes corporeal consumption. Much of the discussion of queer fans of heavy metal, really of anything queer in heavy metal, revolves around the idea of homophobia. For example, a 22 October 2014 essay on the popular website MetalInjection.net was titled "The Problem With Heavy Metal Is Metalheads: Stop Calling Everyone A Faggot."[108] The essay asked metal fans to stop using the word faggot, to stop calling things "gay" as a derogatory term, and to make heavy metal the welcoming place it claimed to be. "Heavy metal fans have been targets for scorn and derision for decades. The metal community is supposed to be a place where misfits and outcasts can find shelter in the face of that intolerance," wrote essayist Shayne Mathis. "When you throw around bigoted slurs, whether you know it or not, you're eroding the community we're all supposed to be a part of."[109] While the use of slurs is certainly a problem in heavy metal, is that going to solve homophobia in heavy metal scenes? The essay also mentions racism and sexism, other major issues in heavy metal scenes and spaces. I suggest, however, that homophobia is a more isolated problem than mainstream metal fans assume. The problem is not the homosexual body, at least not for the majority of fans, performers, and gatekeepers. Heavy metal's queerscape is everywhere, omnipresent, and represented in some of the most important musicians, recordings, and events in heavy metal's storied history. The major issue having to do with bodies in heavy metal is not homophobia but effeminophobia.

Effeminophobia was a term first introduced by scholar Eve Kosofsky Sedgwick in her 1992 essay "How To Bring Your Kids Up Gay." The essay, a critique of psychoanalysis, diagnosis of gender dysphoria, and other gender-based psychological practices, focused on the idea the homosexual body was actually less policed than the effeminate body. Sedgwick explained the need to define the homosexual male body had too frequently hinged on the idea that a "natural" male-ness was rugged, strong, and inherently masculine while a "flawed" male-ness was effeminate.[110] The effeminate, a subject to either be mocked or feared, was the biggest threat. The same concept was extended by Johnson and Samdahl in their study of a lesbian dance night in a gay male bar. Johnson and Samdahl quickly identified the primary issue: the gay men in the bar resented the presence of the females, whether lesbian or not made no difference. In fact, the authors noted the gay men in the bar adopted hypermasculine strategies, such as taking up more physical space or putting down the lesbian patrons as too feminine. "These findings highlight the dialectical relationships between gay and straight, male and female," wrote Johnson and Samdahl, "and demonstrate the importance of studying *gender* as distinct from sexual orientation."[111] In their study of rural, gay-identified men and effeminophobia, Annes and Redlin discovered effeminophobia was the biggest fear among their informants. The men studied explained to researchers that identifying as gay also led them to claim effeminophobia as something that marked them as transgressive and abject. According to Annes and Redlin, rural gay men saw effeminate behavior as a marker of "queens," female-ness, rampant sexuality, and the lack of a need to settle down.[112] As Annes and Redlin stated:

> In their stereotypical view of effeminate gay men, they [their informants] link effeminacy and flamboyance performed through the use of external, feminine signifiers. By doing that, they believe effeminate gays bring their sexuality to the public sphere. In fact, by being flamboyant they are immediately categorized as homosexual and others view them only through this feature.[113]

The heavy metal queerscape shares this with every other aspect of heavy metal's geography, musicology, visuals, and performances. It consumes the effeminate body in conflation with racism, sexism, and unchecked hypermasculinity. This is why heavy metal fans tell "I always knew Halford was gay" stories. This is why queer metal fans are so quick to demonstrate how tough, hard, and brutal they are. This is why sexism and the abuse of women – lyrically, verbally and physically – are still a problem. Effeminophobia is rampant.

The issues with effeminophobia are clearly evident in the stories of queer heavy metal fans and in fans regardless of scene or genre. For example, an informant in Sonia Vasan's study of gender in a death metal scene stated she was a death metal fan because "it wasn't so frilly and feminine."[114] The queer fans of heavy metal did not veer from these attitudes either. One masculine gay male fan from the United States wrote he felt "less feminine wearing shirts with gore on them."[115] "Most metal kids try to be extremely unfeminine, so masculine styles of queerness go over better," a trans* intersex fan from the United States explained. A gay male fan from Portugal wrote he had "seen a couple of more feminine guys being pushed and mocked because of their sexuality."[116] "I'm not feminine," one gay male fan from the United Kingdom stated, "so I 'pass' as straight."[117] Another view, one that reveals both the sexism and the homophobia inherent in effeminophobia, comes from a bisexual fan from rural America:

I've been told that, as a 'femme female' I do not fit the stereotype of most women at heavy metal concerts and have felt that as well when attending – as if lipstick and headbanging do not correlate. I do not personally feel manly, masculine nor butch when attending a metal concert – however, I do feel a bit awkward because I stick out a bit.[118]

Perhaps most telling is one statement from an Israeli, trans*-identified leatherman. According to him, his only experience with oppression in heavy metal came from another member of his own community. In this example, effeminophobia is not just the precursor of homophobia and misogyny, it is also revealing transphobia in heavy metal scenes and spaces.

I don't recall any actual activity that was against me in a concert, but I do remember that after I started referring to myself in a male form of speech, I met someone who I knew from long time ago in the entrance to a fetish party. He belongs to the metal community, and he asked me in a really rude tone "why are you talking about yourself in a male form of speech" while referring to me as female and made it sound like an offense. That's the worse thing I remember I got.[119]

The role of effeminophobia is clearly present in the heavy metal queer-scape. Surveyed and interviewed queer fans did not identify serious problems with homophobic behaviors or hate crimes in the scenes and spaces of heavy metal but they did note the importance of masculinity, toughness, and the avoidance of effeminacy in the heavy metal queerscape. The bodies of heavy metal fandom, queer or not, are consuming effeminacy in the role of so-called video vixens or the metal ladies of symphonic metal. At the same time, they are also consuming their own effeminacy in a practice that mirrors "Mein Teil." Queer fans embrace the hypermasculinity of heavy metal when they consume and swallow down effeminacy and in doing so, help to perpetuate the widely held belief that heavy metal is straight, white, and male-bodied alone. In his essay on corporeal consumption, geographer Gill Valentine wrote: "There is a need for more work to examine how the body is produced and contested and the politics of this location."[120] For scholars of heavy metal and scholars of gender, this need still exists. We must, however, work to unchain our understanding of masculinity as attached to the corporeal alone and instead seek to understand the ways in which fear of the effeminate informs the very hypermasculininty claimed as natural.

Consumption, through music, performance, and the body, is integral to the heavy metal queerscape. Queer fans of heavy metal, in their consumption of heavy metal music, not only take in the commodified aspects of sounds and styles. They accept and exchange the ideas, attitudes, behaviors, and languages of heavy metal with the languages and experiences of a queer life. In her study of death metal, Michelle Phillipov wrote:

While we should not ignore the problematic aspects of metal's gendered practices and aesthetics, any approach which takes the 'problem' of gender as the starting point of analysis is limited in the kinds of questions it can consider.[121]

It is exactly this understanding of heavy metal that the queerscape puts on notice. The very core of heavy metal is indeed gender, from the history of its stylistic cues to the corporeal consumption of its effeminate fans. Any approach that does not consider gender is not only limited but is operating with hypermasculine blinders.

NOTES

1. Gordon Brent Ingram, "(On The Beach) Practising Queerscape Architecture," in *Practice Practise Praxis: Serial Repetition, Organizational Behaviour, and Strategic Action in Architecture*, ed. Scott Sorli (Toronto: YYZ Books, 2000), 109.
2. Rosemary Hennessy, "Queer Visibility and Commodity Culture," *Cultural Critique* 29 (Winter 1994–1995): 33.
3. Ibid., 71.
4. Will Straw, "Music as Commodity and Material Culture," *repercussions* (Spring–Fall 1999–2000): 155.
5. Pierre Bordieu, *Distinction: A Social Critique of the Judgment of Taste*, trans. Richard Nice (Cambridge: Harvard University Press, 1984).
6. Julian Tanner, Mark Asbridge, and Scot Worley, "Our favourite melodies: musical consumption and teenage lifestyles," *The British Journal of Sociology* 59, No. 1 (2008): 193.
7. Ibid., 138–139.
8. Arthur S. Alberson, Azamat Junisbai, and Isaac Heacock, "Social status and cultural consumption in the United States," *Poetics* 35 (2007): 193.
9. David Hesmondhalgh, "Towards a critical understanding of music, emotion and self-identity," *Consumption, Markets and Culture* 11, No. 4 (2008): 329.
10. Ingram, "(On the Beach)."
11. Ibid., 21.
12. Leung, 426.
13. Ingram, "(On the Beach)," 115.
14. Howie Abrams and Sacha Jenkins, *The Merciless Book of Heavy Metal Lists* (New York: Abrams Image, 2013): 69.
15. Ibid., 68.
16. Ibid., 15.
17. Steel Panther, "Glory Hole," on *All You Can Eat*, +180 Records, ASIN B00HUGK8P4.
18. Jodie Taylor, "The queerest of the queer: Sexuality, politics and music on the Brisbane scene," *Continuum: Journal of Media and Cultural Studies* 22, No. 5 (October 2008): 662–663.
19. Small, 2.
20. Bruce K. Friesen and Jonathon S. Epstein, "Rock 'n' Roll Ain't Noise Pollution: Artistic Conventions in the Major Subgenres of Heavy Metal Music," *Popular Music and Society* 18, No. 3 (January 1994): 7.

21. Small, 221.
22. Urvashi Vaid, *Virtual Equality: The Mainstreaming of Gay and Lesbian Liberation* (New York: Doubleday, 1996).
23. Esther Newton, *Mother Camp: Female Impersonators in America* (Chicago: University of Chicago Press, 1979); George Chauncey, *Gay New York: Gender, Urban Culture, and the Making of the Gay Male World, 1890–1940* (New York: Basic Books, 1995); Elizabeth Kennedy and Madeline Davis, *Boots of Leather, Slippers of Gold: The History of a Lesbian Community* (New York: Penguin Books, 1994).
24. Peter Lugosi, "Queer consumption and commercial hospitality: Communitas, myths, and the production of liminoid space," *International Journal of Sociology and Social Policy* 27, No. 3 and 4 (2007): 164.
25. Garry Sharpe-Young, *Metal: The Definitive Guide* (New York: Jawbone Press, 2007): 162.
26. Ibid., 222.
27. "Queer Fans of Heavy Metal," respondent No. 25852.
28. "Queer Fans of Heavy Metal," respondent No. 26357.
29. "Queer Fans of Heavy Metal," respondent No. 26952.
30. "Queer Fans of Heavy Metal," respondent No. 144844.
31. "Queer Fans of Heavy Metal," respondent No. 248705.
32. "Queer Fans of Heavy Metal," respondent No. 25970.
33. The Soft Pink Truth, *Why Do All The Heathen Rage?*, Thrill 368, Thrill Jockey Records, 2014, ASIN B00KZI17X6.
34. Sharpe-Young, 262.
35. Walser, 116.
36. "Queer Fans of Heavy Metal," respondent No. 461.
37. Daniel Harris, *The Rise and Fall of Gay Culture* (New York: Hyperion Books, 1997), 8.
38. JD, interview with the author, July 18, 2010, Skype interview.
39. Sharpe-Young, 90.
40. "Queer Fans of Heavy Metal," respondent No. 26.
41. "Playboy Interview: Metallica," *Playboy*, April 2001, posted online http://metallica.awardspace.com/inter.html. Accessed October 30, 2014.
42. Fast, 249.
43. Ibid., 278.
44. Metallica, *Master of Puppets*, Rhino Records, 2013, ASIN B00EBDXTJG; Anthrax, *Among The Living*, Mobile Fidelity Koch, 1987, vinyl reissue 2012, ASIN B0084MVDF2.
45. HW, interview with the author, September 1, 2010, telephone.
46. Jarman-Ivens, 18–20.
47. Ibid., 21.
48. Michel Foucault, "Technologies of the Self," in *Technologies of the Self: A Seminar With Michel Foucault*, ed. Luther H. Martin, Huck Gutman, and Patrick H. Hutton (Amherst: The University of Massachusetts Press, 1988): 18.
49. Irvin C. Schick, *The Erotic Margin: Sexuality and Spatiality in Alteritist Discourse* (New York: Verso, 1999): 9.
50. Tia DeNora, "Music as a technology of the self," *Poetics* 27 (1999): 32.
51. Gordon Brent Ingram, Anne-Marie Bouthillette, and Cornelia Wyngaarden, "Vancouver(as queer)scape: Strategies for mapping public spaces constructed by sexual minorities," *Critical Geography Conference* (Simon Fraser University &

The University of British Columbia). Session: Locating the politics of theory in critical human geography, August 10, 1997, http://gordonbrentingram.ca/scholarship/wp-content/uploads/2008/12/ingram-bouthillette-wyngaarden-1997-vancouver_-as-queer_scape-critical-geography-conference.pdf. Accessed October 25, 2014 : 2.

52. Michel Foucault, *The History of Sexuality: Volume 3 The Care of the Self*, trans. Robert Hurley (New York: Vintage, 1990): 68.
53. JB, interview with the author, July 18, 2010, Skype interview.
54. PS, interview with the author, July 8, 2010, Skype interview.
55. DK, interview with the author, August 20, 2010, Skype interview.
56. TH, interview with the author, August 13, 2010, MSN Messenger interview.
57. Lindsay Abrams, "Mosh Pits Teach Us About the Physics of Collective Behavior," *The Atlantic*, February 13, 2013, http://www.theatlantic.com/health/archive/2013/02/mosh-pits-teach-us-about-the-physics-of-collective-behavior/273087/., Accessed October 21, 2014.
58. ES, interview with the author, July 9, 2010, Skype interview.
59. "Queer Fans of Heavy Metal," respondent No. 25790.
60. DeNora, 37.
61. Suzanne G. Cusick, "On musical performances of gender and sex," in *Audible Traces: Gender, Identity, and Music* (Zürich: Carciofoli, 1999): 27.
62. DeNora, 45.
63. JE, interview with the author, September 9, 2010, Skype interview.
64. CG, interview with the author, July 7, 2010, Skype interview.
65. DK, interview with the author, August 20, 2010, Skype interview.
66. CW, interview with the author, January 5, 2011, Skype interview.
67. Jodie Taylor, *Playing It Queer: Popular Music, Identity and Queer World-making* (New York: Peter Lang, 2012): 62.
68. DeNora, 36.
69. Frederik Dhaenens, Sofie Van Bauwel, and Daniel Biltereyst, "Slashing the Fiction of Queer Theory. Slash. Fiction, Queer Reading, and Transgressing the Boundaries of Screen Studies, Representations, and Audiences," *European Journal of Cultural Studies* 15 (August 2012): 442–456.
70. Caroline, "Winding Road," Rockfic.com, http://www.rockfic.com/viewstory.php?title=Winding+Road&storyid=5874&numchapters=1&category=Iron%20Maiden,%20Judas%20Priest&author=Caroline&m=f&sort=date&ratinglist=&genrelist=&charlist1=&charlist2. Accessed October 30, 2014.
71. Funky Canuck, "Top, Bottom, and Versatile," Rockfic.com, http://www.rockfic.com/viewstory.php?recid=1926&i=1&title=Top,+Bottom+or+Versatile?&author=FunkyCanuck., Accessed October 30, 2014.
72. BaronZemo, "Nemo," Rockfic.com, http://www.rockfic.com/viewstory.php?title=Nemo&storyid=7486&numchapters=1&category=Marilyn%20Manson,%20Metallica&author=BaronZemo&m=f&sort=date&ratinglist=&genrelist=Slash&bandlist=Marilyn%20Manson., Accessed October 30, 2014.
73. Mad Andy, "Perchance To Dream," Rockfic.com, http://www.rockfic.com/viewstory.php?title=Perchance+To+Dream&storyid=198&numchapters=1&category=Motorhead&author=Mad%20Andy&m=f&sort=date&ratinglist=&genrelist=Slash&bandlist=Motorhead. Accessed October 30, 2014.
74. Taylor, 50.

75. DeNora, 37.
76. "Queer Fans of Heavy Metal," respondent No. 118577.
77. "Queer Fans of Heavy Metal," respondent No. 118644.
78. "Queer Fans of Heavy Metal," respondent No. 118865.
79. "Queer Fans of Heavy Metal," respondent No. 125259.
80. "Queer Fans of Heavy Metal," respondent No. 144431.
81. "Queer Fans of Heavy Metal," respondent No. 144535.
82. "Queer Fans of Heavy Metal," respondent No. 145560.
83. "Queer Fans of Heavy Metal," respondent No. 243993.
84. "Queer Fans of Heavy Metal," respondent No. 25522.
85. Kahn-Harris, 43–44.
86. Siobhan Somerville, "Scientific Racism and the Invention of the Homosexual Body," in Roger Lancaster and Micaela DiLeonardo, *The Gender/Sexuality Reader: Culture, History, Political Economy* (New York: Routledge, 1997): 37.
87. Lynda Johnston and Robyn Longhurst, *Space, Place, and Sex: Geographies of Sexualities* (Lanham: Rowman and Littlefield, 2010): 24.
88. Elizabeth Grosz, *Volatile Bodies: Toward A Corporeal Feminism* (Bloomington: University of Indiana Press, 1994): 192.
89. Johnston and Longhurst, 27.
90. Mary Douglas, *Purity and Danger: An Analysis of Concepts of Pollution and Taboo* (New York: Routledge and Kegan Paul, 1966): 35.
91. Ian Christe, *Sound of the Beast: The Complete Headbanging History of Heavy Metal* (New York: HarperCollins, 2004).
92. Judas Priest, *Defenders of the Faith*, Columbia Records, 1984.
93. Daniels, 108.
94. Walser, 116.
95. Michelle Phillipov, *Death Metal and Music Criticism: Analysis At the Limits* (Lanham: Lexington Books, 2012): 96.
96. Ibid.
97. Kahn-Harris, 45.
98. Meshuggah, *Koloss*, Nuclear Blast, 2012.
99. Karley K. Adney, "A Carnivalesque Cannibal: Armin Meiwes, 'Mein Tei,' and Representations of Homosexuality," in *Rammstein On Fire: New Perspectives on the Music and Performances*, eds. John T. Littlejohn and Michael T. Putnam (Jefferson: McFarland and Company, 2014): 134–137.
100. Ibid., 138.
101. Ibid., 139–140.
102. Rammstein, *Reise, Reise*, Motor Music, 2004.
103. Rammstein, "Mein Teil" official video, 4:23, uploaded February 11, 2012, https://www.youtube.com/watch?v=0hy07wSydOM. Accessed October 30, 2014.
104. Adney, 143.
105. Ibid.
106. Kahn-Harris, 49.
107. Love, 30.
108. Shayne Mathis, "The Problem With Heavy Metal Is Metalheads: Stop Calling Everyone A Faggot," Metalinjection.net, http://www.metalinjection.net/editorials/the-problem-with-heavy-metal-is-metalheads-stop-calling-everyone-a-faggot. Accessed October 29, 2014.

109. Ibid.
110. Eve Kosofsky Sedgwick, "How To Bring Your Kids Up Gay," *Social Text* 29 (1991).
111. Corey W. Johnson and Diane M. Samdahl, " 'The Night They Took Over': Misogyny in a Country-Western Gay Bar," *Leisure Sciences: An Interdisciplinary Journal* 27, No. 4 (2005): 346.
112. Alexis Annes and Meredith Redlin, "The Careful Balance of Gender and Sexuality: Rural Gay Men, the Heterosexual Matrix, and 'Effeminophobia'," *Journal of Homosexuality* 59, No. 2 (2012): 264.
113. Ibid., 278.
114. Vasan, 342.
115. "Queer Fans of Heavy Metal," respondent No. 179339.
116. "Queer Fans of Heavy Metal," respondent No. 30294.
117. "Queer Fans of Heavy Metal," respondent No. 45927.
118. "Queer Fans of Heavy Metal," respondent No. 292788.
119. "Queer Fans of Heavy Metal," respondent No. 30506.
120. Gill Valentine, "A Corporeal Geography of Consumption," *Environment and Planning D: Society and Space,* 17 (1999): 349.
121. Phillipov, 63.

Conclusion

D. Jordan Redhawk, a popular author of lesbian romance fiction, published her book *Warlord Metal* in 2001. It is the story of Torrin, a heavy metal guitarist, and Sonny, the sister of a heavy metal band member. The two meet, have a sexual relationship that includes BDSM scenes, and when the book closes, the two plan to be together forever. According to the back cover, *Warlord Metal* tells the story of Torrin and her "ability to make her guitar sing her soul – a sinister and shattered cry."[1] That sinister and shattered cry, the detuned cacophony of epic heavy metal, brings countless queer folks the acceptance, overt sexuality, and sense of belonging they may not find elsewhere. In fact, it is due to queer folks, both as fans and as performers, that heavy metal developed and grew at all. "Gay visibility and integration mitigate the power of the discourse of compulsory heterosexuality," wrote James Joseph Gordon, "making heterosexual identity practices less taken for granted and now more conscious, deliberate and purposeful."[2] Until heavy metal's gatekeepers attend to its queerness, heavy metal's true ability to disrupt the system will go unrealized.

No academic work is without boundaries. *Queerness in Heavy Metal* is an attempt to disrupt the master narrative of metal music studies and its inference that all fans are straight fans listening to patriarchy. It is also an attempt to disrupt the accepted logic in gender and sexuality studies that heavy metal music, its scenes, and its spaces are somehow divorced from the critique offered to any other sector of popular culture. With that said, there remains much to be done in the intersection of heavy metal studies, gender, and sexuality. As Andy Brown pointed out in his essay on the development of metal music studies, there continues to be a lack of study in mainstream hard rock and heavy metal, as well as crossover genres such as rap-rock.[3] I believe there remains a tremendous amount of work in gender and sexuality as it relates to 1980s hair/glam metal, a genre that too often gets relegated to the metal history dustbin and too frequently gets portrayed as simply straight young men rebelling against authority. Scholars in heavy metal studies are currently and increasingly debating the concepts of community, space, and scene in heavy metal, debates that will no doubt inform the study of music regardless of genre. Finally, one cannot forget the very definitions of gender and sexuality are changing tremendously. When

I bought my bootleg copy of "Fairies Wear Boots," I never thought about the double meaning that title would one day hold for me. I certainly never conceived of a time when trans metal performers would fill venues, or queer fans would make disco covers of black metal, or Rob Halford would be the gay Metal God. If scholars of gender and sexuality want to be truly inclusive, they must include discussion of the cultural institutions that seem impenetrable. If metal music studies wishes to continue to develop and earn the academic respectability it deserves, then scholars of heavy metal must combine their interests in the sonic and lyrical with the cultural and the gendered in increasingly cutting-edge ways. In fact, such future work must avoid the boundaries of discipline that trouble not only heavy metal but academic discourse itself. After all, heavy metal has never been about conforming. A July 2014 essay in *Terrorizer* was titled "Heavy Metal Is Gay: Why We Need to Tackle Our Homophobia."[4] The best way for metal scholars to deal with effeminophobia and homophobia (and misogyny, racism, ableism, ageism) is to make it our mission to write the diverse story of heavy metal.

In my interviews with queer fans, I asked the same opening question: if an academic told you there were no queer fans of heavy metal, what would you say? One fan told me: "If you name your study 'A Rainbow in the Dark' I'll be disappointed in you."[5] A female lesbian fan from the United Kingdom wrote: "Usually a lot of what is available is shit and written by people who know nothing about being queer, or heavy metal."[6] "It's about the music and presence," wrote a gay male fan from America, "since it's an underground sort of music, it bonds together those who listen to it."[7] Other fans asked me to help them find a musician or an agent or asked me to put them in touch with other fans. One informant, however, was particularly clear about his uniquely heavy metal answer: "Those scholars? They're not very metal."[8]

NOTES

1. D. Jordan Redhawk, *Warlord Metal* (Austin: Fortitude Press, 2002).
2. James Joseph Dean, "Thinking Intersectionality: Sexualities and the Politics of Multiple Identities," in *Theorizing Intersectionality and Sexuality*, edited by Yvette Taylor, Sally Hines, and Mark E. Casey (New York: Palgrave Macmillan, 2011): 137.
3. Andy R. Brown, "Heavy Genealogy: Mapping the Currents, Contraflows and Conflicts of the Emergent Field of Metal Studies, 1978-2010," *Journal for Cultural Research* 15, No. 3 (2011): 235.
4. Tom, "Heavy Metal is Gay: Why We Need to Tackle Our Homophobia," *Terrorizer*, July 23, 2014, http://www.terrorizer.com/news/features-2/heavy-metal-is-gay-need-tackle-homophobia/.
5. "Queers in Heavy Metal," respondent No. 57860.
6. "Queers in Heavy Metal," respondent No. 25899.
7. "Queers In Heavy Metal," respondent No. 26248.
8. DK, interview with the author, August 20, 2010.

Appendix
Queer Fans of Heavy Metal: Online Survey

STATEMENT OF CONSENT: IDENTIFICATION OF RESEARCHERS

This research is being conducted by Amber R. Clifford, Ph.D., a faculty member of University of Central Missouri. It is part of a long-term project on gender and heavy metal music. This project has been approved by the IRB of University of Central Missouri.

PURPOSE OF THE STUDY

The goal of this study is to gather information about gender, sexuality, and sexual orientation among fans of heavy metal music. The research is aimed at formulating a better understanding of issues of gender among heavy metal fans as well as examining the masculinity heavy metal engenders. Objectives include identifying the lives of GLBTTQQIA+ heavy metal fans within heavy metal spaces.

DESCRIPTION OF RESEARCH METHOD

This study involves completing a short survey. The survey will ask you demographical questions such as sex, sexual orientation, gender identity, country of origin, and age. The questions following are multiple-choice survey questions and open-ended questions regarding life as a queer fan of heavy metal music. This study will take about 20 minutes to finish. All results are anonymous and confidential, unless you select to consent to an interview at the end of the survey. Results will become property of the researcher.

PRIVACY

All of the information collected will be anonymous. We will not record your name or any information that could be used to identify you unless you consent to an interview at the end of the survey. If you feel your privacy is at risk, please feel free to exit the survey now.

EXPLANATION OF RISKS

The risks associated with participating in this study are similar to the risks of everyday life.

REQUEST FOR PARTICIPATION

You are invited to participate in a study on gender identity and sexual orientation among fans of heavy metal music. If you decide not to participate, you will not be penalized in any way. You can also decide to stop at any time without penalty. If you do not wish to answer the questions, you may simply skip them. You may withdraw your data at the end of the study. If you wish to do this, you can simply exit the survey and your answers will not be submitted. Once you turn in the survey materials, there will be no identifying information on your answers or subsequent results.

EXCLUSIONS

You must be at least 18 years of age, identify as GLBTTQQIA+, and be a fan of heavy metal to participate in this study.

EXPLANATION OF BENEFITS

You will benefit from participating in this study by getting first-hand experience in anthropological research. You may also enjoy completing the survey and contributing to the growing scholarship on heavy metal and its fans.

QUESTIONS

If you have any questions about this study, please contact Dr. Clifford. She can be reached at clifford@ucmo.edu or at (660) 543–4877. If you have any questions about your rights as a research participant, please contact the Human Subjects Protection Program at (660) 543–4621.

1. If you would like to participate, please select that you accept the terms of the survey and give your consent to participate in the research study.*

   I accept the terms of the survey and give my consent to participate in the research study.

2. What is your sex?*

3. Please select your country.*

4. What is your gender identity and/or sexual orientation? Check all that apply.*
Lesbian
Gay
Transgender
Bisexual
Queer or Genderqueer
Butch
Femme
Masculine
Effeminate
Leather and/or BDSM

5. How "out" are you?*

6. Where do you live?*

7. Please select your age range.*

8. At what age did you start listening to heavy metal?

9. How would you describe the type(s) of heavy metal you listen to most often?

10. What are your five favorite heavy metal bands?

11. What are the five heavy metal bands you most dislike?

12. Are there any heavy metal bands or performers you consider "more queer" than others? Please list.

13. How do you consume heavy metal music? Check all that apply.
    Traditional radio
    Internet radio
    Listservs and/or chatrooms
    Live concerts
    File sharing/swapping
    CD purchases
    Magazines
    Facebook
    MySpace
    Heavy metal websites
    Friends
    Other

14. Are there any heavy metal performers you think or know are queer (GLBTQ)? Please list.

15. Does listening to heavy metal, attending concerts, or being part of heavy metal culture make you feel more masculine, manly, or butch? If so, why?

16. How do you usually dress when going to a heavy metal concert or show?

17. Why do you listen to heavy metal?

18. Do you have other queer friends who know you listen to metal? If so, what do they say?

19. When you attend a heavy metal concert or show, what do you watch most of the time?

20. Do you consider heavy metal homophobic (hateful towards GLBTTQQIA+ people)? Please explain.

21. Have you ever been harassed or verbally attacked at a heavy metal concert or show due to your sex, gender identity, or sexual orientation? Almost Always Frequently Sometimes Occasionally Hardly Ever

22. Have you ever been physically abused or attacked at a heavy metal show due to your sex, gender identity or sexual orientation? Please share any details if you wish.

23. Are there any heavy metal musicians or bands you consider homophobic? If yes, please list the performers and explain.

24. Have you ever met other queer individuals at heavy metal venues?
    Yes   No

25. Are people to whom you are "out" surprised to find out you listen to heavy metal?
    Yes   No

26. Do you think heavy metal fans and audiences are more tolerant and/or accepting of sex and gender differences than they were 10 years ago?
    Yes   No

    The researcher is interested in interviewing all survey respondents about their experiences as queer fans of heavy metal music. Interviews would last 30–60 minutes. Interviews can take place via telephone, instant message/chat, or in person (when possible). All individuals who agree to an interview will receive an additional consent form.

27. Are you interested in being interviewed about your experiences as a queer fan of heavy metal?*
    Yes   No

28. If you would like to be interviewed, please enter your first name and a valid email address. This information will remain confidential.

29. Do you have any comments for the researcher?

References

2wo. *Voyeurs*. Innerscope Records, ASIN No. B0000061QC. Released March 10, 1998, compact disc.

Abrams, Howie and Sacha Jenkins. *The Merciless Book of Heavy Metal Lists*. New York: Abrams Image, 2013.

Abrams, Lindsay. "Mosh Pits Teach Us About the Physics of Collective Behavior." *The Atlantic*, February 13, 2013. Online. http://www.theatlantic/com/health/archive/2013/02/mosh-pits-teach-us-about-the-physics-of-collective-behavior/273087/. Accessed October 21, 2014.

Adney, Karley K. "A Carnivalesque Cannibal: Armin Meiwes, 'Mein Teil,' and Representations of Homosexuality." In *Rammstein On Fire: New Perspectives on the Music and Performances*. Jefferson: McFarland and Company, 2014.

Albertson, Arthur S., Azamat Junisbai, and Isaac Heacock. "Social status and cultural consumption in the United States." *Poetics* 35, 2007: 191–212.

Anderson-Minshall, Diane. "Agony and Ecstasy." *The Advocate*. October 29, 2011. http://www.advocate.com/print-issue/advance/2011/10/19/heavy-metal-rocker-comes-out-transgender?page=0,0.

Andromeda. *Chimera*. Massacre Records, ASIN No. B000DZIBSA. Released January 21, 2006, compact disc.

Annes, Alexis and Meredith Redlin. "The Careful Balance of Gender and Sexuality: Rural Gay Men, the Heterosexual Matrix, and 'Effeminophobia'." *Journal of Homosexuality* 59, No. 2, 2012: 256–288.

Anthrax. *Among the Living*. Mobile Fidelity Koch, ASIN No. B0084MVDF2. Released March 22, 1987, compact disc.

Arell, Berndt and Kati Mustala. *Tom of Finland- Unforeseen*. Helsinki: Like, 2006.

Arnett, Jeffrey. *Metalheads: Heavy Metal Music and Adolescent Alienation*. New York: Westview Press, 1996.

Atom and His Package. *Hair: Debatable*. Hopeless Records, ASIN No. B0001JXP6Q. Released April 6, 2004, compact disc.

Atreyu. *Congregation of the Damned*. Hollywood Records, ASIN No. B002NPUCFS. Released October 26, 2009, compact disc.

Auslander, Philip. "I Wanna Be Your Man: Suzi Quatro's Musical Androgyny." *Popular Music* 23, No. 1 (January 2004): 1–16.

Bagby, Dyana. "Love the 'Sinner' Rocker Joan Jett back in spotlight with Warped Tour and her first CD in 10 years." *Southern Voice*. http://joanjettbadrep.com/cgi-bin/fullStory.cgi?archive=200606&story=20060624-01southernvoice.htm, July 20, 2014.

Baltin, Steve. "Judas Priest's Real-Life Rock Star." *Rolling Stone*, September 20, 2001. http://www.rollingstone.com/music/news/judas-priests-real-life-rock-star-20010920#ixzz39jlD74bB.

BaronZemo. "Nemo," Rockfic.com. Online http://www.rockfic.com/viewstory.php?title=Nemo&storyid=7486&numchapters=1&category=Marilyn%20Manson,%20Metallica&author=BaronZemo&m=f&sort=date&ratinglist=&genrelist=Slash&bandlist=Marilyn%20Manson. Accessed October 30, 2014.

Bartkewicz, Anthony. "A Rainbow In The Dark." *Decibel* 23, September 2006: 64–68.

Bashe, Philip. *Heavy Metal Thunder: The Music, Its History, Its Heroes.* Garden City, NY: Dolphin Books, 1985.

Battersby, Matilda. "Man enough to be a woman and still rock 'n' rolling." *The Independent.* May 19, 2012. http://www.independent.co.uk/arts-entertainment/music/features/man-enough-to-be-a-woman-and-still-rocknrolling-7766426.html.

Behind the Music. Behind the Music Remastered: Judas Priest. Episode 5, 15 July 2014. http://www.vh1.com/video/behind-the-music-remastered/full-episodes/behind-the-music-remastered-judas-priest/1631871/playlist.jhtml.

Bell, David and John Binnie. "All Hyped Up and No Place To Go." *Gender, Place & Culture: A Journal of Feminist Geography* 1, No. 1 (1994): 31–47.

Bendix, Trish. " 'Queens of Noise' Is The Most Queer Telling of The Runaways Story Yet." *After Ellen.* August 20, 2013. http://www.afterellen.com/queens-of-noise-is-the-most-queer-telling-of-the-runaways/08/2013/. Accessed August 8, 2014.

Bennett, Chad. "Flaming the Fan: Shame and the Aesthetics of Queer Fandom in Todd Haynes's 'Velvet Goldmine'." *Cinema Journal* 49, No. 2 (Winter 2010): 17–39.

Berelian, Essi. *The Rough Guide to Heavy Metal.* Rough Guide Reference series, edited by Mark Ellingham. New York: Rough Guides, 2005.

Berger, Harris. "Death Metal Tonality and the Act of Listening." *Popular Music* 18, No. 2 (May 1999): 161–178.

Bersani, Leo. "Gay Betrayals." In *Is the Rectum A Grave? And Other Essays.* Chicago: University of Chicago Press, 2010: 36–44.

———. "Is the Rectum a Grave?" In *Is the Rectum A Grave? And Other Essays.* Chicago: University of Chicago Press, 2010: 3–30.

Biddle, Ian and Freya Jarman-Ivens. "Introduction." In *Oh Boy! Making Masculinity in Popular Music.* New York: Routledge, 2007: 1–17.

Binder, Amy. "Racial Rhetoric: Media Depictions of Harm in Heavy Metal and Rap Music." *American Sociological Review* 58, No. 6 (December 1993): 753–767.

Black Sabbath. *Mob Rules.* Universal Japan, ASIN No. B005S1Y728. Released December 27, 2011, compact disc.

Bordieu, Pierre. *Distinction: A Social Critique of the Judgment of Taste.* Trans. Richard Nice. Cambridge: Harvard University Press, 1984.

Brook, James, Chris Carlsson, and Nancy J. Peters. *Reclaiming San Francisco: History, Politics, Culture.* San Francisco: City Lights, 1998.

Brooks, Daphne. *Bodies in Dissent: Spectacular Performances of Race and Freedom, 1850–1910.* Durham: Duke University Press, 2006.

Brown, Andy R. "Heavy Genealogy: Mapping the Currents, Contraflows and Conflicts of the Emergent Field of Metal Studies, 1978–2010." *Journal for Cultural Research* 15, No. 3 (2011): 213–242.

Brown, August. "Cynic's Paul Masvidal, Sean Reinert are out as ready to be loud." *Los Angeles Times*, May, 8, 2012. http://www.latimes.com/entertainment/music/la-et-c1-gay-heavy-metal-20140508-story.html#page=1.

Brown, Michael P. *Closet Space: Geographies of Metaphor From the Body to the Globe*. London: Routledge 2000.

Browne, Kath, Jason Lim, and Gavin Brown (eds). *Geographies of Sexualities: Theory, Practice, and Politics*. London: Ashgate, 2007.

Bryson, Bethany. "'Anything But Heavy Metal': Symbolic Exclusion and Musical Dislikes." *American Sociological Review* 61, No. 5 (October 1996): 884–899.

Butler, Judith. *Gender Trouble: Feminism and the Subversion of Identity*. New York: Routledge, 1999.

Califa, Pat. "A Personal View of the History of the Lesbian S/M Community and Movement in San Francisco." In *Coming to Power: Writings and Graphics on Lesbian S/M*, edited by Samois. Boston: Alyson Publications, 1981; 3d 1987: 245–283.

Caroline. "Winding Road," Rockfic.com. Online. http://www.rockfic.com/viewstory.php?title=Winding+Road&storyid=5874&numchapters=1&category=Iron%20Maiden,%20Judas%20Priest&author=Caroline&m=f&sort=date&ratinglist=&genrelist=&charlist1=&charlist2. Accessed October 30, 2014.

Chauncey, George. *Gay New York: Gender, Urban Culture, and the Making of a Gay Male World, 1890–1940*. New York: Basic Books, 1995.

Christe, Ian. *Sound of the Beast: The Complete Headbanging History of Heavy Metal*. New York: Harper Collins, 2004.

Ciminelli, David and Ken Knox. *Homocore: The Loud and Raucous Rise of Queer Rock*. Los Angeles: Alyson Books, 2005.

Cohen, Sara. "Men Making A Scene: Rock Music and the Production of Gender." In *Sexing the Groove: Popular Music and Gender*, edited by Sheila Whiteley, 17–36. London: Routledge, 1997.

Cole, Shawn. *'Don We Now Our Gay Apparel': Gay Men's Dress in the Twentieth Century*. New York: Berg, 2000.

Collins, John. *Gene Vincent and Eddie Cochran: Rock 'n' Roll Revolutionaries*. London: Virgin Books Limited, 2004.

Cuirmale, L. and M. "Gay Leather Fetish History." Accessed June 24, 2014. http://www.cuirmale.nl/index.htm.

Currie, James. "Music After All." *Journal of the American Musicological Society* 62, No. 1 (Spring 2009): 145–203.

Cusick, Suzanne G. "On musical performances of gender and sex." In *Audible Traces: Gender, Identity, and Music*. Zurich: Carciofoli, 1999.

Cutler, Bert. "Partner Selection, Power Dynamics, and Sexual Bargaining in Self-Defined BDSM Couples." Ph.D. diss., Institute for Advanced Study of Sexuality, 2003.

Dana. "The Metal God, Rob Halford, Explains Why He Trademarked Name." Accessed July 21, 2011. http://eddietrunk.com/the-metal-god-rob-halford-explains-why-he-trademarked-name/.

Daniels, Neil. *The Story of Judas Priest: Defenders of the Faith*. London: Omnibus, 2010.

Davies, Helen. "All Rock and Roll Is Homosocial: The Representation of Women in the British Rock Music Press." *Popular Music* 20, No. 3 (October 2001): 301–319.

Dawson, Ashley. " 'Do Doc Martens Have A Special Smell?' Homocore, Skinhead Eroticism, and Queer Agency." In *Reading Rock and Roll: Authenticity, Appropriation, Aesthetics,* edited by Kevin J.H. Dettmar and William Richey, 125–143. New York: Columbia University Press, 1999.

Dean, James Joseph. "Thinking Intersectionality: Sexualities and the Politics of Multiple Identities." In *Theorizing Intersectionality and Sexuality,* edited by Yvette Taylor, Sally Hines, and Mark E. Casey, 119–139. New York: Palgrave Macmillan, 2011.

DeChaine, D. Robert. "Mapping Subversion: Queercore Music's Playful Discourse of Resistance." *Popular Music and Society* 21, No. 4 (1997): 7–37.

Dehyle, Donna. "From Break Dancing to Heavy Metal." *Youth and Society* 30, No. 1 (September 1998): 3–31.

DeLong, Marilyn, Kelly Sage, Juyeon Park, and Monica Sklar. "From Renegade to Regular Joe: The Black Leather Jacket's Value for Bikers." *International Journal of Motorcycle Studies* 2, No. 2 (Fall 2010). http://ijms.nova.edu/Fall2010/IJMS_Artcl.DeLongetal.html.

DeNora, Tia. "Music as a technology of the self." *Poetics* 27 (1999): 31–56.

Denski, Stan and David Sholle. "Metal Men and Glamour Boys: Gender Performance in Heavy Metal." In *Men, Masculinity, and the Media*, edited by Steve Cray, 41–60. London: Sage 1992.

Deseret, Jean-Ulrick. "Queer Space." In *Queers in Space: Communities/Public Places/Sites of Resistance*, edited by Gordon Brett Ingram, Anne-Marie Bouthillette, and Yolanda Ritter, 17–26. Seattle: Berg Press, 1997.

Dhaenens, Frederik, Sofie Van Bauwel, and Daniel Biltereyst. "Slashing the Fiction of Queer Theory: Slash Fiction, Queer Reading, and Transgressing the Boundaries of Screen Studies, Representations, and Audiences." *European Journal of Cultural Studies*, 15, August 2012: 442–456.

Douglas, Mary. *Purity and Danger: An Analysis of Concepts of Pollution and Taboo.* New York: Routledge and Kegan Paul, 1966.

Dulaney, William L. "A Brief History of 'Outlaw' Motorcycle Clubs." *International Journal of Motorcycle Studies* 1, No. 3 (November 2005). http://ijms.nova.edu/November2005/IJMS_Artcl.Dulaney.html.

Duncan, James S., Nuala C. Johnson, and Richard H. Schein, eds. *A Companion to Cultural Geography*. Oxford: Blackwell 2004.

Dunn, Sam. *Metal: A Headbanger's Journey*. Film. Directed by Sam Dunn, Scott McFayden, and Jessica Joy Wise. Banger Productions, 2006.

Edwards, J. Stephen. "Motorcycle Leathers and the Construction of Masculine Identities Among Homosexual Men." Accessed July 1, 2013. http://www.somegraymatter.com/motorcycle.htm.

Eells, Josh. "The Secret Life of Transgender Rocker Tom Gabel." *Rolling Stone* May 31, 2012. http://www.rollingstone.com/music/news/the-secret-life-of-transgender-rocker-tom-gabel-20120531?page=5.

Elliott, Cass. *Dream A Little Dream*. MCA Records, ASIN No. B000002P3T. Released February 11, 1997, compact disc.

Erbe, Marcus. " 'This Isn't Over Till I Say It's Over': Narratives of Male Frustration in Deathcore and Beyond." Paper presented at the International Congress on Heavy Metal and Gender, Cologne, Germany, October 2009.

Exivious. *Vik In the Closet*. YouTube video, 0:47. May 14, 2014. https://www.youtube.com/watch?v=4wPGmcTnCUg.

Face Culture. "Interview Gaahl from Wardruna and Gorgoroth talks about being gay (part 7)." YouTube, 5:01, April 7, 2009. https://www.youtube.com/watch?v=2AZ2oIuxmYE&list=RD2AZ2oIuxmYE#t=6.

F*cking C*nts. "10 ways to recognize a macho cunt (no, you're not 'men')." Accessed July 1, 2014. http://f-ckingc-nts.com/people/10-ways-to-recognize-a-macho-cunt-no-youre-not-men/.

Farren, Mick. *The Black Leather Jacket*. New York: Abbeville Press, 1985.

Fast, Susan. "Rethinking Issues of Gender and Sexuality in Led Zeppelin: A Woman's View of Pleasure and Power in Hard Rock." *American Music* 17, No. 3 (Autumn 1999): 245–299.

Fejes, Andreas and Magnus Dahlstedt. *The Confessing Society: Foucault, Confession, and Practices of Lifelong Learning*. New York: Routledge, 2013.

Foucault, Michel. *The History of Sexuality: Volume 1 The Care of the Self*. Trans. Robert Hurley. New York: Vintage, 1990.

———. "Technologies of the Self." In *Technologies of the Self: A Seminar With Michel Foucault*. Edited by Luther H. Martin, Huck Gutman, and Patrick H. Hutton. Amherst: The University of Massachusetts Press, 1988: 16–49.

Freeman, Elizabeth. "Queer Belongings: Kinship Theory and Queer Theory." In *A Companion to Lesbian, Gay, Transgender, and Queer Studies*, edited by George E. Haggerty and Molly McGarry, 295–314. London: Blackwell, 2007.

Friedman, Michael. "The Evolving Role of LGBT Musicians in Heavy Metal Music." *Psychology Today Online*, April 1, 2014. http://www.psychologytoday.com/blog/brick-brick/201404/the-evolving-role-lgbt-musicians-in-heavy-metal-music.

Friesen, Bruce K. and Jonathon S. Epstein. "Rock 'n' Roll Ain't Noise Pollution: Artistic Convention in the Major Subgenres of Heavy Metal Music." *Popular Music and Society*, 18, No. 3, 1994: 1–17.

Frith, Simon. "Music and Identity." In *Questions of Cultural Identity*, edited by Stuart Hall and Paul du Gay, 108–122. New York: Sage, 1996.

Frith, Simon and Angela McRobbie. "Rock and Sexuality." In *On Record: Pop, Rock, and the Written Word*, edited by Simon Frith and Andrew Goodwin, 371–390. New York: Pantheon 1990.

Frois, Catarina. *The Anonymous Society: Identity, Transformation and Anonymity in 12 Step Associations*. Newcastle: Cambridge Scholars Publishing, 2009.

Funky Canuck. "Top, Bottom, and Versatile." Rockfic.com. http://www.rockfic.com/viewstory.php?recid=1926&i=1&title=Top,+Bottom+or+Versatile?&author=-FunkyCanuck. Accessed October 30, 2014.

Garber, Marjorie. *Vested Interests: Cross-Dressing and Cultural Anxiety*. New York: Harper Perennial, 1997.

Gardiner, Mark E. "The Real 'Wild Ones': The 1947 Hollister Motorcycle Riot." Accessed August 14, 2014. http://www.salinasramblersmc.org/History/Classic_Bike_Article.htm.

Gay Metal Society. *GMS Headbanger*. Chicago, Illinois, June 1995. http://archive.qzap.org/index.php/Detail/Object/Show/object_id/84.

"Get a Hard On For Hard Ton." *Boyz*, March 18, 2010: 12–13.

Giles, Geoffrey J. "The Denial of Homosexuality: Same-Sex Incidents in Himmler's SS and Police," *Journal of the History of Sexuality* 11, No. 1 (2002): 256–290.

Gill, John. *Queer Noises: Male and Female Homosexuality in Twentieth Century Music*. Minneapolis: University of Minnesota Press, 1995.

Glasser, Larissa. "Interview: An Interview with Annah Moore," *Transgender Tapestry* 112 (Summer 2007): 34–37.

———. An Interview With Randi Elise B. *Transgender Tapestry*, 96, Winter 2001. http://www.ifge.org/index.php?name=News&file=articlesid=94&theme=Printer.

"Gorgoroth Frontman Opens Up About His Sexual Orientation: 'I've Never Made Any Secret About It'." Blabbermouth.net, October 29, 2008. http//www.blabbermouth.net/news.gorgoroth-frontman-opens-up-about-his-sexual-orientation-ive-never-made-any-secret-about-it/.

Green, Stephanie. "12 Tips For Surviving Your First European Heavy Metal Festival." *Matador Network*, May 26, 2009. http://matadornetwork.com/nights/12-tips-for-surviving-your-first-european-heavy-metal-festival/.

Grossberg, Lawrence. "Is There a Fan In the House? The Affective Sensibility of Fandom." In *The Adoring Audience: Fan Culture and Popular Media*, edited by Lisa A. Lewis, 50–68. London: Routledge 1992, 50–68.

———. "Reflections of a Disappointed Music Scholar." In *Rock Over The Edge: Transformations in Popular Music Culture*, edited by Roger Beebe, Denise Fulbrook, and Ben Saunders, 25–60. Durham: Duke UP 2002.

Grosz, Elizabeth. *Volatile Bodies: Toward A Corporeal Feminism*. Bloomington: University of Indiana Press, 1994.

Halberstam, Judith. *Female Masculinity*. Durham: Duke UP 1998.

———. *The Queer Art of Failure*. Durham: Duke University Press, 2014.

Hall, Stuart. "The Spectacle of the 'Other'." In *Representation: Cultural Representations and Signifying Practices*, edited by Stuart Hall. London: Sage, 1997: 223–290.

Halnon, Karen Bettez. "Metal Carnival and Dis-alienation: The Politics of Grotesque Realism." *Symbolic Interaction* 29, No. 1 (Winter 2006): 33–48.

Halperin, David. *Saint Foucault: Towards A Gay Hagiography*. New York: Oxford University Press, 1995.

Harrell, Jeff. "From Otep, with rage. *South Bend Tribune*, April 4, 2013. http://articles.southbendtribune.com/2013-04-04/entertainment/38287380_1_otep-shamaya-metal-band-band-members/2.

Harris, Daniel. *The Rise and Fall of Gay Culture*. New York: Hyperion Books, 1997.

Hartmann, Graham. "Gruhamed." *Loudwire*, May 14, 2014. http://loudwire.com/periphery-cut-ties-vik-guitars-homophobic-remarks-against-cynic/?trackback=tsmclip.

Hasmondhalgh, David. "Towards a critical understanding of music, emotion and self-identity." *Consumption, Markets and Culture* 11, No. 4, 2008: 329–343.

Healy, Murray. *Gay Skins: Class, Masculinity and Queer Appropriation*. London: Cassel, 1996.

Hebdidge, Dick. "Style As Homology and Signifying Practice." In *On Record: Pop, Rock, and the Written Word*, edited by Simon Frith and Andrew Goodwin, 46–55. New York: Pantheon 1990.

Hennen, Peter. *Faeries, Bears and Leathermen: Men in Community Queering the Masculine*. Chicago: University of Chicago Press, 2008.

Hennessy, Rosemary. "Queer Visibility and Commodity Culture." *Cultural Critique* 29 (Winter 1994–1995): 31–76.

Herring, Scott. *Queering the Underworld: Slumming, Literature, and the Undoing of Lesbian and Gay History*. Chicago: University of Chicago Press, 2007.

Herzog, Kenny. "Joan Jett: 'I've Gotta Grow Up'." *Spin*, October 3, 2013. http://www.spin.com/articles/joan-jett-unvarnished-new-album-interview.

Hess, Amanda. "Top 5 Gay Metal Icons." *The Sexist*, August 26, 2008. www.washingtoncitypaper.com/blogs/sexist/2009/08/26/top-5-gay-metal-icons/.

Hickam, Brian and Jeremy Wallach. "Female Authority and Dominion: Discourse and Distinctions of Heavy Metal Scholarship." *Journal for Cultural Research* 15, No. 3 (2011): 255–277.

Hill, Rosemary Lucy. "Hard Rock and Metal in the Subcultural Context: What Fans Listening to the Music Can Tell Us." *Leisure Studies Association Newsletter* 98 (July 2014): 66–71.

Hooven, Valentine III. "Tom of Finland: A Short Biography." Accessed July 1, 2014. http://www.tomoffinlandfoundation.org/foundation/touko.html.

Huffer, Lynne. *Mad For Foucault: Rethinking the Foundations of Queer Theory*. New York: Columbia University Press, 2010.

HX magazine. "Mincing Metal: Hanson Jobb and Udo Von DuYu rock out as Pink Steel." *HX Magazine*, June 16, 2004, 24–25.

Ibbison, Robin. "Rawk and a Hard Place." *Gay Times* (n.d.): 54–56.

Ingram, Gordon Brent. "Mapping the Shifting Queerscape: A Century of Homo-erotic Space-Taking and Placemaking in Pacific Canada." Paper presented to the Do Ask Do Tell: Outing Pacific Northwest History conference, Washington State Historical Museum, Tacoma, Washington, 1998. http://gordonbrentingram.ca/scholarship/wp-content/uploads/2008/12/ingram-1998-mapping-the-shifting-queerscape-space-taking-placemaking-in-pacific-canada-presented-in-tacoma.pdf.

———. "Marginality and the Landscapes of Erotic Alien(n)ations." In *Queers In Space: Communities, Public Places, Sites of Resistance*, edited by Yolanda Retter, Anne-Marie Bouthillette, and Gordon Brent Ingram, 27–52. New York: Bay Press 1997.

———. "(On The Beach) Practising Queerscape Architecture." In *Practice Practise Praxis: Serial Repetition, Organizational Behaviour, and Strategic Action in Architecture*, ed. Scott Sorli. Toronto:YYZ Books, 2000.

———. "Ten Arguments For a Theory of Queers in Public Space." Paper presented to the Queer Frontiers Conference, International Lesbian and Gay Archives, University of Southern California, Los Angeles, California,1995. http://gordonbrentingram.ca/scholarship/wp-content/uploads/2008/12/ingram-1995-ten-arguments-for-a-theory-of-queers-in-public-space-presented-at-queer-frontiers-los-angeles.pdf.

Ingram, Gordon Brent, Anne-Marie Bouthillette, and Cornelia Wyngaarden. "Vancouver (as queer)scape: Strategies for mapping public spaces constructed by sexual minorities." Critical Geography Conference. Simon Fraser University and the University of British Columbia. Session: Locating the politics of theory in critical human geography, August 10, 1997. http://gordonbrentingram.ca/scholarship/wp-content/uploads/2008/12/ingram-bouthillette-wyngaarden-1997-vancouver_-as-queer_scape-critical-geography-conference.pdf. Accessed October 25, 2014.

"Interview: Joan Jett, Queen of Noise." *The Morton Report*, September 13, 2011. http://www.themortonreport.com/entertainment/music/interview-joan-jett-queen-of-noise/.

Jarman-Ivens, Freya. *Queer Voices: Technologies, Vocalities, and the Musical Flow*. Palgrave Macmillan Critical Studies in Gender, Sexuality, and Culture series, edited by Patricia T. Clough and R. Danielle Egan. New York: Palgrave Macmillan, 2011.

Jeremy. "Music in Your Toybag." Unpublished. Vertical file: Music-General, Leather Archives and Museum, Chicago, Illinois.

Jett, Joan. "Bad Reputation/Jezebel." Boardwalk Records, 1981. Vinyl.

———. "Do You Wanna Touch Me (Oh Yeah)/Victim of Circumstance." Boardwalk Records, 1981. Vinyl.

———. *Fetish*. Polygram, ASIN B00000J7QA. Released June 8, 1999. Compact disc.

———. "Oh Woe Is Me/Crimson and Clover." Boardwalk Records, 1982.

"Joan Jett and The Blackhearts: Crimson and Clover." YouTube video, 3:10. Posted February 8, 2007. https://www.youtube.com/watch?v=hdhonK8NMm8.

Johnson, Corey W. and Diane M. Samdahl. " 'The Night They Took Over': Misogyny in a Country-Western Bar." *Leisure Sciences: An Interidsiciplinary Journal* 27, No. 4, 2005: 331–348.

Johnston, Lynda and Robyn Longhurst. *Space, Place, and Sex: Geographies of Sexualities*. Lanham: Rowman and Littlefield, 2010.

Jon. "Unleashing Satan: An Evening with Gaahl." Accessed July 4, 2014. http://www.metalblast.net/interviews/unleashing-satan-an-evening-with-gaahl/.

Judas Priest. *British Steel*. Columbia Records, ASIN No. B009139040. Released April 14, 1980, vinyl.

———. *Defenders of the Faith*. Columbia Records, ASIN No. B00005CBTI. Released January 4, 1984, vinyl.

Jugulator. "The Judas Priest History." Accessed July 25, 2014. http://www.jugulator.net/judas_priest_history.htm.

Kahn-Harris, Keith. *Extreme Metal: Metal and Culture on the Edge*. London: Berg Publishers, 2007.

Keehnen, Owen. *We're Here: We're Queer: The Gay 90s and Beyond*. Chicago: Prairie Avenue Productions, 2011.

Kennedy, Elizabeth and Madeline Davis. *Boots of Leather, Slippers of Gold: The History of a Lesbian Community*. New York: Penguin Books, 1994.

Kennedy, Kathleen. "Results of a Misspent Youth: Joan Jett's Performance of Female Masculinity." *Women's History Review* 11, No. 1 (2002): 89–114.

"Kerry King: Ex-Soulfly Drummer Joe Nunez's Mother Wouldn't Let Him Play In Slayer!" *Blabbermouth*, June 10, 2002. http://www.blabbermouth.net/news/kerry-king-ex-soulfly-drummer-joe-nunez-s-mother-wouldn-t-let-him-play-in-slayer/#QXe2FeSy7eBm18AT.99.

"Kinky Music Hall of Fame." *Brat Attack* 1, No. 3 (n.d.): 41.

Kitteringham, Sarah. "Extreme Conditions Demand Extreme Responses: The Treatment of Women in Black Metal, Death Metal, Doom Metal, and Grindcore." MA thesis, University of Calgary, 2014.

Klypchak, Brad. *Performed Identity: Heavy Metal Musicians Between 1984 and 1991*. Berlin GE: VDM Verlag Dr Mueller, 2007.

Kotarba, Joseph A., Jennifer L. Fackler, and Kathryn M. Nowotny. "An Ethnography of Emerging Latino Music Scenes." *Symbolic Interaction* 32, No. 4 (Fall 2009): 310–333.

Krenske, Leigh and Jim McKay. " 'Hard and Heavy': Gender and Power in Heavy Metal Music Subculture." *Gender, Place and Culture* 7, No. 3 (2000): 287–304.

Kruse, Holly. "Subcultural Identity in Alternative Music Culture." *Popular Music* 12, No. 1 (January 1993): 33–41.

Kun, Josh. *Audiotopia: Music, Race and America*. Berkeley: University of California Press, 2005.

LaBruce, Bruce. *J.D.s #1, 1985*. Queer 'Zine Archive Project. Accessed June 13, 2013. http://archive.qzap.org/index.php/Detail/Object/Show/object_id/308.

———. *J.D.s #3 1987*. Queer 'Zine Archive Project. Accessed June 13, 2013. http://archive.qzap.org/index.php/Detail/Object/Show/object_id/345.

LaShure, C. "What Is Liminality?" *Liminality: The Space In Between*. Accessed July 19, 2014. http://www.liminality.org/about/whatisliminality.

Leonard, Marion. *Gender in the Music Industry: Rock, Discourse and Girl Power*. London: Ashgate, 2007.

Leung, Helen Hok-sze. "Queerscapes in Contemporary Hong Kong Cinema." *Positions* 9, No. 2 (2001): 428–447.

Lim, Jason. "Queer Critique and the Politics of Affect." In *Geographies of Sexualities: Theory, Practices, and Politics*, edited by Kath Browne, Jason Lim, and Gavin Brown, 53–67. London: Ashgate, 2007.

Lionnet, Françoise and Shu-mei Shih, eds. *Minor Transnationalism*. Durham: Duke University Press, 2005.

Logos, Yer. "Live: Cavern Club, Liverpool (evening)." *The Beatles* Bible. Accessed June 24, 2014. http://www.beatlesbible.com/1962/07/01/live-cavern-club-liverpool-189/.

Love, Heather. *Feeling Backward: Loss and the Politics of Queer History*. Cambridge: Harvard University Press, 2007.

Lugosi, Peter. "Queer consumption and hospitality: Communitas, myths, and the production of liminoid space." *International Journal of Sociology and Social Policy*, 27, Nos. 3 and 4, 2007: 163–174.

Mad Andy. "Perchance To Dream." Rockfic.com. Online. http://www.rockfic.com/viewstory.php?title=Perchance+To+Dream&storyid=198&numchapters=1&category=Motorhead&author=Mad%20Andy&m=f&sort=date&ratinglist=&genrelist=Slash&bandlist=Motorhead. Accessed October 30, 2014.

Marilyn Manson. *Born Villain*. Downtown Records, ASIN B007KIZ6IG. Released May 1, 2012, compact disc.

Marti, Kris Scott. "Interview with Otep Shamaya." *After Ellen*, January 31, 2005. http://www.afterellen.com/interview-with-otep-shamaya/01/2005/.

Matheu, Robert and Brian Bowe. *Creem: America's Only Rock 'N' Roll Magazine*. New York: Harper Collins, 1988.

Mathis, Shayne. "The Problem with Heavy Metal Is Metalheads: Stop Calling Everyone A Faggot." Metalinjection.net. Online. http://www.metalinjection.net/editorials/the-problem-with-heavy-metal-is-metalheads-stop-calling-everyone-a-faggot. Accessed October 29, 2014.

McCormick, Neil. "Suzi Quatro interview: 'When I zip up, it just feels like me.'" *The Telegraph*, July 27, 2013. http://www.telegraph.co.uk/culture/music/10191291/Suzi-Quatro-interview-When-I-zip-up-it-just-feels-like-me.html.

McDonnell, Evelyn. "With Her New Album and L.A. Acclaim, Former Runaway Joan Jett Proves She Never Left." *Los Angeles Times,* October 26, 2013. http://articles.latimes.com/print/2013/oct/26/entertainment/la-et-ms-joan-jett-20131027.

McRobbie, Angela. "Settling Accounts With Subcultures: A Feminist Critique." In *On Record: Pop, Rock, and the Written Word*, edited by Simon Frith and Andrew Goodwin, 66–80. New York: Pantheon 1990.

Meshuggah. *Koloss*. Nuclear Blast, ASIN No. B006ZT47MM. Released March 26, 2012, compact disc.

Metallica. *Master of Puppets*. Rhino Records, ASIN No. B00EBDXTJG. Released February 24, 1986, compact disc.

———.*Ride the Lightning*. Megaforce Records, ASIN No. B00EBDXSOW. Released July 27, 1984, compact disc.

MTV. *Superrock*. YouTube video, 4:37. February 25, 1998. https://www.youtube.com/watch?v=UaOVLTmjUo0.

MTV News. "Judas Priest Speaks About Rob Halford's Sexual Openness." MTV News online, February 5, 1998. http://www.mtv.com/news/articles/1429869/judas-priest-speaks-about-rob-halfords-sexual-openness.jhtml.

Muñoz, José Esteban. *Disidentifications: Queers of Color and the Performance of Politics*. Minneapolis: University of Minnesota Press 1999.

National Public Radio. "Judas Priest Lead Singer Rob Halford." *Fresh Air*, broadcast June 21, 2005. http://www.npr.org/templates/story/story.php?storyId=4712606.

Neilstein, Vince. "Keith Caputo Is Now A Woman ... Sort Of." *MetalSucks.net*, July 15, 2011. http://www.metalsucks.net/2011/07/15/keith-caputo-is-now-a-woman-sort-of/.

Newton, Esther. *Mother Camp: Female Impersonation in America*. Chicago: University of Chicago Press, 1979.

Olson, Mark J.V. " 'Everybody Loves Our Town': Scenes, Spatiality, Migrancy." In *Mapping the Beat: Popular Music and Contemporary Theory*, edited by Thomas Swiss, John Sloop, and Andrew Herman, 269–289. Malden, MA: Blackwell 1998, 269–289.

Otep. *Sevas Tra*. Capital Records, June 18, 2002. Compact disc.

Parks, Andrew. "Daddy's Little Girl." *Decibel* 45 (July 2008): 54–59.

Pasbani, Robert. "Vik Guitars Owner Posts Homophobic Remarks, Gets Denounced by Members of Periphery, Scar Symmetry." *MetalInjection,* May 13, 2014. http://www.metalinjection.net/latest-news/drama/vik-guitars-owner-homophobic-remarks-gets-denounced-by-periphery-scar-symmetry.

Patterson, Dayal. "The Terror of Stagnation: Gaahl of Wardruna Interviewed." *The Quietus*, May 30, 2013. http://www.thequietus.com/articles/12384-gaahl-wardruna-gorgoroth-interview.

Peraino, Judith A. *Listening to Sirens: Musical Technologies of Queer Identity from Homer to Hedwig*. Berkeley: University of California Press, 2006.

Peterson, Richard A. and Andy Bennett. "Introducing Music Scenes." In *Music Scenes: Local, Translocal, and Virtual*, edited by Andy Bennett and Richard A. Peterson, 1–15. Nashville: Vanderbilt University Press, 2004.

Petridis, Alexis. "Judas Priest's Rob Halford: 'I've Become the Stately Homo of Heavy Metal.' " *The Guardian* July 3, 2014. http://theguardian.com/music/2014/jul/03/judas-priest-rob-halford-quentin-crisp-interview-redeemer-of-souls/print. Accessed August 6, 2014.

Phillipov, Michelle. *Death Metal and Music Criticism: Analysis At the Limits*. Lanham: Lexington Books, 2012.

Pink Steel. "About." Accessed August 17, 2014. http://www.pinksteel.com/home.html.

———. "Lyrics." Accessed August 13, 2014. http://pinksteel.com/lyrics.html.

Playboy. "Playboy Interview: Metallica." *Playboy*, April 2001. Online. http://metallica.awardspace.com/inter.html. Accessed October 30, 2014.

Preston, John. "Introduction." In *The Leatherman's Handbook: The Original*. New York: LT Publications, 1994.

Priest, Annika. "Gender Bender Divas Centrestage at Midsumma." *Melbourne Leader*, January 13, 2010. http://www.melbourne-leader,whereilive.com.au/lifestyle/story/gender-bender-divas/.

Probyn, Elspeth. "Queer Belongings: The Politics of Departure." In *Sexy Bodies: The Strange Carnalities of Feminism*, edited by Elizabeth Grosz and Elspeth Probyn, 1–18. London: Routledge, 1995.

Puar, Jasbir K. "Queer Times, Queer Assemblages." *Social Text* 23, No. 3 (Fall-Winter 2005): 121–139.

Radford, Chad. "Torche's Steve Brooks talks about Atlanta, Harvey Milk and what makes metal so gay." *Creative Loafing Atlanta*, July 31, 2009. http://clatl.com/cribnotes/archives/2009/07/31/torches-steve-brooks-talks-about-atlanta-harvey-milk-and-what-makes-metal-so-gay, posted July 31, 2009.

Rafalovich, Adam. "Broken and Becoming God-Sized: Contemporary Metal Music and Masculine Individualism." *Symbolic Interaction* 29, No. 1 (Winter 2006): 19–32.

Rammstein. *Liebe ist fur alle da*. Universal Records, ASIN No. B002OOG6RQ. Released October 20, 2009, compact disc.

———. "Mein Teil" official video, 4:23. YouTube. Uploaded February 11, 2012. Online. https://www.youtube.com/watch?v=0hy07wSydOM. Accessed October 30, 2014.

———. *Reise, Reise*. Motor Music, ASIN No. B0002XDODU. Released November 16, 2004, compact disc.

———. *Sennsucht*. Slash Records, ASIN No. B0000057C5. Released January 13, 1998, compact disc.

Redhawk, D. Jordan. *Warlord Metal*. Austin: Fortitude Press, 2002.

Revolver. "Revolver Golden Gods Turns 6!6!6!." *Revolver* 114 (April-May 2014): 15–16.

———. "The Hottest Chicks In Metal: Otep Shamaya." *Revolver*, October 2009, 32.

Reynolds, Simon and Joy Press. *The Sex Revolts: Gender, Rebellion, and Rock 'n' Roll*. Cambridge: Harvard UP 1995.

Reznor, Trent. *The Downward Spiral*. Nothing/TVT/Interscope Records, ASIN No. B000001Y5Z. Released March 8, 1994, compact disc.

———. "Happiness is Slavery." Directed by Jon Reiss, 1992. Accessed June 18, 2014. Vimeo video. http://vimeo.com/3556108.

Rock Star. Directed by Stephen Herek. Hollywood: Warners Brothers, 2001.

"Rock Star: Quotes." *Internet Movie Database*. Accessed August 17, 2014. http://www.imdb.com/title/tt0202470/quotes?ref_=tt_ql_3.

Rubin, Gayle. "The Miracle Mile: South of Market and Gay Male Leather 1962–1997." In *Reclaiming San Francisco: History, Politics, Culture*. James Brook, Chris Carllson, and Nancy J. Peters (eds). San Francisco: City Lights, 1998: 247–272.

Saxey, Esther. *Homoplot: The Coming-Out Story and Gay, Lesbian and Bisexual Identity*. New York: Peter Lang, 2008.

Schick, Irvin C. *The Erotic Margin: Sexuality and Spatiality in Alterist Discourse*. New York: Verso, 1999.

Schippers, Mimi. "Social Organization of Sexuality and Gender in Alternative Hard Rock: An Analysis of Intersectionality." *Gender and Society* 14, No. 6 (December 2000): 747–764.

Sedgwick, Eve Kosofsky. "How To Bring Your Kids Up Gay." *Social Text*, 29, 1991: 18–27.

Shapiro, Gregg. "Otep Ascending: An Interview With Out Metal Goddess Otep." *Outlook Weekly*, April 10- April 16, 2008: 26.

———. "Heavy Metal Queen Raging Against Conformity." *Xtra*, April 10, 2008: 41.

Sharpe-Young, Garry. *Metal: The Definitive Guide*. New York: Jawbone Press, 2007.

Small, Christopher. *Musicking: The Meanings of Performing and Listening*. Connecticut: Wesleyan University Press, 1998.

The Soft Pink Truth. *Why Do All The Heathen Rage?* Thrill 368/Thrill Jockey Records, ASIN B00KZI7X6. Released June 20, 2014, compact disc.

Somerville, Siobhan. "Scientific Racism and the Invention of the Homosexual Body." In Roger Lancaster and Micaela DiLeonardo. *The Gender/Sexuality Reader: Culture, history, Political Economy*. New York: Routledge, 1997: 37–52.

St. John, Graham. *Victor Turner and Contemporary Cultural Performance*. New York: Berghan Books, 2008.

Steel Panther. *All You Can Eat*. +180 Records, ASIN B00HUGK8P4. Released April 1, 2014, compact disc.

Steele, Victoria. *Fetish: Fashion, Sex and Power*. New York: Oxford University Press, 1996.

Stosuy, Brandon. "Queer As Fuck: The Soft Pink Truth's Black Metal." *Pitchfork*, May 29, 2014. http://pitchfork.com/features/show-no-mercy/9417-soft-pink-truth/.

Straw, Will. "Music as Commodity and Material Culture." *Repercussions* (Spring-Fall 1999–2000): 147–171.

————. "Sizing Up Record Collections: Gender and Connoisseurship in Rock Music Culture." In *Sexing the Groove: Popular Music and Gender*, edited by Sheila Whiteley, 3–16. London: Routledge 1997.

Street-Jammer, Richard. "Rob Halford's Raw Deal." *Invisible Oranges*, November 8, 2011. http://www.invisibleoranges.com/2011/11/rob-halfords-raw-deal/.

Stuart, Johnny. *Rockers!* London: Plexus, 1987.

Tanner, Julian, Mark Asbridge, and Scot Worley. "Our favourite melodies: musical consumption and teenage lifestyles." *The British Journal of Sociology* 59, No. 1, 2008: 117–144.

Taylor, Jodie. *Playing It Queer: Popular Music, Identity, and Queer World-making.* New York: Peter Lang, 2012.

————. "The queerest of the queer: Sexuality, politics and music on the Brisbane scene." *Journal of Media and Cultural Studies,* 22, No. 5, 2008: 651–665.

"The Cliks: Their *Snakehouse* Strikes Like A Viper." *Diva,* January 2008: 21.

Thompson, Mark ed. *Leatherfolk: Radical Sex, People, Politics, and Practice.* Los Angeles: Daedalus Publishing Company, 1991; 3d, 2004.

Tom. "Heavy Metal is Gay: Why We Need to Tackle Our Homophobia." *Terrorizer,* July 23, 2014. http://www.terrorizer.com/news/features-2/heavy-metal-is-gay-need-tackle-homophobia/.

Townsend, Larry. *The Leatherman's Handbook: The Original.* New York: LT Publications, 1994.

Turner, Victor. "Liminality and Communitas." In *The Ritual Process: Structure and Anti-Structure.* Chicago: Aldine Publishing, 1969.

Vaid, Urvashi. *Virtual Equality: The Mainstreaming of Gay and Lesbian Liberation.* New York: Doubleday, 1996.

Valentine, Gill. "A Corporeal Geography of Consumption." *Environment and Planning D: Society and Space* 17, 1999: 329–351.

————. "Creating Transgressive Space: The Music of kd lang." *Transactions of the Institute of British Geographers* (new series) 20, No. 4, 1995: 474–485.

Varandela, Inma. "Gaahl Hates Your Sweatpants." *Vice United States,* February 28, 2011. http://www.vice.com/print.gaahl-hates-your-sweatpants-730-v18n3.

Waksman, Steve. *Instruments of Desire: The Electric Guitar and the Shaping of Musical Experience.* Harvard University Press, 1999.

Walker, Steve. "Obituary: Larry Parnes." Accessed June 20, 2014. http://www.rockabilly.nl/references/messages/larry_parnes.htm.

Wallach, Jeremy, Harris Berger, and Paul D. Greene. "Affective Overdrive, Scene Dynamics, and Identity in the Global Metal Scene." In *Metal Rules the Globe: Heavy Metal Music Around the World,* edited by Jeremy Wallach, Harris Berger, and Paul D. Greene, 3–33. Durham: Duke University Press, 2011.

Walser, Robert. *Running with the Devil: Power, Gender, and Madness in Heavy Metal Music.* Middletown, CT:L Wesleyan University Press 1982.

Waxlax, Bianca. "Q&A with Rob Halford: Heavy Metal Star Talks About Being Openly Gay, His New CD and His San Diego Gig." *San Diego Gay and Lesbian News,* December 14, 2010. http://www.sdgln.com/news/2010/12/14/qa-rob-halford-heavy-metal-star-talks-about-being-openly-gay-his-new-cd.

Weinstein, Deena. *Heavy Metal: The Music and Its Culture.* New York: DaCapo Press, 1991, revised edition 2000.

Weston, Kath. "Theory, Theory, Who's Got The Theory?" *GLQ* 2 (1995): 347–349.

————. "The Virtual Anthropologist." In *Anthropological Locations: Bounds and Grounds of a Field Science*, edited by Akhil Gupta and James Ferguson, 163–184. Berkeley: University of California Press, 1997.

Whisper. "Music in the Scene." Chicago: Mad Productions, 1998.

Whiteley, Sheila. "Introduction." In *Sexing the Groove: Popular Music and Gender*, edited by Sheila Whiteley, xiii-1. London: Routledge 1997.

————. *Sexing the Groove: Popular Music and Gender*. London: Routledge, 1997.

Wieder, Judy. "Heavy Metal Rob Halford: Between a Rock and a Hard Place," *The Advocate*, May 12, 1998: 56–61, 64–69.

Wiederhorn, Jon. "Judas Priest Turn Their Backs on 'Rock Star' Movie." *MTV News*, June 28, 2001. http://www.mtv.com/news/1444846/judas-priest-turn-their-backs-on-rock-star-movie/.

Wilkins, Amy C. " 'So Full of Myself as a Chick': Goth Women, Sexual Independence, and Gender Egalitarianism." *Gender and Society* 18, No. 3 (June 2004): 328–349.

Zanes, R. J. Warren. "Too Much Mead? Under the Influence (Of Participant Observation)." In *Reading Rock and Roll: Authenticity, Appropriation, Aesthetics*, edited by Kevin J.H Dettmat and William Richey, 37–71. New York: Columbia University Press, 1999.

Index